LANGUAGE AND LANGUAGE LEARNING

The Edinburgh Course in
Applied Linguistics

Volume 1

LANGUAGE AND LANGUAGE LEARNING

General Editors: RONALD MACKIN *and* PETER STREVENS

The Edinburgh Course in Applied
Linguistics

Edited by J. P. B. ALLEN *and* S. PIT CORDER

VOLUME ONE

Readings for
Applied Linguistics

LONDON
OXFORD UNIVERSITY PRESS
1973

Oxford University Press, Ely House, London W.1

GLASGOW NEW YORK TORONTO MELBOURNE WELLINGTON
CAPE TOWN IBADAN NAIROBI DAR ES SALAAM LUSAKA ADDIS ABABA
DELHI BOMBAY CALCUTTA MADRAS KARACHI LAHORE DACCA
KUALA LUMPUR SINGAPORE HONG KONG TOKYO

Library Edition ISBN 0 19 437122 0

Paperbound Edition ISBN 0 19 437057 7

Reproduced and printed by photolithography and bound in
Great Britain at The Pitman Press, Bath

Contents

Acknowledgements

The editors and publishers wish to thank the following for permission to use extracts from the sources mentioned:

Peter Owen Ltd and The Philosophical Library Inc, New York (*Course in General Linguistics* by F. de Saussure, translated by Wade Birkin); Oxford University Press (*Personality and Language in Society* by J. R. Firth); Appleton-Century-Crofts Inc (*Verbal Behaviour* by B. F. Skinner); Harcourt Brace Jovanovich Inc (*Language and Mind* by Noam Chomsky); E & S Livingstone ('Paralanguage' by D. Abercrombie from *British Journal of Disorders of Communication*); Clarendon Press, Oxford and Harvard University Press (*How to do Things with Words* by J. L. Austin); Professor Roman Jakobson ('Linguistics and Poetics' from *Style and Language* edited by T. A. Sebeok); The Editors of the Educational Review and Professor M. A. K. Halliday ('Relevant Models of Language' from the *Educational Review*); Longman Group Ltd and D. Chrystal and D. Davy (*Investigating British Style*); Research Center for the Language Sciences, Indiana University ('Linguistic Diversity in South Asia' by C. A. Ferguson and J. D. Gumperz from the *International Journal of American Linguistics*); M.I.T. Press ('Science and Linguistics' by B. L. Whorf from *Language, Thought and Reality* edited by J. B. Carroll); Mental Health Research Institute and Professor J. Fishman ('A Systematization of the Whorfian Hypothesis' from *Behavioral Science*); Julius Groos Verlag ('Linguistic Relativity, Contrastive Linguistics and Language Learning' by J. B. Carroll from the *International Review of Applied Linguistics in language teaching*); Cambridge University Press and Professor W. S. Allen (*On the Linguistic Study of Languages*); Edinburgh University Press (*The Scientific Study of Language* by Professor J. Lyons); Chicago Linguistic Society ('On Achieving Agreement in Linguistics' by V. H. Yngve from *Papers from the Fifth Regional Meeting of the Chicago Linguistic Society*); Martin Joos (*Readings in Linguistics*); University of Chicago Press and the Trustees of the Bloomfield Estate ('Linguistic Aspects of Science' by L. Bloomfield from the *International Encyclopaedia of Unified Science*); University of Chicago Press and C. F. Hockett ('A Note on "Structure" ' from *Readings in Linguistics* edited by M. Joos); The University of Wisconsin Press (*Prolegomena to a Theory of Language* by L. Hjelmslev, translated by F. J. Whitfield); Longman Group Ltd and Indiana University Press (*The Linguistic Sciences and Language Teaching* by M. A. K. Halliday, P. D. Strevens and A. McIntosh); M.I.T. Press (*Aspects of the Theory of Syntax* by A. N. Chomsky); Linguistic Society of America and Professor J. J. Katz ('Mentalism in Linguistics' from *Language*); Northeast Conference on the Teaching of Foreign Languages ('Linguistic Theory' by A. N. Chomsky from *Language Teaching: Broader Contexts*); Georgetown University Press ('Syntax and the Consumer' by Professor M. A. K. Halliday from the *Monograph Series of Language and Linguistics*); Oxford University Press, The British Council and Professor W. F. Mackey ('Applied Linguistics: its Meaning and Use' from *English Language Teaching*); Harvard Educational Review and P. S. Rosenbaum (*On the Role of Linguistics in The Teaching of English*); McGraw-Hill Book Company ('Applied Linguistics and Generative Grammar' from *Trends in Language Teaching* edited by A. Valdman); Cambridge University Press ('Advanced Study and the Experienced Teacher' by S. P. Corder from *Teachers of English as a Second Language* edited by G. L. Perren).

Editors' Preface

This first volume of the Edinburgh Course in Applied Linguistics contains a set of readings, the majority of which have been written in the last 15 years. Some of the readings consist of complete articles or lectures; others are extracts from longer papers or books. Some of the texts were intended for specialist audiences—linguists, psychologists, sociolinguists, applied linguists or language teachers—others were directed towards an informed lay readership.

The readings have been selected with three aims in mind, and these aims are reflected in the way the readings are grouped. The first group (sections I–IV) has been chosen to present a broad range of views about the way language can be approached as an object of scientific investigation. The second group (sections V–VI) concentrates on presenting a number of alternative and sometimes sharply conflicting accounts of the scope, methods and philosophical foundations of the approach to the study of language known generally as 'structural linguistics'.

In preparing the four textbooks in this series we have assumed that the reader already possesses or is concurrently acquiring a knowledge of linguistic, psycholinguistic and sociolinguistic theory. It is important nevertheless to emphasize that those who study language and how it is acquired do not all start out from the same point, and do not necessarily share the same views as to the nature of the scientific process or the scope of what they are investigating.

The Applied Linguist is a 'consumer' of theories, in that he attempts to make use of the explanations they provide about the nature of language in order to plan and execute language teaching programmes. He is not a creator of theories—that is the role of the theoretician. However, the Applied Linguist must be a *discriminating* consumer; that is, he must be able to decide what is or is not a relevant theoretical approach for his purposes. In order to make this decision he must not only be familiar with a wide range of possible theories about language; he must also understand what phenomena the theorists attempt to explain, the methods they adopt and the philosophical presuppositions which lie behind their theories. These are matters which, though rarely made explicit in introductory textbooks in linguistics, are important to applied linguists, and they provide the main theme of the group of readings in sections V–VI.

The last group of readings (section VII) offers a variety of accounts of the relation of theory to application. In this sense it has to do with the philosophical bases of Applied Linguistics itself.

The aim of this volume is to present in as clear and direct a form as possible a set of arguments or points of view. The origin, authority or evidence for these points of view is here a secondary consideration. We have therefore, in most cases, omitted the notes and bibliographical references with which many of the original texts were provided. The interested reader may follow up these matters by consulting the works in their original form.

Department of Linguistics, Edinburgh   J. P. B. Allen
January, 1973   S. Pit Corder

Various Views of Language

If someone sets up in business as a teacher of physics, he would probably be able to give a fairly concise answer to the question: *What is physics?* Or if he set up as a teacher of swimming he could give a pretty confident account of what being able to swim involves. It might seem reasonable, therefore, that a language teacher should be able to give a fairly coherent answer to the apparently simple question: *What is language?* Questions of the form: *What is . . .?* usually expect as an answer some sort of a definition. *What is physics?*—The study of the properties of matter and energy; *What is swimming?*—It's when you propel yourself through the water by moving your arms and legs. But there are a lot of questions of the form: *What is . . .?* to which the only answer seems to be a tautology: e.g. *What is speed?*—Rapidity of movement, *What is time?*—Duration, or like: *What is life?* to which the only answer seems to be: *Well, it depends on how you look at it.* Is the question: *What is language?* a question of this sort? Is language something you know? We regularly talk about people knowing French or Arabic. Is it something you acquire and possess? We talk about a child acquiring his mother tongue, and Shakespeare was said to have had small Latin and less Greek. Or something you do? We speak and read; we make speeches. Or a skill? We may do any of these well or badly. Is language something we use? We use words or tones of voice to convey our meaning and intentions. Or something which happens? We speak of a conversation, a discussion or an argument taking place, and Mr. Smith's speech being the event of the evening. Or is language a thing? We talk about language as a tool; we speak of its structure and how it works. We even talk about its birth, growth and decline, and about living and dead languages as if they had an independent organic existence. Is language, then, knowledge, behaviour, skill, an event or an object? To judge only by the way we talk about it, the answer seems to be that it can be regarded as any or all of these things. No one way of looking at it is uniquely right, nor is one way of looking at it sufficient. There is no single, adequate definition, or comprehensive description of it. You cannot satisfactorily classify it or uniquely identify it by pointing to it. If this is the case then all ways of regarding language are likely to be relevant to the teaching of it, and any disregard of one aspect will imply that something important may be missing in the teaching.

If language is knowledge then learning it will share some of the characteristics of learning, say, chemistry; if it is skilful behaviour, it will be something we acquire through practice; if it is an object we may get to know it through descriptions or through use, while if it is a social event we shall wish to participate in the social interaction in which it is manifest.

1 HERMANN PAUL
Language and Organisms: An Analogy

It is a well established fact in comparative linguistics that several different languages have developed out of what is essentially one single language, and that these different languages for their part have not remained unitary but have split up into a series of dialects. Consequently it is not surprising that in regard to this process more than anywhere else an analogy with the development of natural organisms should be drawn. It is a matter of surprise, however, that the Darwinians among linguistic scholars have not actively favoured this point of view. The parallelism is in fact both justified and instructive within certain limits. Following this line of thought we can not only set up a correspondence between the language of an individual (i.e. the whole of the linguistic apparatus available to him), and the individual animal or plant, but also between dialects, languages and families of languages on the one hand and orders, species and classes of fauna or flora on the other.

In the first instance it is a matter of recognizing the equivalence of the relationship in one important respect. The great 'revolution' which zoology has undergone in recent times has been based to a considerable extent upon the recognition that only the isolated individual possesses real existence and that the orders, genera and species are nothing more than conceptual groupings and distinctions made by the human mind, which may turn out to be purely arbitrary and that the distinctions between individuals and between groupings are matters not of kind but of degree. We must adopt a similar standpoint with regard to differences in dialect: we should really distinguish as many languages as there are individual speakers. When we group together the separate languages of any particular set of individuals and exclude those of any other particular set of speakers, we are merely disregarding certain differences by doing so whilst giving weight to certain others. There is in this activity a certain scope for arbitrariness. There is no particular reason why one should

H. Paul: Extract from *Prinzipien der Sprachgeschichte*, Chapter II, Section 22, 7th Ed. Tûbingen, 1966, pp. 37–39. [Editors' translation.]

make a classification of individual languages at all and one should accept the fact that, however many groupings one distinguishes, there will always remain a certain number of individuals whose language could equally well be included in either of two closely related classes. A clear distinction will only be possible in the case where communication between two groups has been interrupted for a period of several generations.

To speak, therefore, of the splitting of what was formerly a single language into different dialects is a very inadequate way of describing what actually happens. In fact, at any particular moment, as many dialects are spoken in any speech community as there are speakers, and these dialects each have their own historical development and are in a state of continual change. Dialect division is nothing more than the growth of individual differences beyond a certain point.

Another respect in which we can draw a parallel is the following: The development of an individual animal organism is dependent on two factors: on the one hand it is conditioned by the characteristics of its parents who, through the process of inheritance, start it off developing in a particular direction. On the other hand are all the chance influences of climate, nutrition and environmental pressures, etc. to which an individual is subject throughout his life. The substantial similarity to its parents is established by the first influence and (within certain limits) the differences by the other. In the same way an idiolect is formed under the influence of the speech of members of the social group on the one hand, which we can regard as the equivalent of the parents, and on the other by the quite unrelated and unique experiences of his mental and physical life. It is generally agreed that the first is by far the most powerful determinant. Firstly, because any change in the character of the individual which causes it to deviate from the direction which it first acquired will be handed on to a following generation and this leads to a more marked differentiation amongst types. So also in the history of language. Furthermore we can assert in the case of language as in the case of animal organisms that the lower on the philogenetic scale, the stronger the effect of the second factor in relation to the first will be.

On the other hand, we must not overlook the considerable differences that exist between the creation of languages and organisms. In the case of the latter the influence of the 'parents' ceases at a fixed point, and from then on only the general direction acquired is *relevant* whereas in the case of the idiolect the influence of the individual idiolects of members of the community continues throughout, even though the effect is more powerful in the idiolect of childhood and becomes weaker as it grows and becomes stronger. The animal organism is the creation of an individual or a pair, whereas the creation of a language of an individual is the product of the idiolects of a large number of individuals—all those.

in fact, with whom one comes into verbal contact throughout one's life, even if in very varying degrees of closeness. And what makes the matter even more complicated, the different individual idiolects can in this creative process play both an active and a passive role. The parents can be the children of their own children. We must finally bear in mind that even when we are speaking of the speech of an individual we are not dealing with something concrete but with an abstraction unless, of course, we are referring to the whole system of mental concepts associated with language and their innumerable internal associations.

Social 'intercourse' is the sole creator of speech in the individual. Genetic factors only come into the picture in as much as they determine the physical and mental characteristics of the individual speaker which, as we have already said, certainly is a factor in the formation of language but a subordinate one in comparison to the effect of social interaction.

2 F. DE SAUSSURE
Language: 'A well-defined object'

1 Definition of language

What is both the integral and concrete object of linguistics? The question is especially difficult; later we shall see why; here I wish merely to point up the difficulty.

Other sciences work with objects that are given in advance and that can then be considered from different viewpoints; but not linguistics. Someone pronounces the French word *nu* 'bare': a superficial observer would be tempted to call the word a concrete linguistic object; but a more careful examination would reveal successively three or four quite different things, depending on whether the word is considered as a sound, as the expression of an idea, as the equivalent of Latin *nudum*, etc. Far from it being the object that antedates the viewpoint, it would seem that it is the viewpoint that creates the object; besides, nothing tells us in advance that one way of considering the fact in question takes precedence over the others or is in any way superior to them.

Moreover, regardless of the viewpoint that we adopt, the linguistic phenomenon always has two related sides, each deriving its values from the other. For example:

1 Articulated syllables are acoustical impressions perceived by the ear, but the sounds would not exist without the vocal organs; an *n*, for example, exists only by virtue of the relation between the two sides. We simply cannot reduce language to sound or detach sound from oral articulation; reciprocally, we cannot define the movements of the vocal organs without taking into account the acoustical impression.

2 But suppose that sound were a simple thing: would it constitute speech? No, it is only the instrument of thought; by itself, it has no existence. At this point a new and redoubtable relationship arises: a sound, a complex acoustical-vocal unit, combines in turn with an

F. de Saussure: Extract from *Course in General Linguistics*, Chapter III, 'The Object of Linguistics', Peter Owen, London, 1959, pp. 7–17.

idea to form a complex physiological-psychological unit. But that is still not the complete picture.

3 Speech has both an individual and a social side, and we cannot conceive of one without the other. Besides:

4 Speech always implies both an established system and an evolution; at every moment it is an existing institution and a product of the past. To distinguish between the system and its history, between what it is and what it was, seems very simple at first glance; actually the two things are so closely related that we can scarcely keep them apart. Would we simplify the question by studying the linguistic phenomenon in its earliest stages—if we began, for example, by studying the speech of children? No, for in dealing with speech, it is completely misleading to assume that the problem of early characteristics differs from the problem of permanent characteristics. We are left inside the vicious circle.

From whatever direction we approach the question, nowhere do we find the integral object of linguistics. Everywhere we are confronted with a dilemma: if we fix our attention on only one side of each problem, we run the risk of failing to perceive the dualities pointed out above; on the other hand, if we study speech from several viewpoints simultaneously, the object of linguistics appears to us as a confused mass of heterogeneous and unrelated things. Either procedure opens the door to several sciences—psychology, anthropology, normative grammar, philology, etc.—which are distinct from linguistics, but which might claim speech, in view of the faulty method of linguistics, as one of their objects.

As I see it there is only one solution to all the foregoing difficulties: *from the very outset we must put both feet on the ground of language and use language as the norm of all other manifestations of speech.* Actually, among so many dualities, language alone seems to lend itself to independent definition and provide a fulcrum that satisfies the mind.

But what is language [*langue*]? It is not to be confused with human speech [*langage*], of which it is only a definite part, though certainly an essential one. It is both a social product of the faculty of speech and a collection of necessary conventions that have been adopted by a social body to permit individuals to exercise that faculty. Taken as a whole, speech is many-sided and heterogeneous; straddling several areas simultaneously—physical, physiological, and psychological—it belongs both to the individual and to society; we cannot put it into any category of human facts, for we cannot discover its unity.

Language, on the contrary, is a self-contained whole and a principle of classification. As soon as we give language first place among the facts of speech, we introduce a natural order into a mass that lends itself to no other classification.

One might object to that principle of classification on the ground that since the use of speech is based on a natural faculty whereas language is something acquired and conventional, language should not take first place but should be subordinated to the natural instinct.

That objection is easily refuted.

First, no one has proved that speech, as it manifests itself when we speak, is entirely natural, i.e. that our vocal apparatus was designed for speaking just as our legs were designed for walking. Linguists are far from agreement on this point. For instance Whitney, to whom language is one of several social institutions, thinks that we use the vocal apparatus as the instrument of language purely through luck, for the sake of convenience: men might just as well have chosen gestures and used visual symbols instead of acoustical symbols. Doubtless his thesis is too dogmatic; language is not similar in all respects to other social institutions. Moreover, Whitney goes too far in saying that our choice happened to fall on the vocal organs; the choice was more or less imposed by nature. But on the essential point the American linguist is right: language is a convention, and the nature of the sign that is agreed upon does not matter. The question of the vocal apparatus obviously takes a secondary place in the problem of speech.

One definition of *articulated speech* might confirm that conclusion. In Latin, *articulus* means a member, part, or subdivision of a sequence; applied to speech, articulation designates either the subdivision of a spoken chain into syllables or the subdivision of the chain of meanings into significant units; *gegliederte Sprache* is used in the second sense in German. Using the second definition, we can say that what is natural to mankind is not oral speech but the faculty of constructing a language, i.e. a system of distinct signs corresponding to distinct ideas.

Broca discovered that the faculty of speech is localized in the third left frontal convolution; his discovery has been used to substantiate the attribution of a natural quality to speech. But we know that the same part of the brain is the centre of *everything* that has to do with speech, including writing. The preceding statements, together with observations that have been made in different cases of aphasia resulting from lesion of the centres of localization, seem to indicate: (1) that the various disorders of oral speech are bound up in a hundred ways with those of written speech; and (2) that what is lost in all cases of aphasia or agraphia is less the faculty of producing a given sound or writing a given sign than the ability to evoke by means of an instrument, regardless of what it is, the signs of a regular system of speech. The obvious implication is that beyond the functioning of the various organs there exists a more general faculty which governs signs and which would be the linguistic faculty proper. And this brings us to the same conclusion as above.

To give language first place in the study of speech, we can advance a final argument: the faculty of articulating words—whether it is natural or not—is exercised only with the help of the instrument created by a collectivity and provided for its use; therefore, to say that language gives unity to speech is not fanciful.

2 Place of language in the facts of speech

In order to separate from the whole of speech the part that belongs to language, we must examine the individual act from which the speaking-circuit can be reconstructed. The act requires the presence of at least two persons; that is the minimum number necessary to complete the circuit Suppose that two people, A and B, are conversing with each other:

Suppose that the opening of the circuit is in A's brain, where mental facts (concepts) are associated with representations of the linguistic sounds (sound-images) that are used for their expression. A given concept unlocks a corresponding sound-image in the brain; this purely *psychological* phenomenon is followed in turn by a *physiological* process: the brain transmits an impulse corresponding to the image to the organs used in producing sounds. Then the sound waves travel from the mouth of A to the ear of B: a purely *physical* process. Next, the circuit continues in B, but the order is reversed: from the ear to the brain, the physiological transmission of the sound-image; in the brain, the psychological association of the image with the corresponding concept. If B then speaks, the new act will follow—from his brain to A's—exactly the same course as the first act and pass through the same successive phases, which I shall diagram as overleaf.

The preceding analysis does not purport to be complete. We might also single out the pure acoustical sensation, the identification of that sensation with the latent sound-image, the muscular image of phonation, etc. I have included only the elements thought to be essential, but the drawing brings out at a glance the distinction between the physical (sound waves), physiological (phonation and audition), and psychological parts (word-images and concepts). Indeed, we should not fail to note that the word-image stands apart from the sound itself and that it is just as psychological as the concept which is associated with it.

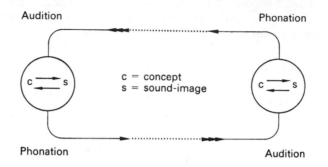

The circuit that I have outlined can be further divided into:

a an outer part that includes the vibrations of the sounds which travel from the mouth to the ear, and an inner part that includes everything else;

b a psychological and a nonpsychological part, the second including the physiological productions of the vocal organs as well as the physical facts that are outside the individual;

c an active and a passive part: everything that goes from the associative centre of the speaker to the ear of the listener is active, and everything that goes from the ear of the listener to his associative centre is passive;

d finally, everything that is active in the psychological part of the circuit is executive ($c \rightarrow s$), and everything that is passive is receptive ($s \rightarrow c$).

We should also add the associative and co-ordinating faculty that we find as soon as we leave isolated signs; this faculty plays the dominant role in the organization of language as a system.

But to understand clearly the role of the associative and co-ordinating faculty, we must leave the individual act, which is only the embryo of speech, and approach the social fact.

Among all the individuals that are linked together by speech, some sort of average will be set up: all will reproduce—not exactly of course, but approximately—the same signs united with the same concepts.

How does the social crystallization of language come about? Which parts of the circuit are involved? For all parts probably do not participate equally in it.

The nonpsychological part can be rejected from the outset. When we hear people speaking a language that we do not know, we perceive the sounds but remain outside the social fact because we do not understand them.

Neither is the psychological part of the circuit wholly responsible: the executive side is missing, for execution is never carried out by the collectivity. Execution is always individual, and the individual is always its master: I shall call the executive side *speaking* [*parole*].

Through the functioning of the receptive and co-ordinating faculties, impressions that are perceptibly the same for all are made on the minds of speakers. How can that social product be pictured in such a way that language will stand apart from everything else? If we could embrace the sum of word-images stored in the minds of all individuals, we could identify the social bond that constitutes language. It is a storehouse filled by the members of a given community through their active use of speaking, a grammatical system that has a potential existence in each brain, or, more specifically, in the brains of a group of individuals. For language is not complete in any speaker; it exists perfectly only within a collectivity.

In separating language from speaking we are at the same time separating: (1) what is social from what is individual; and (2) what is essential from what is accessory and more or less accidental.

Language is not a function of the speaker; it is a product that is passively assimilated by the individual. It never requires premeditation, and reflection enters in only for the purpose of classification, which we shall take up later.

Speaking, on the contrary, is an individual act. It is wilful and intellectual. Within the act, we should distinguish between: (1) the combinations by which the speaker uses the language code for expressing his thought; and (2) the psychophysical mechanism that allows him to exteriorize those combinations.

Note that I have defined things rather than words; these definitions are not endangered by certain ambiguous words that do not have identical meanings in different languages. For instance, German *Sprache* means both 'language' and 'speech'; *Rede* almost corresponds to 'speaking' but adds the special connotation of 'discourse'. Latin *sermo* designates both 'speech' and 'speaking', while *lingua* means 'language', etc. No word corresponds exactly to any of the notions specified above; that is why all definitions of words are made in vain; starting from words in defining things is a bad procedure.

To summarize, these are the characteristics of language:

1 Language is a well-defined object in the heterogeneous mass of speech facts. It can be localized in the limited segment of the speaking-circuit where an auditory image becomes associated with a concept.

It is the social side of speech, outside the individual who can never create nor modify it by himself; it exists only by virtue of a sort of contract signed by the members of a community. Moreover, the individual must always serve an apprenticeship in order to learn the functioning of language; a child assimilates it only gradually. It is such a distinct thing that a man deprived of the use of speaking retains it provided that he understands the vocal signs that he hears.

2 Language, unlike speaking, is something that we can study separately. Although dead languages are no longer spoken, we can easily assimilate their linguistic organisms. We can dispense with the other elements of speech; indeed, the science of language is possible only if the other elements are excluded.

3 Whereas speech is heterogeneous, language, as defined, is homogeneous. It is a system of signs in which the only essential thing is the union of meanings and sound-images, and in which both parts of the sign are psychological.

4 Language is concrete, no less so than speaking; and this is a help in our study of it. Linguistic signs, though basically psychological, are not abstractions; associations which bear the stamp of collective approval—and which added together constitute language—are realities that have their seat in the brain. Besides, linguistic signs are tangible; it is possible to reduce them to conventional written symbols, whereas it would be impossible to provide detailed photographs of acts of speaking [*actes de parole*]; the pronunciation of even the smallest word represents an infinite number of muscular movements that could be identified and put into graphic form only with great difficulty. In language, on the contrary, there is only the sound-image, and the latter can be translated into a fixed visual image. For if we disregard the vast number of movements necessary for the realization of sound-images in speaking, we see that each sound-image is nothing more than the sum of a limited number of elements or phonemes that can in turn be called up by a corresponding number of written symbols. The very possibility of putting the things that relate to language into graphic form allows dictionaries and grammars to represent it accurately, for language is a storehouse of sound-images, and writing is the tangible form of those images.

3 Place of language in human facts: semiology

The foregoing characteristics of language reveal an even more important characteristic. Language, once its boundaries have been marked off within the speech data, can be classified among human phenomena, whereas speech cannot.

We have just seen that language is a social institution; but several features set it apart from other political, legal, etc. institutions. We must call in a new type of facts in order to illuminate the special nature of language.

Language is a system of signs that express ideas, and is therefore comparable to a system of writing, the alphabet of deaf-mutes, symbolic rites, polite formulas, military signals, etc. But it is the most important of all these systems.

A *science that studies the life of signs within society* is conceivable; it would be a part of social psychology and consequently of general psychology; I shall call it *semiology* (from Greek *sēmeîon* 'sign'). Semiology would show what constitutes signs, what laws govern them. Since the science does not yet exist, no one can say what it would be; but it has a right to existence, a place staked out in advance. Linguistics is only a part of the general science of semiology; the laws discovered by semiology will be applicable to linguistics, and the latter will circumscribe a well-defined area within the mass of anthropological facts.

To determine the exact place of semiology is the task of the psychologist. The task of the linguist is to find out what makes language a special system within the mass of semiological data. This issue will be taken up again later; here I wish merely to call attention to one thing: if I have succeeded in assigning linguistics a place among the sciences, it is because I have related it to semiology.

Why has semiology not yet been recognized as an independent science with its own object like all the other sciences? Linguists have been going around in circles: language, better than anything else, offers a basis for understanding the semiological problem; but language must, to put it correctly, be studied in itself; heretofore language has almost always been studied in connexion with something else, from other viewpoints.

There is first of all the superficial notion of the general public: people see nothing more than a name-giving system in language, thereby prohibiting any research into its true nature.

Then there is the viewpoint of the psychologist, who studies the sign-mechanism in the individual; this is the easiest method, but it does not lead beyond individual execution and does not reach the sign, which is social.

Or even when signs are studied from a social viewpoint, only the traits that attach language to the other social institutions—those that are more or less voluntary—are emphasized; as a result, the goal is by-passed and the specific characteristics of semiological systems in general and of language in particular are completely ignored. For the distinguishing characteristic of the sign—but the one that is least apparent at first sight—is that in some way it always eludes the individual or social will.

In short, the characteristic that distinguishes semiological systems from all other institutions shows up clearly only in language where it manifests itself in the things which are studied least, and the necessity or specific value of a semiological science is therefore not clearly recognized. But to me the language problem is mainly semiological, and all developments derive their significance from that important fact. If we are to discover the true nature of language we must learn what it has in common with all other semiological systems; linguistic forces that seem very important at first glance (e.g. the role of the vocal apparatus) will receive only secondary consideration if they serve only to set language apart from the other systems. This procedure will do more than to clarify the linguistic problem. By studying rites, customs, etc. as signs, I believe that we shall throw new light on the facts and point up the need for including them in a science of semiology and explaining them by its laws.

3 J. R. FIRTH
Personality and Language in Society

Antoine Meillet stated as a basic principle (in the Saussurean sense of *langue*) that 'chaque langue forme un système où tout se tient'. A language is a system in which all the constituent units are held together in function by the whole. To get at such a language as a system, you must assume it holds together in *a state*. Hence the Russian objection that this theory leads to static structural formalism, to mechanical structure, to mechanical materialism in linguistics, which is according to them clearly superseded by the dialectical materialism given to the world in the name of Marx, Engels, Lenin, and Stalin.

The Russian critics understand de Saussure and represent his theory quite fairly as static mechanical structuralism. Moreover, they are right in believing that true Saussureans, like true Durkheimians, regard the structures formulated by linguistics or sociology as *in rebus*. The structure is existent and is treated as a thing. As Durkheim said, such social facts must be regarded 'comme des choses'. This is structural realism, or social realism.

In this country such theory has not taken root in professional linguistics. Even Malinowski pursued what I call *personality studies* in his ethnographic work. For my own part and for a number of my colleagues, I venture to think linguistics is a group of related techniques for the handling of language events. We regard our group of disciplines as designed for systematic empirical analysis and as autonomous in the sense that they do not necessarily have a point of departure in another science or discipline such as psychology, sociology, or in a school of metaphysics.

In the most general terms we study language as part of the social process, and what we may call the systematics of phonetics and phonology, of grammatical categories or of semantics, are ordered schematic constructs, frames of reference, a sort of scaffolding for the handling of events. The study of the social process and of single human beings is simultaneous and of equal validity, and for both, structural hypotheses are proved by

J. R. Firth: Extract from 'Personality and Language in Society' in *Papers in Linguistics* 1934–1951, Oxford University Press, 1957, pp. 180–7.

their own social functioning in the scientific process of dealing with events. Our schematic constructs must be judged with reference to their combined tool power in our dealings with linguistic events in the social process. Such constructs have no ontological status and we do not project them as having being or existence. They are neither immanent nor transcendent, but just language turned back on itself. By means of linguistics we hope to state facts systematically, and especially to make *statements of meaning*.

A key concept in the technique of the London group is the concept of the *context of situation*. The phrase 'context of situation' was first used widely in English by Malinowski. In the early thirties, when he was especially interested in discussing problems of languages, I was privileged to work with him.

Malinowski's context of situation is a bit of the social process which can be considered apart and in which a speech event is central and makes all the difference, such as a drill sergeant's welcome utterance on the square, '*Stand at—ease!*' The context of situation for Malinowski is an ordered series of events considered as *in rebus*.

My view was, and still is, that 'context of situation' is best used as a suitable schematic construct to apply to language events, and that it is a group of related categories at a different level from grammatical categories but rather of the same abstract nature. A context of situation for linguistic work brings into relation the following categories:

A The relevant features of participants: persons, personalities.
   (i) The verbal action of the participants.
   (ii) The non-verbal action of the participants.
B The relevant objects.
C The effect of the verbal action.

Contexts of situation and types of language function can then be grouped and classified. A very rough parallel to this sort of context can be found in language manuals providing the learner with a picture of a railway station and the operative words for travelling by train. It is very rough. But it is parallel with the grammatical rules, and is based on the repetitive routines of initiated persons in the society under description.

If I give you one brief sentence with the information that it represents a typical Cockey event, you may even be able to provide a typical context of situation in which it would be the verbal action of one of the participants. The sentence is:

'Ahng gunna gi' wun fer Ber'.'
(I'm going to get one for Bert.)

What is the minimum number of participants? Three? Four? Where might it happen? In a pub? Where is Bert? Outside? Or playing darts? What are the relevant objects? What is the effect of the sentence? 'Obvious!' you say. So is the convenience of the schematic construct called 'context of situation'. It makes sure of the sociological component.

The context of situation is a convenient abstraction at the social level of analysis and forms the basis of the hierarchy of techniques for the statement of meanings. The statement of meaning cannot be achieved by one analysis, at one level, in one fell swoop. Having made the first abstraction and having treated the social process of speaking by applying the above-mentioned set of categories grouped in the context of situation, descriptive linguistics then proceeds by a method rather like the dispersion of light of mixed wavelengths into a spectrum.

At this point, linguistics treats the verbal process of a speaking personality by writing down, let us say, a *sentence*. The technique of syntax is concerned with the word process in the sentence. The technique of phonology states the phonematic and prosodic processes within the word and sentence. The phonetician links all this with the processes and features of utterance. The sentence must also have its relations with the processes of the context of situation. Descriptive linguistics is thus a sort of hierarchy of techniques by means of which the meaning of linguistic events may be, as it were, dispersed in a spectrum of specialized statements.

We are now a long way from de Saussure's mechanistic structuralism based on a given language as a function of a speaking mass, stored in the collective conscience, and from the underdog, considered merely as the speaking subject, whose speech was not the 'integral and concrete object of linguistics'. The unique object of Saussurean linguistics is *'la langue'*, which exists only in the *collectivité*. Now it is at this point that I wish to stress the importance of the study of persons, even one at a time, and of introducing the notions of personality and language as in some sense vectors of the continuity of repetitions in the social process, and the persistence of personal forces.

The greatest English philologist of the nineteenth century was, I think, the Oxford phonetician, Sweet. He was never weary of asserting that language existed only in the individual. Others would say that all the essentials of linguistics can be studied in language operating between two persons. I am not subscribing to any theories of 'existence', and one must abandon the individual and look to the development and continuity of personality born of nature and developed in nurture. Language is part of the nurture, and part of the personality.

Before making any further use of the word 'personality' and its cognates, I propose briefly to review some of the contexts of its occurrence, and indicate the limitations within which it may be profitably employed in general linguistics.

Let us begin with Johnson's dictionary. For his first entry on *person*, he uses a citation from Locke: 'a person is a thinking intelligent being that has reason and reflection and can consider itself as itself, the same thinking thing in different times and places'. In another entry Johnson emphasizes the idea of being 'present in person', not through a representative. There is also the notion of responsibility which is made explicit in the phrase 'a responsible person'.

The meaning of *person* in the sense of a man or woman represented in fictitious dialogue, or as a character in a play, is relevant if we take a sociological view of the *personae* or parts we are called upon to play in the routine of life. Every social person is a bundle of *personae*, a bundle of parts, each part having its lines. If you do not know your lines, you are no use in the play. It is very good for you and society if you are cast for your parts and remember your lines.

To 'personate' in Johnson's sense is not so good. It is to feign. We must not personate unless it be professionally as a performer. The word 'impersonate' is not entered by Johnson in his dictionary. I have the impression that in England there has been a certain amount of impersonation in the matter of what is called public school pronunciation and what is wrongly described as the Oxford Accent.

In America the Schools of Speech use the dramatic method and presumably train people to produce themselves better, which is useful education. Happily only a few persons need become impersonators.

In defining *personality*, Johnson again quotes Locke: 'this *personality* extends itself beyond present existence to what is past, only by consciousness whereby it imputes to itself past actions just upon the same grounds that it does the present'.

If we accept the view expressed in Johnson's citation of Locke, we must consider language, like personality, as a systematic linking of the past with the present and with the future. Just as life itself is directed towards the maintenance of the general pattern of the bodily system, so also personality and language are usually maintained by the continuous and consistent activity of the bodily system, personality and language through life, language through the generations.

There is the element of habit, custom, tradition, the element of the past, and the element of innovation, of the moment, in which the future is being born. When you speak you fuse these elements in verbal creation, the outcome of your language and of your personality. What you say may be said to have style, and in this connexion a vast field of research in stylistics awaits investigation in literature and speech.

The continuity of the person, the development of personality, are paralleled by the continuity and development of language in a variety of forms. Human beings do vastly more than this. By means of language we can pass on our acquired learning and experience through the generations.

Following these lines of thought we see two very different streams linking the generations and linking people. The first is breeding, biological heredity, physical inheritance. This I shall refer to as *nature*. Physical inheritance, and the unification or integration of bodily activity by the nervous system and the endocrine organs, has a great deal to do with *personality*, and sex is a main determinant. In most societies social roles by sex are formally recognized in speech.

The second stream is *nurture*, and this includes the learning of the languages of the community. You weave *nurture* into *nature*, and you do this with the most powerful magic—speech.

In order to live, the young human has to be progressively incorporated into a social organization, and the main condition of that incorporation is sharing the local magic—that is, the language.

Allow me to misapply to speech and language Rousseau's famous sentence, 'Man is born free and is everywhere in chains'. The bonds of family, neighbourhood, class, occupation, country, and religion are knit by speech and language. We take eagerly to the magic of language because only by apprenticeship to it can we be admitted to association, fellowship, and community in our social organization which ministers to our needs and gives us what we want or what we deserve. The emphasis is on society and fellowship, in which a man may find his personality.

The various forms of local and familiar speech may be stated by means of constructs, so-called cultural systems, the elements of which we may regard as values to the people, who by continuing to give utterance to them maintain them or modify them by their activity. They are not to be measured by values in other cultural systems such as those of the A B C. These values do not necessarily conflict and a healthy personality can carry more than one set without developing morbid symptoms. A useful distinction can be drawn between speech fellowship and language community. The speech of those whose sounds, intonation, grammar, idiom, and usage are similar in structure and have similar function is a bond of fellowship based on the sharing of a truly common experience. A speech fellowship sees itself and hears itself as different from those who do not belong. Such speech, besides being a bond among the fellows, is a bar to the outsider. Local dialects, regional and occupational dialects, as well as the accents of the big English public schools, are speech fellowships. Within such speech fellowships a speaker is phonetically and verbally content because when he speaks to one of his fellows he is also speaking to himself. That can be the most deeply satisfying form of self-expression. No wonder the true proletarian despises 'fancy talk' or any form of impersonation, except when it has entertainment value.

Members of various speech fellowships may, however, belong to larger speech or language communities without conflict of values. Both sets of values deserve respect. The vast enterprises of the English-speaking world, operated by English, go on without a standardization of accent. You may estimate the relative values of what is called an Oxford accent, an Aberdonian accent, a Boston, a New York, or an Australian accent, but the main thing is a wider language community with room for diversity of personality. The genesis of correctness deserves study in all the fellowship groups, and not only in what is called a standard language. The genesis of correctness in several forms of speech is possibly part of the social process and part of the personal process. It is true that in everyday life we generally say what the other fellow expects us, one way or the other, to say, but this expectancy is the measure even of our most delightful surprises, and good personal style is highly valued.

Our studies of speech and language, and indeed a good deal of our educational methodology, have been dominated far too much by logic and psychology. Individual psychology tends to emphasize a kind of experience which is incommunicable or at any rate is not usually shared. And logic has given us bad grammar and taken the heart out of language.

My intention is to link language studies with social human nature, to think of persons rather than individuals. Linguistics may learn something from the sciences which treat human beings as separate natural entities in their psycho-biological characters, but it is mainly interested in persons and personalities as active participators in the creation and maintenance of cultural values, among which languages are its main concern.

Language and personality partake of both *nature* and *nurture* and are the expression of both. I am not now using the word 'language' in any Saussurean sense. I use the word 'language' without article, in three principal senses according to context:

1 The urges and drives in our nature which impel us to make use of sounds, gestures, signs, and symbols.

In the first sense, then, *language* is a *natural tendency*.

2 As a result of nurture, traditional systems or habits of speech are learnt and maintained by social activity.

Language in the second sense is everywhere actively maintained by *persons*, that is, by people who are members of society. Language in this sense must be *systemic*, because it owes its genesis and its continuance to human bodily systems living in society.

3 We may apply the word *language* collectively to the myriads of personal uses or the millions of speech events in social life. Or, alternatively, we may use the word—*speech*.

When we use *the article* or *any determining expression* such as *a language, the language, the English language*, we intend to refer to a specific set of language habits, some of which may be inadequately stated in grammars and dictionaries. I have suggested that language is systemic. Most grammars and dictionaries are systematic statements of fact—but quite a number are not. Even when they are systematic, they can sometimes fail to represent the language systems, in the sense in which I have used the expression *systemic*.

We may assume that any social person speaking in his own personality will behave systematically, since experienced language is universally systemic. Therefore, we may study his speech and ask the question, 'What is systemic?' We must not expect to find one closed system. But we may apply systematic categories to the statement of the facts. We must separate from the mush of general goings-on those features of repeated events which appear to be parts of a patterned process, and handle them systematically by stating them by the spectrum of linguistic techniques. The systemic statements of meaning produced by such techniques need not be given existent status.

A few specific language systems are stated in grammars and dictionaries and other works of linguistic science. But the vast majority of languages are not recorded. Such language systems can, however, be regarded as actively and consistently maintained by persons in the social process.

4 Verbal Behaviour

B. F. SKINNER

What happens when a man speaks or responds to speech is clearly a question about human behaviour and hence a question to be answered with the concepts and techniques of psychology as an experimental science of behaviour. At first blush, it may not seem to be a particularly difficult question. Except on the score of simplicity, verbal behaviour has many favourable characteristics as an object of study. It is usually easily observed (if it were not, it would be ineffective as verbal behaviour); there has never been any shortage of material (men talk and listen a great deal); the facts are substantial (careful observers will generally agree as to what is said in any given instance); and the development of the practical art of writing has provided a ready-made system of notation for reporting verbal behaviour which is more convenient and precise than any available in the non-verbal field. What is lacking is a satisfactory causal or functional treatment. Together with other disciplines concerned with verbal behaviour, psychology has collected facts and sometimes put them in convenient order, but in this welter of material it has failed to demonstrate the significant relations which are the heart of a scientific account. For reasons which, in retrospect, are not too difficult to discover, it has been led to neglect some of the events needed in a functional or causal analysis. It has done this because the place of such events has been occupied by certain fictional causes which psychology has been slow in disavowing. In examining some of these causes more closely, we may find an explanation of why a science of verbal behaviour has been so long delayed.

It has generally been assumed that to explain behaviour, or any aspect of it, one must attribute it to events taking place inside the organism. In the field of verbal behaviour this practice was once represented by the doctrine of the expression of ideas. An utterance was felt to be explained by setting forth the ideas which it expressed. If the speaker had had a different idea, he would have uttered different words or words in a

B. F. Skinner: Extract from 'Verbal Behaviour', Chapter I, *A Functional Analysis of Verbal Behaviour*, Appleton-Century-Crofts, New York, 1957, pp. 5–7.

different arrangement. If his utterance was unusual, it was because of the novelty or originality of his ideas. If it seemed empty, he must have lacked ideas or have been unable to put them into words. If he could not keep silent, it was because of the force of his ideas. If he spoke haltingly, it was because his ideas came slowly or were badly organized. And so on. All properties of verbal behaviour seem to be thus accounted for.

Such a practice obviously has the same goal as a causal analysis, but it has by no means the same results. The difficulty is that the ideas for which sounds are said to stand as signs cannot be independently observed. If we ask for evidence of their existence, we are likely to be given a restatement in other words; but a restatement is no closer to the idea than the original utterance. Restatement merely shows that the idea is not identified with a single expression. It is, in fact, often defined as something common to two or more expressions. But we shall not arrive at this 'something' even though we express an idea in every conceivable way.

Another common answer is to appeal to images. The idea is said to be what passes through the speaker's mind, what the speaker sees and hears and feels when he is 'having' the idea. Explorations of the thought processes underlying verbal behaviour have been attempted by asking thinkers to describe experiences of this nature. But although selected examples are sometimes convincing, only a small part of the ideas said to be expressed in words can be identified with the kind of sensory event upon which the notion of image rests. A book on physics is much more than a description of the images in the minds of physicists.

There is obviously something suspicious in the ease with which we discover in a set of ideas precisely those properties needed to account for the behaviour which expresses them. We evidently construct the ideas at will from the behaviour to be explained. There is, of course, no real explanation. When we say that a remark is confusing because the idea is unclear, we seem to be talking about two levels of observation although there is, in fact, only one. It is the *remark* which is unclear. The practice may have been defensible when inquiries into verbal processes were philosophical rather than scientific, and when a science of ideas could be imagined which would some day put the matter in better order; but it stands in a different light today. It is the function of an explanatory fiction to allay curiosity and to bring inquiry to an end. The doctrine of ideas has had this effect by appearing to assign important problems of verbal behaviour to a psychology of ideas. The problems have then seemed to pass beyond the range of the techniques of the student of language, or to have become too obscure to make further study profitable.

Perhaps no one today is deceived by an 'idea' as an explanatory fiction. Idioms and expressions which seem to explain verbal behaviour in terms of ideas are so common in our language that it is impossible to avoid them, but they may be little more than moribund figures of speech. The basic formulation, however, has been preserved. The immediate successor to 'idea' was 'meaning', and the place of the latter is in danger of being usurped by a newcomer, 'information'. These terms all have the same effect of discouraging a functional analysis and of supporting, instead, some of the practices first associated with the doctrine of ideas.

One unfortunate consequence is the belief that speech has an independent existence apart from the behaviour of the speaker. Words are regarded as tools or instruments, analogous to the tokens, counters, or signal flags sometimes employed for verbal purposes. It is true that verbal behaviour usually produces objective entities. The sound-stream of vocal speech, the words on a page, the signals transmitted on a telephone or telegraph wire—these are records left by verbal behaviour. As objective facts, they may all be studied, as they have been from time to time in linguistics, communication engineering, literary criticism, and so on. But although the formal properties of the records of utterances are interesting, we must preserve the distinction between an activity and its traces. In particular we must avoid the unnatural formulation of verbal behaviour as the 'use of words'. We have no more reason to say that a man 'uses the word *water*' in asking for a drink than to say that he 'uses a reach' in taking the offered glass. In the arts, crafts, and sports, especially where instruction is verbal, acts are sometimes named. We say that a tennis player uses a drop stroke, or a swimmer a crawl. No one is likely to be misled when drop strokes or crawls are referred to as things, but words are a different matter. Misunderstanding has been common, and often disastrous.

5 Language and Mind

NOAM CHOMSKY

One difficulty in the psychological sciences lies in the familiarity of the phenomena with which they deal. A certain intellectual effort is required to see how such phenomena can pose serious problems or call for intricate explanatory theories. One is inclined to take them for granted as necessary or somehow 'natural'.

Effects of this familiarity of phenomena have often been discussed. Wolfgang Köhler, for example, has suggested that psychologists do not open up 'entirely new territories' in the manner of the natural sciences, 'simply because man was acquainted with practically all territories of mental life a long time before the founding of scientific psychology . . because at the very beginning of their work there were no entirely un-known mental facts left which they could have discovered'. The most elementary discoveries of classical physics have a certain shock value—man has no intuition about elliptical orbits or the gravitational constant. But 'mental facts' of even a much deeper sort cannot be 'discovered' by the psychologist, because they are a matter of intuitive acquaintance and, once pointed out, are obvious.

There is also a more subtle effect. Phenomena can be so familiar that we really do not see them at all, a matter that has been much discussed by literary theorists and philosophers. For example, Viktor Shklovskij in the early 1920s developed the idea that the function of poetic art is that of 'making strange' the object depicted. 'People living at the seashore grow so accustomed to the murmur of the waves that they never hear it. By the same token, we scarcely ever hear the words which we utter. . . . We look at each other, but we do not see each other any more. Our perception of the world has withered away; what has remained is mere recognition'. Thus, the goal of the artist is to transfer what is depicted to the 'sphere of new perception'; as an example, Shklovskij cites a story by Tolstoy in which social customs and institutions are 'made strange' by the device

A. N. Chomsky: Extract from *Language and Mind*, Section 2, Harcourt, Brace & World, 1968, pp. 21–24.

of presenting them from the viewpoint of a narrator who happens to be a horse.

The observation that 'we look at each other, but we do not see each other any more' has perhaps itself achieved the status of 'words which we utter but scarcely ever hear'. But familiarity, in this case as well, should not obscure the importance of the insight.

Wittgenstein makes a similar observation, pointing out that 'the aspects of things that are most important for us are hidden because of their simplicity and familiarity (one is unable to notice something—because it is always before one's eyes)'. He sets himself to 'supplying . . . remarks on the natural history of human beings: we are not contributing curiosities however, but observations which no one has doubted, but which have escaped remark only because they are always before our eyes'.

Less noticed is the fact that we also lose sight of the need for explanation when phenomena are too familiar and 'obvious'. We tend too easily to assume that explanations must be transparent and close to the surface. The greatest defect of classical philosophy of mind, both rationalist and empiricist, seems to me to be its unquestioned assumption that the properties and content of the mind are accessible to introspection; it is surprising to see how rarely this assumption has been challenged, insofar as the organization and function of the intellectual faculties are concerned, even with the Freudian revolution. Correspondingly, the far-reaching studies of language that were carried out under the influence of Cartesian rationalism suffered from a failure to appreciate either the abstractness of those structures that are 'present to the mind' when an utterance is produced or understood, or the length and complexity of the chain of operations that relate the mental structures expressing the semantic content of the utterance to the physical realization.

A similar defect mars the study of language and mind in the modern period. It seems to me that the essential weakness in the structuralist and behaviourist approaches to these topics is the faith in the shallowness of explanations, the belief that the mind must be simpler in its structure than any known physical organ and that the most primitive of assumptions must be adequate to explain whatever phenomena can be observed. Thus, it is taken for granted without argument or evidence (or is presented as true by definition) that a language is a 'habit structure' or a network of associative connexions, or that knowledge of language is merely a matter of 'knowing how', a skill expressible as a system of dispositions to respond. Accordingly, knowledge of language must develop slowly through repetition and training, its apparent complexity resulting from the proliferation of very simple elements rather than from deeper principles of mental organization that may be as inaccessible to introspection as the mechanisms of digestion or co-ordinated movement.

Although there is nothing inherently unreasonable in an attempt to account for knowledge and use of language in these terms, it also has no particular plausibility or *a priori* justification. There is no reason to react with uneasiness or disbelief if study of the knowledge of language and use of this knowledge should lead in an entirely different direction.

I think that in order to achieve progress in the study of language and human cognitive faculties in general it is necessary first to establish 'psychic distance' from the 'mental facts' to which Köhler referred, and then to explore the possibilities for developing explanatory theories, whatever they may suggest with regard to the complexity and abstractness of the underlying mechanisms. We must recognize that even the most familiar phenomena require explanation and that we have no privileged access to the underlying mechanisms, no more so than in physiology or physics. Only the most preliminary and tentative hypotheses can be offered concerning the nature of language, its use, and its acquisition. As native speakers, we have a vast amount of data available to us. For just this reason it is easy to fall into the trap of believing that there is nothing to be explained, that whatever organizing principles and underlying mechanisms may exist must be 'given' as the data is given. Nothing could be further from the truth, and an attempt to characterize precisely the system of rules we have mastered that enables us to understand new sentences and produce a new sentence on an appropriate occasion will quickly dispel any dogmatism on this matter. The search for explanatory theories must begin with an attempt to determine these systems of rules and to reveal the principles that govern them.

The person who has acquired knowledge of a language has internalized a system of rules that relate sound and meaning in a particular way. The linguist constructing a grammar of a language is in effect proposing a hypothesis concerning this internalized system. The linguist's hypothesis, if presented with sufficient explicitness and precision, will have certain empirical consequences with regard to the form of utterances and their interpretations by the native speaker. Evidently, knowledge of language—the internalized system of rules—is only one of the many factors that determine how an utterance will be used or understood in a particular situation. The linguist who is trying to determine what constitutes knowledge of a language—to construct a correct grammar—is studying one fundamental factor that is involved in performance, but not the only one. This idealization must be kept in mind when one is considering the problem of confirmation of grammars on the basis of empirical evidence. There is no reason why one should not also study the interaction of several factors involved in complex mental acts and underlying actual performance, but such a study is not likely to proceed very far unless the separate factors are themselves fairly well understood.

In a good sense, the grammar proposed by the linguist is an explanatory theory; it suggests an explanation for the fact that (under the idealization mentioned) a speaker of the language in question will perceive, interpret, form, or use an utterance in certain ways and not in other ways. One can also search for explanatory theories of a deeper sort. The native speaker has acquired a grammar on the basis of very restricted and degenerate evidence; the grammar has empirical consequences that extend far beyond the evidence. At one level, the phenomena with which the grammar deals are explained by the rules of the grammar itself and the interaction of these rules. At a deeper level, these same phenomena are explained by the principles that determine the selection of the grammar on the basis of the restricted and degenerate evidence available to the person who has acquired knowledge of the language, who has constructed for himself this particular grammar. The principles that determine the form of grammar and that select a grammar of the appropriate form on the basis of certain data constitute a subject that might, following a traditional usage, be termed 'universal grammar'. The study of universal grammar, so understood, is a study of the nature of human intellectual capacities. It tries to formulate the necessary and sufficient conditions that a system must meet to qualify as a potential human language, conditions that are not accidentally true of the existing human languages, but that are rather rooted in the human 'language capacity', and thus constitute the innate organization that determines what counts as linguistic experience and what knowledge of language arises on the basis of this experience. Universal grammar, then, constitutes an explanatory theory of a much deeper sort than particular grammar, although the particular grammar of a language can also be regarded as an explanatory theory.

In practice, the linguist is always involved in the study of both universal and particular grammar. When he constructs a descriptive, particular grammar in one way rather than another on the basis of what evidence he has available, he is guided, consciously or not, by certain assumptions as to the form of grammar, and these assumptions belong to the theory of universal grammar. Conversely, his formulation of principles of universal grammar must be justified by the study of their consequences when applied in particular grammars. Thus, at several levels the linguist is involved in the construction of explanatory theories, and at each level there is a clear psychological interpretation for his theoretical and descriptive work. At the level of particular grammar, he is attempting to characterize knowledge of a language, a certain cognitive system that has been developed —unconsciously, of course—by the normal speaker-hearer. At the level of universal grammar, he is trying to establish certain general properties of human intelligence. Linguistics, so characterized, is simply the subfield of psychology that deals with these aspects of mind.

The Functions of Language

Most attempts to define language include some statement of what language is for. For example, Sapir's definition: 'Language is a purely human and non-instinctive method of communicating ideas, emotions and desires by means of a system of voluntarily produced symbols'. The more traditional formulations tend to limit the function of language to the expression of thoughts. The Port Royal grammar says simply: 'Words were invented to communicate our thoughts'.

Common to all such formulations is the notion of communication. Of course, no one suggests that man communicates exclusively by means of language. Abercrombie shows that we also communicate voluntarily by means of gesture, posture, facial expression and tones of voice. But any idea of communication necessarily implies the communication of something, and it is here the difficulty arises. What is it that is communicated by language? Thoughts, ideas, desires, emotions? These are concepts which are not readily defined except in the terms of some psychological theory. If we adopt the extreme view in which language behaviour is ultimately to be accounted for as an automatic and mechanical response to environmental stimuli, as Skinner seems to do, then such terms as *idea*, *thought*, *desire* and *emotion* are devoid of meaning (as is the term *meaning*, itself) and the question: *What is language for?* is itself a meaningless question.

If, however, we adopt a point of view in which language is regarded as *creative* and *stimulus free* (as Chomsky does in Section 7 and as Sapir evidently does in the quoted definition), the way is open to giving some account of the functions of language.

The restricted view of the functions of language, as limited to the expression of thought, derives from the fact that the study of language was for a long time a philosophical preoccupation, and philosophers tended, because of their concern with truth-value and logic, to confine their interest to a limited range of sentence types, those which expressed propositions. Whilst it is possible to make judgements about the truth or falsity of a proposition expressed by a declarative sentence, it is clearly not so in the case of imperative and interrogative sentences.

Austin points out, however, that there are many sentences of a declarative form which are not in fact descriptions of states of affairs, but merely 'masquerade' as such, and about which, therefore, the question of their truth or falsity does not arise. Such sentences, he suggests, are 'acts', not just the act of saying something, which is trivially true of all speech, but the performance of a certain type of act such as 'promising' or 'betting'. Acts of this sort are typically, and in some cases uniquely, performed through speech. On the basis of the conditions under which the act is performed, what the intention of the speaker is, and what the effect of the act is, he proposes a number of classes of speech act or functions of language.

Jakobson arrives at a rather different account from Austin's, approaching the subject through an analysis of the speech event. But he points out that it is probably rare that any speech act fulfills only one function. It is rather a case of one function being predominant on any particular occasion.

Whilst Halliday's analysis is substantially the same as Jakobson's, its special interest lies in its relevance to language teaching. His principal concern is, of course, with the teaching of the mother tongue and the dangers inherent in a teacher's inadequate conception of the range of functions of language.

The learner of a second language will normally have acquired all these linguistic functions in his mother tongue. We may ask whether he will require to use the second language in the same range of functions. We may come to the conclusion that he will not. It may be that certain functions assume a larger relative importance in a second language than in a first, that there will be certain acts he will more often perform in the new language. It is commonplace nowadays to say that we must adapt our teaching materials to the needs of the learner. One way of describing these needs is in terms of the uses that he will have for the second language.

6 Paralinguistic Communication

DAVID ABERCROMBIE

We speak with our vocal organs, but we converse with our entire bodies; conversation consists of much more than a simple interchange of spoken words. The term *paralanguage* is increasingly commonly used to refer to non-verbal communicating activities which accompany verbal behaviour in conversation. Anyone with a professional interest in spoken language is likely, sooner or later, to have to take an interest in paralanguage too.

I do not, all the same, like the term paralanguage very much, although I have used it for my title, and although it has been widely adopted. It seems to me potentially misleading: it can give the impression that, because there exists a (more or less) homogeneous entity called *language*, there must be, existing beside it, a comparably homogeneous entity called *paralanguage*. I believe this is not so. (The word *paralinguistics*, I regret to say, has already emerged as a name for a new subject, the study of paralanguage; and we may be sure that *paralinguist*, or *paralinguistician*, will not be far behind to designate the person who practises it.) These non-verbal, though conversational, activities to which the word para-language refers are far too diverse, too little codified, too uninvestigated, and too insufficiently understood, to be given the air of unity which a noun confers on them; so, having used 'Paralanguage' for the title of my paper, I shall, as far as I can, from now on avoid it. The adjective *paralinguistic* (which was the first of all these terms to be coined) seems to me, however, much more innocuous, with less power to mislead; and I shall therefore prefer to speak of paralinguistic phenomena, or behaviour, or activities, rather than of paralanguage.

Paralinguistic phenomena are neither idiosyncratic and personal, on the one hand, nor generally human, on the other. They must, therefore, be culturally determined, and so, as one would expect, they differ from social group to social group. They differ a great deal, and the differences go with language differences, even with dialect differences within

David Abercrombie: Extract from 'Paralanguage', *British Journal of Disorders of Communication*, Vol. 3, No. 1, 1968, pp. 55–9.

languages, though they sometimes cut across linguistic boundaries. These aspects of human behaviour are bound therefore to interest language teachers, psychiatrists, anthropologists, speech therapists, and of course linguists and phoneticians too. Their systematic investigation started comparatively recently, though a desultory interest in them is of long standing. However, a great deal has been done during the last few years —particularly, interestingly enough, by, or in collaboration with, psychiatrists; and I would like here to summarize, sometimes critically, what has so far been accomplished in this area.

Paralinguistic phenomena are non-linguistic elements in conversation. They occur alongside spoken language, interact with it, and produce together with it a total system of communication. They are not necessarily continuously simultaneous with spoken words. They may also be inter-spersed among them, or precede them, or follow them; but they are always integrated into a conversation considered as a complete linguistic inter-action. The study of paralinguistic behaviour is part of the study of conversation: the conversational use of spoken language cannot be properly understood unless paralinguistic elements are taken into account.

All animals communicate with each other by means of noises, bodily movements, and postures, and human beings are no exception; they too communicate by acts which are not different in kind. But human beings have language as well, and these more primitive communicative acts have often become entangled with spoken language when used in conversation, and hence become paralinguistic. Of course, plenty of other 'animal-like' communicative acts are used in various circumstances by human beings, but not as part of conversation: they are then not paralinguistic. This is perhaps a good point to try to delimit the application of 'paralinguistic' rather more strictly than some writers have done. Paralinguistic activities must (a) communicate, and (b) be part of a conversational interaction. These two requirements rule out several sorts of activity which have at times been put together with paralinguistic activities. They rule out, for example, a nervous twitch of the eyelid which some people have while talking, since it does not communicate, and many personal mannerisms and tics, since they do not either; and they rule out, for example, the act of taking one's hat off, or a 'wolf whistle', which communicate but do not enter into conversation. (They may initiate one.) Moreover to be accounted paralinguistic an element in conversation must, at least potentially, be consciously controllable: hoarseness may communicate the fact that one has a cold, but it is not a paralinguistic element in conversation.

We see then that paralinguistic behaviour is non-verbal communication, but not all non-verbal communication is paralinguistic. I have just limited the application of the word, compared to the way it is used by some other writers; I should now like to widen its current application in an important respect. This is connected with a second reason why I do not like the noun *paralanguage* being used in this field. It inevitably runs the risk of being brought into association with that rather special meaning given to the word *language* by certain linguists today who, following Bloomfield, say it can only be 'the noise you make with your face'. If language is this, then —it will be said—paralanguage too must be facial noises. And in fact this is the way the word paralanguage is used by most people nowadays. When systematic investigation of the field first started, in America, the word *metalinguistic* was (not very happily) chosen for these non-linguistic elements in conversation, and they were divided into two classes, called *kinesics* and *vocalizations* (another rather unhappy term)—roughly, elements due to movements and elements due to sounds. When the term *paralanguage* was introduced it was applied only to what earlier had been called vocalizations, and kinesics pursued a largely independent existence. This has been a pity. Parallels between the two have been obscured, and kinesics has expanded to include the study of all human bodily movement and posture, whether paralinguistic or not.

I would therefore go back to the early days, and apply the word paralinguistic to both movements and sounds. It is convenient for descriptive purposes to have this dichotomy of paralinguistic elements into *visible movements and postures* and *audible movements and postures* (as many have pointed out, there is a strong gestural aspect about sounds produced by the vocal organs), but it should not be taken to imply difference of function between them in conversation. I do not think there is any. (I would suggest it might be an advantage to restrict the word *kinesics* to the study of non-conversational bodily movements of all kinds.)

If we start examining visible paralinguistic elements, we find another dichotomy, a functional one, useful here, which I suggested some years ago. This dichotomy is into those elements which *can* be *independent* of the verbal elements of conversation, and those which *must* be *dependent* on them. A participant in a conversation may nod his head, for example, at the same time as he says the word 'yes'; or he may nod but say nothing —the nod will still communicate. This, therefore, is an *independent* paralinguistic element—it *can* occur alone, though it does not have to. Manual gestures of emphasis, on the other hand, must always accompany spoken words, and communicate nothing without them. These therefore are *dependent* paralinguistic elements.

Much of dependent visible paralinguistic behaviour comes under the heading of posture—the general way in which the whole body is disposed, either when sitting or standing during conversation. Posture goes through a series of changes while people converse: legs are crossed or uncrossed, participants lean forward or back, elbows are placed on tables, and so on.

These changes in posture have a punctuative role in conversation: they indicate the beginnings and endings of contributions to the interaction, show when a point has been made, make clear the relations of participants to each other at any given moment. They are not, as might be supposed, random. The number of postures used in any given culture appears to be limited, and their configurations are determined culturally: Englishmen, we are told by Scheflen, cross their legs differently from Americans. (The study of posture already has its own name in some quarters: 'body semantics'.)

Conversations take place most commonly in the world, perhaps, while the participants are standing up. The distance at which they stand from each other is then of paralinguistic importance, and moreover may vary greatly from culture to culture. Each person unconsciously adopts the conversational proximity appropriate to situations in his own culture; the use of the wrong distance—whether too close or too far away—can give offence. (The study of the proximity of conversationalists also already has a name: 'proxemics'.)

It is probably necessary to distinguish at least three more dependent ingredients in visible paralinguistic communication, each making its own contribution to the interaction: gesture, facial expression, and eye contacts between the participants. Gesture is superimposed on posture, involves less of the body at any one time, and changes more rapidly. The amount of gesture that accompanies the verbal elements of conversation varies very much between cultures, as has often been pointed out, and so do the gesture-movements themselves. Much of facial expression is probably idiosyncratic and not to be accounted paralinguistic, though some of it undoubtedly is in some cultures. It is characteristic of other cultures that changes in facial expression are absent in conversation ('dead-pan'). The role of eye-contacts in conversation is only recently beginning to be understood.

Gesture and facial expression supply the independent visible elements in paralinguistic communication: shrugs, nods, winks, and so on. ('Gesture languages' or 'sign languages', whether of the deaf or of American Indians, are, as their name indicates, linguistic and not paralinguistic; they are systems of communication which are structured as language.)

The same dichotomy, into independent and dependent elements, is useful for handling audible elements of paralinguistic behaviour also. Independent elements are what are usually called *interjections*, and examples are easy to find in all languages. They are characterized by the fact that they do not follow the normal phonological rules of the language. In English we have recognized ways of spelling many of them—tut tut, whew, uh-huh, ahem, humph, sh, ugh—though one could not pronounce them from the spelling unless one already knew what the interjection was.

Dependent audible elements, which are extremely varied, might all be put together under another popular term, *tones of voice*. They are produced by variations from the social *linguistic* norm in features of voice dynamics—loudness, tempo, register, tessitura, and others; and also by 'talking through' sobs, yawning, laughter, and so on. A large number of categories have been developed for dealing with them.

I have simply tried here to indicate briefly the state of our knowledge of paralinguistic phenomena at the present time. Their investigation has perhaps not made the progress it should in some directions, and this is for diverse reasons: because of the initial unfortunate separation of the visible and the audible components; because of over-categorization—too much taxonomy without enough to classify; and because linguists have left too much of the work to others. There is an urgent need for the comparative study, over as much of the world as possible, of the full range of paralinguistic phenomena—the kind of thing for which the linguistic field-worker is best fitted. Fact-finding, not theorizing, is what is wanted at this present juncture. True, fact-finding needs a theoretical framework within which to be conducted, but at this stage categories should be kept flexible, not allowed to proliferate, and regarded mainly as heuristic rather than explanatory. The difficulties—and the expense—of investigation should not, of course, be underrated. Talking films seem essential for obtaining data, and they would probably have to be clandestinely taken, 'candid camera' fashion, to be of real value, which raises difficult moral problems about invasion of privacy. There is also the problem of devising a notation adequate for a paralinguistic text parallel with the linguistic one.

At this point it is appropriate to ask, what sort of things are all these paralinguistic elements communicating in a conversational exchange? The answer sometimes given is that they are communicating attitudes and emotions, the linguistic side of the interchange being more 'referential'. But this is not really satisfactory. Paralinguistic elements are often clearly referential—many independent gestures, for instance, which can even be translated directly into words such as 'tomorrow', or 'money'. And on the other hand linguistic elements in a conversation may often communicate attitudes or emotions.

It seems to me a possible hypothesis, in the present state of our knowledge, that in all cultures conversation communicates more or less the same total of 'meaning' of all kinds—sense, feeling, tone, intention; or however one wants to divide up referential and emotive components. Where cultural groups differ, however, is in the way the total information is distributed over the linguistic and the paralinguistic elements of the conversation. For instance, Jules Henry reports that among the

Kaingang of Brazil concepts of degree and intensity are communicated by such things as changes in pitch, facial expression and bodily posture, though we communicate these things by formal linguistic devices. On the other hand in Dakota, an American Indian language, an emotional state such as annoyance, which with us would be communicated in conversation by facial expression or tone of voice, has formal linguistic expression by means of a particle added at the end of the sentence (of normal phonological structure, and therefore not an interjection).

Almost anything can be communicated linguistically, and almost anything paralinguistically. What is to be regarded as linguistic and what as paralinguistic depends not on the nature of what is communicated, but on how it is communicated—whether by formal systems and structures, in which case it is linguistic, or not, in which case it is paralinguistic.

7 J. L. AUSTIN
Speech Acts

LECTURE I

What I shall have to say here is neither difficult nor contentious; the only merit I should like to claim for it is that of being true, at least in parts. The phenomenon to be discussed is very widespread and obvious, and it cannot fail to have been already noticed, at least here and there, by others. Yet I have not found attention paid to it specifically.

It was for too long the assumption of philosophers that the business of a 'statement' can only be to 'describe' some state of affairs, or to 'state some fact', which it must do either truly or falsely. Grammarians, indeed, have regularly pointed out that not all 'sentences' are (used in making) statements:* there are, traditionally, besides (grammarians') statements, also questions and exclamations, and sentences expressing commands or wishes or concessions. And doubtless philosophers have not intended to deny this, despite some loose use of 'sentence' for 'statement'. Doubtless, too, both grammarians and philosophers have been aware that it is by no means easy to distinguish even questions, commands, and so on from statements by means of the few and jejune grammatical marks available, such as word order, mood, and the like: though perhaps it has not been usual to dwell on the difficulties which this fact obviously raises. For how do we decide which is which? What are the limits and definitions of each?

But now in recent years, many things which would once have been accepted without question as 'statements' by both philosophers and grammarians have been scrutinized with new care. This scrutiny arose

J. L. Austin: Extract from *How to do things with words*, Lecture I and Lecture XII, Oxford University Press, 1962, pp. 1–11 and 147–63.

* It is, of course, not really correct that a sentence ever *is* a statement: rather, it is *used* in *making a statement*, and the statement itself is a 'logical construction' out of the makings of statements. [Author's footnote.]

somewhat indirectly—at least in philosophy. First came the view, not always formulated without unfortunate dogmatism, that a statement (of fact) ought to be 'verifiable', and this led to the view that many 'statements' are only what may be called pseudo-statements. First and most obviously, many 'statements' were shown to be, as Kant perhaps first argued systematically, strictly nonsense, despite an unexceptionable grammatical form: and the continual discovery of fresh types of nonsense, unsystematic though their classification and mysterious though their explanation is too often allowed to remain, has done on the whole nothing but good. Yet we, that is, even philosophers, set some limits to the amount of nonsense that we are prepared to admit we talk: so that it was natural to go on to ask, as a second stage, whether many apparent pseudo-statements really set out to be 'statements' at all. It has come to be commonly held that many utterances which look like statements are either not intended at all, or only intended in part, to record or impart straightforward information about the facts: for example, 'ethical propositions' are perhaps intended, solely or partly, to evince emotion or to prescribe conduct or to influence it in special ways. Here too Kant was among the pioneers. We very often also use utterances in ways beyond the scope at least of traditional grammar. It has come to be seen that many specially perplexing words embedded in apparently descriptive statements do not serve to indicate some specially odd additional feature in the reality reported, but to indicate (not to report) the circumstances in which the statement is made or reservations to which it is subject or the way in which it is to be taken and the like. To overlook these possibilities in the way once common is called the 'descriptive' fallacy; but perhaps this is not a good name, as 'descriptive' itself is special. Not all true or false statements are descriptions, and for this reason I prefer to use the word 'Constative'. Along these lines it has by now been shown piecemeal, or at least made to look likely, that many traditional philosophical perplexities have arisen through a mistake—the mistake of taking as straightforward statements of fact utterances which are *either* (in interesting non-grammatical ways) nonsensical *or else* intended as something quite different.

Whatever we may think of any particular one of these views and suggestions, and however much we may deplore the initial confusion into which philosophical doctrine and method have been plunged, it cannot be doubted that they are producing a revolution in philosophy. If anyone wishes to call it the greatest and most salutary in its history, this is not, if you come to think of it, a large claim. It is not surprising that beginnings have been piecemeal, with *parti pris*, and for extraneous aims; this is common with revolutions.

Preliminary isolation of the performative*

The type of utterance we are to consider here is not, of course, in general a type of nonsense; though misuse of it can, as we shall see, engender rather special varieties of 'nonsense'. Rather, it is one of our second class—the masqueraders. But it does not by any means necessarily masquerade as a statement of fact, descriptive or constative. Yet it does quite commonly do so, and that, oddly enough, when it assumes its most explicit form. Grammarians have not, I believe, seen through this 'disguise', and philosophers only at best incidentally. It will be convenient, therefore, to study it first in this misleading form, in order to bring out its characteristics by contrasting them with those of the statement of fact which it apes.

We shall take, then, for our first examples some utterances which can fall into no hitherto recognized *grammatical* category save that of 'statement', which are not nonsense, and which contain none of those verbal danger-signals which philosophers have by now detected or think they have detected (curious words like 'good' or 'all', suspect auxiliaries like 'ought' or 'can', and dubious constructions like the hypothetical): all will have, as it happens, humdrum verbs in the first person singular present indicative active. Utterances can be found, satisfying these conditions, yet such that

A they do not 'describe' or 'report' or constate anything at all, are not 'true or false'; and

B the uttering of the sentence is, or is a part of, the doing of an action, which again would not *normally* be described as saying something.

This is far from being as paradoxical as it may sound or as I have meanly been trying to make it sound: indeed, the examples now to be given will be disappointing.

Examples:

(E. *a*) 'I do (sc. take this woman to be my lawful wedded wife)'—as uttered in the course of the marriage ceremony.

(E. *b*) 'I name this ship the *Queen Elizabeth*'—as uttered when smashing the bottle against the stem.

(E. *c*) 'I give and bequeath my watch to my brother'—as occurring in a will.

(E. *d*) 'I bet you sixpence it will rain tomorrow'.

In these examples it seems clear that to utter the sentence (in, of course, the appropriate circumstances) is not to *describe* my doing of what I should be said in so uttering to be doing or to state that I am doing it:

* Everything said in these sections is provisional, and subject to revision in the light of later sections. [Author's footnote.]

it is to do it. None of the utterances cited is either true or false: I assert this as obvious and do not argue it. It needs argument no more than that 'damn' is not true or false: it may be that the utterance 'serves to inform you'—but that is quite different. To name the ship *is* to say (in the appropriate circumstances) the words 'I name, etc.'. When I say, before the registrar or altar, etc., 'I do', I am not reporting on a marriage: I am indulging in it.

What are we to call a sentence or an utterance of this type? I propose to call it a *performative sentence* or a performative utterance, or, for short, 'a performative'. The term 'performative' will be used in a variety of cognate ways and constructions, much as the term 'imperative' is. The name is derived, of course, from 'perform', the usual verb with the noun 'action': it indicates that the issuing of the utterance is the performing of an action—it is not normally thought of as just saying something.

A number of other terms may suggest themselves, each of which would suitably cover this or that wider or narrower class of performatives: for example, many performatives are *contractual* ('I bet') or *declaratory* ('I declare war') utterances. But no term in current use that I know of is nearly wide enough to cover them all. One technical term that comes nearest to what we need is perhaps 'operative', as it is used strictly by lawyers in referring to that part, i.e. those clauses, of an instrument which serves to effect the transaction (conveyance or what not) which is its main object, whereas the rest of the document merely 'recites' the circumstances in which the transaction is to be effected. But 'operative' has other meanings, and indeed is often used nowadays to mean little more than 'important'. I have preferred a new word, to which, though its etymology is not irrelevant, we shall perhaps not be so ready to attach some preconceived meaning.

Can saying make it so?

Are we then to say things like this:

'To marry is to say a few words', or
'Betting is simply saying something'?

Such a doctrine sounds odd or even flippant at first, but with sufficient safeguards it may become not odd at all.

A sound initial objection to them may be this; and it is not without some importance. In very many cases it is possible to perform an act of exactly the same kind *not* by uttering words, whether written or spoken, but in some other way. For example, I may in some places effect marriage by cohabiting, or I may bet with a totalisator machine by putting a coin in a slot. We should then, perhaps, convert the propositions above, and put it that 'to say a few certain words is to marry' or 'to marry is, in some cases, simply to say a few words' or 'simply to say a certain something is to bet'.

But probably the real reason why such remarks sound dangerous lies in another obvious fact, to which we shall have to revert in detail later, which is this. The uttering of the words is, indeed, usually a, or even *the*, leading incident in the performance of the act (of betting or what not), the performance of which is also the object of the utterance, but it is far from being usually, even if it is ever, the *sole* thing necessary if the act is to be deemed to have been performed. Speaking generally, it is always necessary that the *circumstances* in which the words are uttered should be in some way, or ways, *appropriate*, and it is very commonly necessary that either the speaker himself or other persons should *also* perform certain *other* actions, whether 'physical' or 'mental' actions or even acts of uttering further words. Thus, for naming the ship, it is essential that I should be the person appointed to name her, for (Christian) marrying, it is essential that I should not be already married with a wife living, sane and undivorced, and so on: for a bet to have been made, it is generally necessary for the offer of the bet to have been accepted by a taker (who must have done something, such as to say 'Done'), and it is hardly a gift if I *say* 'I give it you' but never hand it over.

So far, well and good. The action may be performed in ways other than by a performative utterance, and in any case the circumstances, including other actions, must be appropriate. But we may, in objecting, have something totally different, and this time quite mistaken, in mind, especially when we think of some of the more awe-inspiring performatives such as 'I promise to . . .'. Surely the words must be spoken 'seriously' and so as to be taken 'seriously'? This is, though vague, true enough in general—it is an important commonplace in discussing the purport of any utterance whatsoever. I must not be joking, for example, nor writing a poem. But we are apt to have a feeling that their being serious consists in their being uttered as (merely) the outward and visible sign, for convenience or other record or for information, of an inward and spiritual act: from which it is but a short step to go on to believe or to assume without realizing that for many purposes the outward utterance is a description, *true or false*, of the occurrence of the inward performance. The classic expression of this idea is to be found in the *Hippolytus* (l. 612), where Hippolytus says

ἡ γλῶσσ' ὀμώμοχ' ἡ δὲ φρὴν ἀνώμοτός,

i.e. 'my tongue swore to, but my heart (or mind or other backstage artiste) did not'. Thus, 'I promise to . . .' obliges me—puts on record my spiritual assumption of a spiritual shackle.

It is gratifying to observe in this very example how excess of profundity, or rather solemnity, at once paves the way for immorality. For one who says 'promising is not merely a matter of uttering words! It is an inward and spiritual act!' is apt to appear as a solid moralist standing out against a generation of superficial theorizers: we see him as he sees himself, surveying the invisible depths of ethical space, with all the distinction of a specialist in the *sui generis*. Yet he provides Hippolytus with a let-out, the bigamist with an excuse for his 'I do' and the welsher with a defence for his 'I bet'. Accuracy and morality alike are on the side of the plain saying that *our word is our bond*.

If we exclude such fictitious inward acts as this, can we suppose that any of the other things which certainly are normally required to accompany an utterance such as 'I promise that . . .' or 'I do (take this woman . . .)' are in fact described by it, and consequently do by their presence make it true or by their absence make it false? Well, taking the latter first, we shall next consider what we actually do say about the utterance concerned when one or another of its normal concomitants is *absent*. In no case do we say that the utterance was false but rather that the utterance —or rather the *act*, e.g. the promise—was void, or given in bad faith, or not implemented, or the like. In the particular case of promising, as with many other performatives, it is appropriate that the person uttering the promise should have a certain intention, viz. here to keep his word: and perhaps of all concomitants this looks the most suitable to be that which 'I promise' does describe or record. Do we not actually, when such intention is absent, speak of a 'false' promise? Yet so to speak is *not* to say that the utterance 'I promise that . . .' is false, in the sense that though he states that he does, he doesn't, or that though he describes he misdescribes—misreports. For he *does* promise: the promise here is not even *void*, though it is given *in bad faith*. His utterance is perhaps misleading, probably deceitful and doubtless wrong, but it is not a lie or a misstatement. At most we might make out a case for saying that it implies or insinuates a falsehood or a mis-statement (to the effect that he does intend to do something): but that is a very different matter. Moreover, we do not speak of a false bet or a false christening; and that we *do* speak of a false promise need commit us no more than the fact that we speak of a false move. 'False' is not necessarily used of statements only.

LECTURE XII

We have left numerous loose ends, but after a brief résumé we must plough ahead. How did the 'constatives'–'performatives' distinction look in the light of our later theory? In general and for all utterances that we have considered (except perhaps for swearing), we have found:

1   Happiness/unhappiness dimension,

1*a* An illocutionary force,

2   Truth/falsehood dimension,

2*a* A locutionary meaning (sense and reference).

The doctrine of the performative/constative distinction stands to the doctrine of locutionary and illocutionary acts in the total speech act as the *special* theory to the *general* theory. And the need for the general theory arises simply because the traditional 'statement' is an abstraction, an ideal, and so is its traditional truth or falsity. But on this point I could do no more than explode a few hopeful fireworks. In particular, the following morals are among those I wanted to suggest:

A The total speech act in the total speech situation is the *only actual* phenomenon which, in the last resort, we are engaged in elucidating.

B Stating, describing, etc., are *just two* names among a very great many others for illocutionary acts; they have no unique position.

C In particular, they have no unique position over the matter of being related to facts in a unique way called being true or false, because truth and falsity are (except by an artificial abstraction which is always possible and legitimate for certain purposes) not names for relations, qualities, or what not, but for a dimension of assessment —how the words stand in respect of satisfactoriness to the facts, events, situations, etc., to which they refer.

D By the same token, the familiar contrast of 'normative or evaluative' as opposed to the factual is in need, like so many dichotomies, of elimination.

E We may well suspect that the theory of 'meaning' as equivalent to 'sense and reference' will certainly require some weeding-out and reformulating in terms of the distinction between locutionary and illocutionary acts (*if this distinction is sound*: it is only adumbrated here). I admit that not enough has been done here: I have taken the old 'sense and reference' on the strength of current views; I would also stress that I have omitted any direct consideration of the illocutionary force of statements.

Now we said that there was one further thing obviously requiring to be done, which is a matter of prolonged fieldwork. We said long ago that we needed a list of 'explicit performative verbs'; but in the light of the more general theory we now see that what we need is a list of *illocutionary forces* of an utterance. The old distinction, however, between *primary* and *explicit* performatives will survive the sea-change from the performative/constative distinction to the theory of speech-acts quite successfully. For we have since seen reason to suppose that the sorts of test suggested for the explicit performative verbs ('to say . . . is to . . .', etc.) will do, and in fact do better for sorting out those verbs which make explicit, as we shall now say, the illocutionary force of an utterance, or what illocutionary act it is that we are performing in issuing that utterance. What will *not* survive the transition, unless perhaps as a marginal limiting case, and hardly surprisingly because it gave trouble from the start, is the notion of the purity of performatives: this was essentially based upon a belief in the dichotomy of performatives and constatives, which we see has to be abandoned in favour of more general *families* of related and overlapping speech acts, which are just what we have now to attempt to classify.

Using then the simple test (with caution) of the first person singular present indicative active form, and going through the dictionary (a concise one should do) in a liberal spirit, we get a list of verbs of the order of the third power of 10. I said I would attempt some general preliminary classification and make some remarks on these proposed classes. Well, here we go. I shall only give you a run around, or rather a flounder around.

I distinguish five more general classes: but I am far from equally happy about all of them. They are, however, quite enough to play Old Harry with two fetishes which I admit to an inclination to play Old Harry with, viz. (1) the true/false fetish, (2) the value/fact fetish. I call then these classes of utterance, classified according to their illocutionary force, by the following more-or-less rebarbative names:

1 Verdictives.
2 Exercitives.
3 Commissives.
4 Behabitives (a shocker this).
5 Expositives.

We shall take them in order, but first I will give a rough idea of each.

The first, verdictives, are typified by the giving of a verdict, as the name implies, by a jury, arbitrator, or umpire. But they need not be final; they may be, for example, an estimate, reckoning, or appraisal. It is essentially giving a finding as to something—fact, or value—which is for different reasons hard to be certain about.

The second, exercitives, are the exercising of powers, rights, or influence. Examples are appointing, voting, ordering, urging, advising, warning, etc.

The third, commissives, are typified by promising or otherwise undertaking; they *commit* you to doing something, but include also declarations or announcements of intention, which are not promises, and also rather vague things which we may call espousals, as for example, siding with. They have obvious connexions with verdictives and exercitives.

The fourth, behabitives, are a very miscellaneous group, and have to do with attitudes and *social behaviour*. Examples are apologizing, congratulating, commending, condoling, cursing, and challenging.

The fifth, expositives, are difficult to define. They make plain how our utterances fit into the course of an argument or conversation, how we are using words, or, in general, are expository. Examples are 'I reply', 'I argue', 'I concede', 'I illustrate', 'I assume', 'I postulate'. We should be clear from the start that there are still wide possibilities of marginal or awkward cases, or of overlaps.

The last two classes are those which I find most troublesome, and it could well be that they are not clear or are cross-classified, or even that some fresh classification altogether is needed. I am not putting any of this forward as in the very least definitive. Behabitives are troublesome because they seem too miscellaneous altogether: and expositives because they are enormously numerous and important, and seem both to be included in the other classes and at the same time to be unique in a way that I have not succeeded in making clear even to myself. It could well be said that all aspects are present in all my classes.

1 Verdictives

Examples are:

acquit	convict	find (as a matter of fact)
hold (as a matter of law)	interpret as	understand
read it as	rule	calculate
reckon	estimate	locate
place	date	measure
put it at	make it	take it
grade	rank	rate
assess	value	describe
characterize	diagnose	analyse

Further examples are found in appraisals or assessments of character, such as 'I should call him industrious'.

Verdictives consist in the delivering of a finding, official or unofficial, upon evidence or reasons as to value or fact, so far as these are distinguishable. A verdictive is a judicial act as distinct from legislative or executive acts, which are both exercitives. But some judicial acts, in the wider sense that they are done by judges instead of for example, juries, really are exercitive. Verdictives have obvious connexions with truth and falsity as regards soundness and unsoundness or fairness and unfairness. That the content of a verdict is true or false is shown, for example, in a dipute over an umpire's calling 'Out', 'Three strikes', or 'Four balls'.

Comparison with exercitives

As official acts, a judge's ruling makes law; a jury's finding makes a convicted felon; an umpire's giving the batsman out, or calling a fault or a no-ball, makes the batsman out, the service a fault, or the ball a no-ball. It is done in virtue of an official position: but it still purports to be correct or incorrect, right or wrong, justifiable or unjustifiable on the evidence. It is not made as a decision in favour or against. The judicial act is, if you like, executive, but we must distinguish the executive utterance, 'You shall have it', from the verdict, 'It is yours', and must similarly distinguish the assessing from the awarding of damages.

Comparison with commissives

Verdictives have an effect, in the law, on ourselves and on others. The giving of a verdict or an estimate does, for example, commit us to certain future conduct, in the sense that any speech-act does and perhaps more so, at least to consistency, and maybe we know to what it will commit us. Thus to give a certain verdict will commit us or, as we say, commits us, to awarding damages. Also, by an interpretation of the facts we may commit ourselves to a certain verdict or estimate. To give a verdict may very well be to espouse also; it may commit us to standing up for someone, defending him, etc.

Comparison with behabitives

To congratulate may imply a verdict about value or character. Again, in one sense of 'blame' which is equivalent to 'hold responsible', to blame is a verdictive, but in another sense it is to adopt an attitude towards a person and is thus a behabitive.

Comparison with expositives

When I say 'I interpret', 'I analyse', 'I describe', 'I characterize', this, in a way, is to give a verdict, but is essentially connected with verbal matters and clarifying our exposition. 'I call you out' must be distinguished from 'I call that "out" '; the first is a verdict *given* the use of words, like 'I should describe that as cowardly'; the second is a verdict *about* the use of words, as 'I should describe that as "cowardly" '.

2 Exercitives

An exercitive is the giving of a decision in favour of or against a certain course of action, or advocacy of it. It is a decision that something is to be so, as distinct from a judgement that it is so: it is advocacy that it should be so, as opposed to an estimate that it is so; it is an award as opposed to an assessment; it is a sentence as opposed to a verdict. Arbitrators and judges make use of exercitives as well as issuing verdictives. Its consequences may be that others are 'compelled' or 'allowed' or 'not allowed' to do certain acts.

It is a very wide class; examples are:

appoint	degrade	demote
dismiss	excommunicate	name
order	command	direct
sentence	fine	grant
levy	vote for	nominate
choose	claim	give
bequeath	pardon	resign
warn	advise	plead
pray	entreat	beg
urge	press	recommend
proclaim	announce	quash
countermand	annul	repeal
enact	reprieve	veto
dedicate	declare closed	declare open

Comparison with verdictives

'I hold', 'I interpret', and the like, may, if official, be exercitive acts. Furthermore, 'I award' and 'I absolve' are exercitives, which will be based on verdicts.

Comparison with commissives

Many exercitives such as *permit, authorize, depute, offer, concede, give, sanction, stake*, and *consent* do in fact commit one to a course of action. If I say 'I declare war' or 'I disown', the whole purpose of my act is to commit me personally to a certain course of action. The connexion between an exercitive and committing oneself is as close as that between meaning and implication. It is obvious that appointing and naming do commit us, but we would rather say that they confer powers, rights, names, etc., or change or eliminate them.

Comparison with behabitives

Such exercitives as 'I challenge', 'I protest', 'I approve', are closely connected with behabitives. Challenging, protesting, approving, commending, and recommending, may be the taking up of an attitude or the performing of an act.

Comparison with expositives

Such exercitives as 'I withdraw', 'I demur', and 'I object', in the context of argument or conversation, have much the same force as expositives.

Typical contexts in which exercitives are used are in:

1 filling offices and appointments, candidatures, elections, admissions, resignations, dismissals, and applications.
2 advice, exhortation, and petition,
3 enablements, orders, sentences, and annulments,
4 the conduct of meetings and business,
5 rights, claims, accusations, etc.

3 Commissives

The whole point of a commissive is to commit the speaker to a certain course of action. Examples are:

promise	covenant	contract
undertake	bind myself	give my word
am determined to	intend	declare my intention
mean to	plan	purpose
propose to	shall	contemplate
envisage	engage	swear
guarantee	pledge myself	bet
vow	agree	consent
dedicate myself to	declare for	side with
adopt	champion	embrace
espouse	oppose	favour

Declarations of intention differ from undertakings, and it might be questioned whether they should be classed together. As we have a distinction between urging and ordering, so we have a distinction between intending and promising. But both are covered by the primary performative 'shall'; thus we have the locutions 'shall probably', 'shall do my best to', 'shall very likely', and 'promise that I shall probably'.

There is also a slide towards 'descriptives'. At the one extreme I may *just* state that I have an intention, but I may also declare or express or announce my intention or determination. 'I declare my intention' undoubtedly does commit me; and to say 'I intend' is generally to declare or announce. The same thing happens with espousals, as, for example, in 'I dedicate my life to . . .'. In the case of commissives like 'favour', 'oppose', 'adopt the view', 'take the view', and 'embrace', you cannot state that you favour, oppose, etc., generally, without announcing that you do so. To say 'I favour X' may, according to context, be to *vote* for X, to *espouse* X, or to *applaud* X.

Comparison with verdictives
Verdictives commit us to actions in two ways:

   a to those necessary for consistency with and support of our verdict,
   b to those that may be, or may be involved in, the consequences of a
      verdict.

Comparison with exercitives
Exercitives commit us to the consequences of an act, for example of
naming. In the special case of permissives we might ask whether they
should be classified as exercitives or as commissives.

Comparison with behabitives
Reactions such as resenting, applauding, and commending do involve
espousing and committing ourselves in the way that advice and choice do.
But behabitives commit us to *like* conduct, by implication, and not to
that actual conduct. Thus if I blame, I adopt an attitude to someone
else's past conduct, but can commit myself only to avoiding like conduct.

Comparison with expositives
Swearing, promising, and guaranteeing that something is the case work
like expositives. Calling, defining, analysing, and assuming form one
group, and supporting, agreeing, disagreeing, maintaining, and defending
form another group of illocutions which seem to be both expositive and
commissive.

4 Behabitives
Behabitives include the notion of reaction to other people's behaviour
and fortunes and of attitudes and expressions of attitudes to someone
else's past conduct or imminent conduct. There are obvious connexions
with both stating or describing what our feelings are and expressing, in
the sense of venting our feelings, though behabitives are distinct from
both of these.

   Examples are:

   1 For apologies we have 'apologize'.
   2 For thanks we have 'thank'.
   3 For sympathy we have 'deplore', 'commiserate', 'compliment',
     'condole', 'congratulate', 'felicitate', 'sympathize'.
   4 For attitudes we have 'resent', 'don't mind', 'pay tribute', 'criticize',
     'grumble about', 'complain of', 'applaud', 'overlook', 'commend',
     'deprecate', and the non-exercitive uses of 'blame', 'approve', and
     'favour'.

5 For greetings we have 'welcome', 'bid you farewell'.

6 For wishes we have 'bless', 'curse', 'toast', 'drink to', and 'wish' (in its strict performative use).

7 For challenges we have 'dare', 'defy', 'protest', 'challenge'.

In the field of behabitives, besides the usual liability to infelicities, there is a special scope for insincerity.

There are obvious connexions with commissives, for to commend or to support is both to react to behaviour and to commit oneself to a line of conduct. There is also a close connexion with exercitives, for to approve may be an exercise of authority or a reaction to behaviour. Other border line examples are 'recommend', 'overlook', 'protest', 'entreat', and 'challenge'.

5 Expositives

Expositives are used in acts of exposition involving the expounding of views, the conducting of arguments, and the clarifying of usages and of references. We have said repeatedly that we may dispute as to whether these are not verdictive, exercitive, behabitive, or commissive acts as well; we may also dispute whether they are not straight descriptions of our feelings, practice, etc., especially sometimes over matters of suiting the action to the words, as when I say 'I turn next to', 'I quote', 'I cite', 'I recapitulate', 'I repeat that', 'I mention that'.

Examples which may well be taken as verdictive are: 'analyse', 'class', 'interpret', which involve exercise of judgement. Examples which may well be taken as exercitive are: 'concede', 'urge', 'argue', 'insist', which involve exertion of influence or exercise of powers. Examples which may well be taken as commissive are: 'define', 'agree', 'accept', 'maintain', 'support', 'testify', 'swear', which involve assuming an obligation. Examples which may well be taken as behabitive are: 'demur', 'boggle at', which involve adopting an attitude or expressing a feeling.

For good value, I shall give you some lists to indicate the extent of the field. Most central are such examples as 'state', 'affirm', 'deny', 'emphasize', 'illustrate', 'answer'. An enormous number, such as 'question', 'ask', 'deny', etc., seem naturally to refer to conversational interchange: but this is no longer necessarily so, and all, of course, have reference to the communicational situation.

Here then is a list of expositives:

1	affirm	describe
	deny	class
	state	identify

2   remark
     mention
     ? interpose

3   inform
     apprise
     tell
     answer
     rejoin
3a   ask

4   testify
     report
     swear
     conjecture
     ? doubt
     ? know
     ? believe

5   accept
     concede
     withdraw
     agree
     demur to
     object to
     adhere to

     recognize
     repudiate
5a   correct
     revise

6   postulate
     deduce
     argue
     neglect
     ? emphasize

7   begin by
     turn to
     conclude by
7a   interpret
     distinguish
     analyse
     define
7b   illustrate
     explain
     formulate
7c   mean
     refer
     call
     understand
     regard as

To sum up, we may say that the verdictive is an exercise of judgement, the exercitive is an assertion of influence or exercising of power, the commissive is an assuming of an obligation or declaring of an intention, the behabitive is the adopting of an attitude, and the expositive is the clarifying of reasons, arguments, and communications.

I have as usual failed to leave enough time in which to say why what I have said is interesting. Just one example then. Philosophers have long been interested in the word 'good' and, quite recently, have begun to take the line of considering how we use it, what we use it to do. It has been suggested, for example, that we use it for expressing approval, for commending, or for grading. But we shall not get really clear about this word 'good' and what we use it to do until, ideally, we have a complete list of those illocutionary acts of which commending, grading, etc., are isolated specimens—until we know how many such acts there are and what are their relationships and inter-connexions. Here, then, is an instance of one possible application of the kind of general theory we have been considering; no doubt there are many others. I have purposely not embroiled the general theory with philosophical problems (some of which are complex enough almost to merit their celebrity); this should not be taken to mean that I am unaware of them. Of course, this is bound to be a little boring and dry to listen to and digest; not nearly so much so as to think and write. The real fun comes when we begin to apply it to philosophy.

In these lectures, then, I have been doing two things which I do not altogether like doing. These are:

1 producing a programme, that is, saying what ought to be done rather than doing something;

2 lecturing.

However, as against 1, I should very much like to think that I have been sorting out a bit the way things have already begun to go and are going with increasing momentum in some parts of philosophy, rather than proclaiming an individual manifesto. And as against 2, I should certainly like to say that nowhere could, to me, be a nicer place to lecture in than Harvard.

8 Functions of Language

ROMAN JAKOBSON

Language must be investigated in all the variety of its functions. Before discussing the poetic function we must define its place among the other functions of language. An outline of these functions demands a concise survey of the constitutive factors in any speech event, in any act of verbal communication. The ADDRESSER sends a MESSAGE to the ADDRESSEE. To be operative the message requires a CONTEXT referred to ('referent' in another, somewhat ambiguous, nomenclature), seizable by the addressee, and either verbal or capable of being verbalized; a CODE fully, or at least partially, common to the addresser and addressee (or in other words, to the encoder and decoder of the message); and, finally, a CONTACT, a physical channel and psychological connexion between the addresser and the addressee, enabling both of them to enter and stay in communication. All these factors inalienably involved in verbal communication may be schematized as follows:

CONTEXT

MESSAGE

ADDRESSER --- ADDRESSEE

CONTACT

CODE

Each of these six factors determines a different function of language. Although we distinguish six basic aspects of language, we could, however, hardly find verbal messages that would fulfill only one function. The diversity lies not in a monopoly of some one of these several functions but in a different hierarchical order of functions. The verbal structure of a message depends primarily on the predominant function. But even though a set (*Einstellung*) toward the referent, an orientation toward the CONTEXT —briefly the so-called REFERENTIAL, 'denotative', 'cognitive' function—is

R. Jakobson: Extract from 'Linguistics and Poetics' in *Style and Language*, editor Thomas A. Sebeok, M.I.T. Press, 1960, pp. 353–7.

the leading task of numerous messages, the accessory participation of the other functions in such messages must be taken into account by the observant linguist.

The so-called EMOTIVE or 'expressive' function, focused on the ADDRESSER, aims a direct expression of the speaker's attitude toward what he is speaking about. It tends to produce an impression of a certain emotion whether true or feigned; therefore, the term 'emotive', launched and advocated by Marty has proved to be preferable to 'emotional'. The purely emotive stratum in language is presented by the interjections. They differ from the means of referential language both by their sound pattern (peculiar sound sequences or even sounds elsewhere unusual) and by their syntactic role (they are not components but equivalents of sentences). '*Tut! Tut!* said McGinty': the complete utterance of Conan Doyle's character consists of two suction clicks. The emotive function, laid bare in the interjections, flavours to some extent all our utterances, on their phonic, grammatical, and lexical level. If we analyse language from the standpoint of the information it carries, we cannot restrict the notion of information to the cognitive aspect of language. A man, using expressive features to indicate his angry or ironic attitude, conveys ostensible information, and evidently this verbal behaviour cannot be likened to such nonsemiotic, nutritive activities as 'eating grapefruit' (despite Chatman's bold simile). The difference between [big] and the emphatic prolongation of the vowel [bi: g] is a conventional, coded linguistic feature like the difference between the short and long vowel in such Czech pairs as [vi] 'you' and [vi:] 'knows', but in the latter pair the differential information is phonemic and in the former emotive. As long as we are interested in phonemic invariants, the English /i/ and /i:/ appear to be mere variants of one and the same phoneme, but if we are concerned with emotive units, the relation between the invariant and variants is reversed: length and shortness are invariants implemented by variable phonemes. Saporta's surmise that emotive difference is a non-linguistic feature, 'attributable to the delivery of the message and not to the message', arbitrarily reduces the informational capacity of messages.

A former actor of Stanislavskij's Moscow Theatre told me how at his audition he was asked by the famous director to make forty different messages from the phrase *Segodnja večerom* 'This evening', by diversifying its expressive tint. He made a list of some forty emotional situations, then emitted the given phrase in accordance with each of these situations, which his audience had to recognize only from the changes in the sound shape of the same two words. For our research work in the description and analysis of contemporary Standard Russian (under the auspices of the Rockefeller Foundation) this actor was asked to repeat Stanislavskij's test. He wrote down some fifty situations framing the same elliptic sentence and made of it fifty corresponding messages for a tape record. Most of the messages were correctly and circumstantially decoded by Moscovite listeners. May I add that all such emotive cues easily undergo linguistic analysis.

Orientation toward the ADDRESSEE, the CONATIVE function, finds its purest grammatical expression in the vocative and imperative, which syntactically, morphologically, and often even phonemically deviate from other nominal and verbal categories. The imperative sentences cardinally differ from declarative sentences: the latter are and the former are not liable to a truth test. When in O'Neill's play *The Fountain*, Nano, '(in a fierce tone of command)', says 'Drink!'—the imperative cannot be challenged by the question 'is it true or not?' which may be, however, perfectly well asked after such sentences as 'one drank', 'one will drink', 'one would drink'. In contradistinction to the imperative sentences, the declarative sentences are convertible into interrogative sentences: 'did one drink?' 'will one drink?' 'would one drink?'

The traditional model of language as elucidated particularly by Bühler was confined to these three functions—emotive, conative, and referential —and the three apexes of this model—the first person of the addresser, the second person of the addressee, and the 'third person', properly —someone or something spoken of. Certain additional verbal functions can be easily inferred from this triadic model. Thus the magic, incantatory function is chiefly some kind of conversion of an absent or inanimate 'third person' into an addressee of a conative message. 'May this sty dry up, *tfu, tfu, tfu, tfu*' (Lithuanian spell). 'Water, queen river, daybreak! Send grief beyond the blue sea, to the sea-bottom, like a grey stone never to rise from the sea-bottom, may grief never come to burden the light heart of God's servant, may grief be removed and sink away'. (North Russian incantation.) 'Sun, stand thou still upon Gibeon; and thou, Moon, in the valley of Aj-a-lon. And the sun stood still, and the moon stayed ...' (Josh. 10.12). We observe, however, three further constitutive factors of verbal communication and three corresponding functions of language.

There are messages primarily serving to establish, to prolong, or to discontinue communication, to check whether the channel works ('Hello, do you hear me?'), to attract the attention of the interlocutor or to confirm his continued attention ('Are you listening?' or in Shakespearean diction, 'Lend me your ears!'—and on the other end of the wire 'Um-hum!'). This set for CONTACT, or in Malinowski's terms PHATIC function, may be displayed by a profuse exchange of ritualized formulas, by entire dialogues with the mere purport of prolonging communication. Dorothy Parker caught eloquent examples: ' "Well!" the young man said. "Well!" she said. "Well, here we are," he said. "Here we are," she said, "Aren't we?" "I should say we were," he said, "Eeyop! Here we are." "Well!" she said. "Well!" he said, "well." ' The endeavour to start and sustain communication is typical of talking birds; thus the phatic function of language is the only one they share with human beings. It is also the first verbal function acquired by infants; they are prone to communicate before being able to send or receive informative communication.

A distinction has been made in modern logic between two levels of language, 'object language' speaking of objects and 'metalanguage' speaking of language. But metalanguage is not only a necessary scientific tool utilized by logicians and linguists; it plays also an important role in our everyday language. Like Molière's Jourdain who used prose without knowing it, we practice metalanguage without realizing the metalingual character of our operations. Whenever the addresser and/or the addressee need to check up whether they use the same code, speech is focused on the CODE: it performs a METALINGUAL (i.e. glossing) function. 'I don't follow you—what do you mean?' asks the addressee, or in Shakespearean diction, 'What is't thou say'st?' And the addresser in anticipation of such recapturing questions inquires: 'Do you know what I mean?' Imagine such an exasperating dialogue: 'The sophomore was plucked.' 'But what is *plucked*?' '*Plucked* means the same as *flunked*'. 'And *flunked*?' '*To be flunked* is *to fail in an exam*'. 'And what is *sophomore*?' persists the interrogator innocent of school vocabulary. '*A sophomore* is (or means) a *second-year student*'. All these equational sentences convey information merely about the lexical code of English; their function is strictly metalingual. Any process of language learning, in particular child acquisition of the mother tongue, makes wide use of such metalingual operations; and aphasia may often be defined as a loss of ability for metalingual operations.

We have brought up all the six factors involved in verbal communication except the message itself. The set (*Einstellung*) toward the MESSAGE as such, focus on the message for its own sake, is the POETIC function of language. This function cannot be productively studied out of touch with the general problems of language, and, on the other hand, the scrutiny of language requires a thorough consideration of its poetic function. Any attempt to reduce the sphere of poetic function to poetry or to confine poetry to poetic function would be a delusive oversimplification. Poetic function is not the sole function of verbal art but only its dominant, determining function, whereas in all other verbal activities it acts as a subsidiary, accessory constituent. This function, by promoting the palpability of signs, deepens the fundamental dichotomy of signs and objects. Hence, when dealing with poetic function, linguistics cannot limit itself to the field of poetry.

'Why do you always say *Joan and Margery*, yet never *Margery and*

Joan? Do you prefer Joan to her twin sister?' 'Not at all, it just sounds smoother'. In a sequence of two co-ordinate names, as far as no rank problems interfere, the precedence of the shorter name suits the speaker, unaccountably for him, as a well-ordered shape of the message.

A girl used to talk about 'the horrible Harry'. 'Why horrible?' 'Because I hate him'. 'But why not *dreadful, terrible, frightful, disgusting?*' 'I don't know why, but *horrible* fits him better'. Without realizing it, she clung to the poetic device of paronomasia.

The political slogan 'I like Ike' /ay layk ayk/, succinctly structured, consists of three monosyllables and counts three dipthongs /ay/, each of them symmetrically followed by one consonantal phoneme, /..l..k..k/. The make-up of the three words presents a variation: no consonantal phonemes in the first, two around the diphthong in the second, and one final consonant in the third. A similar dominant nucleus /ay/ was noticed by Hymes in some of the sonnets of Keats. Both cola of the trisyllabic formula 'I like/Ike' rhyme with each other, and the second of the two rhyming words is fully included in the first one (echo rhyme). /layk/— /ayk/, a paronomastic image of a feeling which totally envelops its object. Both cola alliterate with each other, and the first of the two alliterating words is included in the second: /ay/—/ayk/, a paronomastic image of the loving subject enveloped by the beloved object. The secondary, poetic function of this electional catch phrase reinforces its impressiveness and efficacy.

As we said, the linguistic study of the poetic function must overstep the limits of poetry, and, on the other hand, the linguistic scrutiny of poetry cannot limit itself to the poetic function. The particularities of diverse poetic genres imply a differently ranked participation of the other verbal functions along with the dominant poetic function. Epic poetry, focused on the third person, strongly involves the referential function of language; the lyric, oriented toward the first person, is intimately linked with the emotive function; poetry of the second person is imbued with the conative function and is either supplicatory or exhortative, depending on whether the first person is subordinated to the second one or the second to the first.

Now that our cursory description of the six basic functions of verbal communication is more or less complete, we may complement our scheme of the fundamental factors by a corresponding scheme of the functions:

REFERENTIAL

EMOTIVE   POETIC   CONATIVE
                     PHATIC

          METALINGUAL

9 M. A. K. HALLIDAY
'A rich and adaptable instrument'

The teacher of English who, when seeking an adequate definition of language to guide him in his work, meets with a cautious 'well, it depends on how you look at it' is likely to share the natural impatience felt by anyone who finds himself unable to elicit 'a straight answer to a straight question'. But the very frequency of this complaint may suggest that, perhaps, questions are seldom as straight as they seem. The question 'what is language?', in whatever guise it appears, is as diffuse and, at times, disingenuous as other formulations of its kind, for example 'what is literature?' Such questions, which are wisely excluded from examinations, demand the privilege of a qualified and perhaps circuitous answer.

In a sense the only satisfactory response is 'why do you want to know?', since unless we know what lies beneath the question we cannot hope to answer it in a way which will suit the questioner. Is he interested in language planning in multilingual communities? Or in aphasia and language disorders? Or in words and their histories? Or in dialects and those who speak them? Or in how one language differs from another? Or in the formal properties of language as a system? Or in the functions of language and the demands that we make on it? Or in language as an art medium? Or in the information and redundancy of writing systems? Each one of these and other such questions is a possible context for a definition of language. In each case language 'is' something different.

The criterion is one of relevance; we want to understand, and to highlight, those facets of language which bear on the investigation or the task in hand. In an educational context the problem for linguistics is to elaborate some account of language that is relevant to the work of the English teacher. What constitutes a relevant notion of language from his point of view, and by what criteria can this be decided? Much of what has recently been objected to, among the attitudes and approaches to language that are current in the profession, arouses criticism not so

M. A. K. Halliday: Extract from 'Relevant Models of Language', *Educational Review*, Vol. 22, No. 7, 1969, pp. 26–34.

much because it is false as because it is irrelevant. When, for example, the authors of *The Linguistic Sciences and Language Teaching* suggested that teaching the do's and don'ts of grammar to a child who is linguistically unsuccessful is like teaching a starving man how to hold a knife and fork, they were not denying that there is a ritual element in our use of language, with rules of conduct to which everyone is expected to conform; they were simply asserting that the view of language as primarily good manners was of little relevance to educational needs. Probably very few people ever held this view explicitly; but it was implicit in a substantial body of teaching practices, and if it has now largely been discarded this is because its irrelevance became obvious in the course of some rather unhappy experience.

It is not necessary, however, to sacrifice a generation of children, or even one classroomful, in order to demonstrate that particular preconceptions of language are inadequate or irrelevant. In place of a negative and somewhat hit-and-miss approach, a more fruitful procedure is to seek to establish certain general, positive criteria of relevance. These will relate, ultimately, to the demands that we make of language in the course of our lives. We need therefore to have some idea of the nature of these demands; and we shall try to consider them here from the point of view of the child. We shall ask, in effect, about the child's image of language: what is the 'model' of language that he internalizes as a result of his own experience? This will help us to decide what is relevant to the teacher, since the teacher's own view of language must at the very least encompass all that the child knows language to be.

The child knows what language is because he knows what language does. The determining elements in the young child's experience are the successful demands on language that he himself has made, the particular needs that have been satisfied by language for him. He has used language in many ways—for the satisfaction of material and intellectual needs, for the mediation of personal relationships, the expression of feelings and so on. Language in all these uses has come within his own direct experience, and because of this he is subconsciously aware that language has many functions that affect him personally. Language is, for the child, a rich and adaptable instrument for the realization of his intentions; there is hardly any limit to what he can do with it.

As a result, the child's internal 'model' of language is a highly complex one; and most adult notions of language fail to match up to it. The adult's ideas about language may be externalized and consciously formulated, but they are nearly always much too simple. In fact it may be more helpful, in this connexion, to speak of the child's 'models' of language, in the plural, in order to emphasize the many-sidedness of his linguistic experience. We shall try to identify the models of language with which the normal child is endowed by the time he comes to school at the age of five; the assumption being that if the teacher's own 'received' conception of language is in some ways less rich or less diversified it will be irrelevant to the educational task.

We tend to underestimate both the total extent and the functional diversity of the part played by language in the life of the child. His interaction with others, which begins at birth, is gradually given form by language, through the process whereby at a very early age language already begins to mediate in every aspect of his experience. It is not only as the child comes to act on and to learn about his environment that language comes in; it is there from the start in his achievement of intimacy and in the expression of his individuality. The rhythmic recitation of nursery rhymes and jingles is still language, as we can see from the fact that children's spells and chants differ from one language to another: English nonsense is quite distinct from French nonsense, because the one is English and the other French. All these contribute to the child's total picture of language 'at work'.

Through such experiences, the child builds up a very positive impression —one that cannot be verbalized, but is none the less real for that—of what language is and what it is for. Much of his difficulty with language in school arises because he is required to accept a stereotype of language that is contrary to the insights he has gained from his own experience. The traditional first 'reading and writing' tasks are a case in point, since they fail to coincide with his own convictions about the nature and uses of language.

Perhaps the simplest of the child's models of language, and one of the first to be evolved, is what we may call the *instrumental* model. The child becomes aware that language is used as a means of getting things done. About a generation ago, zoologists were finding out about the highly developed mental powers of chimpanzees; and one of the observations described was of the animal that constructed a long stick out of three short ones and used it to dislodge a bunch of bananas from the roof of its cage. The human child, faced with the same problem, constructs a sentence. He says, 'I want a banana'; and the effect is the more impressive because it does not depend on the immediate presence of the bananas. Language is brought in to serve the function of 'I want', the satisfaction of material needs. Success in this use of language does not in any way depend on the production of well-formed adult sentences; a carefully contextualized yell may have substantially the same effect, and although this may not be language there is no very clear dividing line between, say, a noise made on a commanding tone and a full-dress imperative clause.

The old *See Spot run. Run, Spot, run!* type of first reader bore no relation whatsoever to this instrumental function of language. This by itself does not condemn it, since language has many other functions besides that of manipulating and controlling the environment. But it bore little apparent relation to any use of language, at least to any with which the young child is familiar. It is not recognizable as language in terms of the child's own intentions, of the meanings that he has reason to express and to understand. Children have a very broad concept of the meaningfulness of language, in addition to their immense tolerance of inexplicable tasks; but they are not accustomed to being faced with language which, in their own functional terms, has no meaning at all, and the old-style reader was not seen by them as language. It made no connexion with language in use.

Language as an instrument of control has another side to it, since the child is well aware that language is also a means whereby others exercise control over him. Closely related to the instrumental model, therefore, is the *regulatory* model of language. This refers to the use of language to regulate the behaviour of others. Bernstein and his colleagues have studied different types of regulatory behaviour by parents in relation to the process of socialization of the child, and their work provides important clues concerning what the child may be expected to derive from this experience in constructing his own model of language. To adapt one of Bernstein's examples, as described by Turner, the mother who finds that her small child has carried out of the supermarket, unnoticed by herself or by the cashier, some object that was not paid for, may exploit the power of language in various ways, each of which will leave a slightly different trace or after-image of this role of language in the mind of the child. For example, she may say *you mustn't take things that don't belong to you* (control through conditional prohibition based on a categorization of objects in terms of a particular social institution, that of ownership); *that was very naughty* (control through categorization of behaviour in terms of opposition approved/disapproved); *if you do that again I'll smack you* (control through threat of reprisal linked to repetition of behaviour); *you'll make Mummy very unhappy if you do that* (control through emotional blackmail); *that's not allowed* (control through categorization of behaviour as governed by rule), and so on. A single incident of this type by itself has little significance; but such general types of regulatory behaviour, through repetition and reinforcement, determine the child's specific awareness of language as a means of behavioural control.

The child applies this awareness, in his own attempts to control his peers and siblings; and this in turn provides the basis for an essential component in his range of linguistic skills, the language of rules and instructions. Whereas at first he can make only simple unstructured

demands, he learns as time goes on to give ordered sequences of instructions, and then progresses to the further stage where he can convert sets of
instructions into rules, including conditional rules, as in explaining the
principles of a game. Thus his regulatory model of language continues
to be elaborated, and his experience of the potentialities of language in
this use further increases the value of the model.

Closely related to the regulatory function of language is its function
in social interaction, and the third of the models that we may postulate as
forming part of the child's image of language is the *interactional* model.
This refers to the use of language in the interaction between the self and
others. Even the closest of the child's personal relationships, that with his
mother, is partly and, in time, largely mediated through language; his
interaction with other people, adults and children, is very obviously
maintained linguistically. (Those who come nearest to achieving a
personal relationship that is not linguistically mediated, apparently, are
twins.)

Aside, however, from his experience of language in the maintenance
of permanent relationships, the neighbourhood and the activities of the
peer group provide the context for complex and rapidly changing interactional patterns which make extensive and subtle demands on the
individual's linguistic resources. Language is used to define and con-
solidate the group, to include and to exclude, showing who is 'one of us'
and who is not; to impose status, and to contest status that is imposed;
and humour, ridicule, deception, persuasion, all the forensic and theatrical
arts of language are brought into play. Moreover, the young child, still
primarily a learner, can do what very few adults can do in such situations:
he can be internalizing language while listening and talking. He can be,
effectively, both a participant and an observer at the same time, so that his
own critical involvement in this complex interaction does not prevent
him from profiting linguistically from it.

Again there is a natural link here with another use of language, from
which the child derives what we may call the *personal* model. This
refers to his awareness of language as a form of his own individuality.
In the process whereby the child becomes aware of himself, and in
particular in the higher stages of that process, the development of his
personality, language plays an essential role. We are not talking here
merely of 'expressive' language—language used for the direct expression
of feelings and attitudes—but also of the personal element in the interactional function of language, since the shaping of the self through
interaction with others is very much a language-mediated process. The
child is enabled to offer to someone else that which is unique to himself,
to make public his own individuality; and this in turn reinforces and
creates this individuality. With the normal child, his awareness of himself

is closely bound up with speech: both with hearing himself speak, and with having at his disposal the range of behavioural options that constitute language. Within the concept of the self as an actor, having discretion, or freedom of choice, the 'self as a speaker' is an important component.

Thus for the child language is very much a part of himself, and the 'personal' model is his intuitive awareness of this, and of the way in which his individuality is identified and realized through language. The other side of the coin, in this process, is the child's growing understanding of his environment, since the environment is, first of all, the 'non-self', that which is separated out in the course of establishing where he himself begins and ends. So, fifthly, the child has a *heuristic* model of language, derived from his knowledge of how language has enabled him to explore his environment.

The heuristic model refers to language as a means of investigating reality, a way of learning about things. This scarcely needs comment, since every child makes it quite obvious that this is what language is for by his habit of constantly asking questions. When he is questioning, he is seeking not merely facts but explanations of facts, the generalizations about reality that language makes it possible to explore. Again, Bernstein has shown the importance of the question-and-answer routine in the total setting of parent-child communication and the significance of the latter, in turn, in relation to the child's success in formal education: his research has demonstrated a significant correlation between the mother's linguistic attention to the child and the teacher's assessment of the child's success in the first year of school.

The young child is very well aware of how to use language to learn, and may be quite conscious of this aspect of language before he reaches school; many children already control a metalanguage for the heuristic function of language, in that they know what a 'question' is, what an 'answer' is, what 'knowing' and 'understanding' mean, and they can talk about these things without difficulty. Mackay and Thompson have shown the importance of helping the child who is learning to read and write to build up a language for talking about language; and it is the heuristic function which provides one of the foundations for this, since the child can readily conceptualize and verbalize the basic categories of the heuristic model. To put this more concretely, the normal five-year-old either already uses words such as *question, answer* in their correct meanings or, if he does not, is capable of learning to do so.

The other foundation for the child's 'language about language' is to be found in the imaginative function. This also relates the child to his environment, but in a rather different way. Here, the child is using language to create his own environment; not to learn about how things are but to make them as he feels inclined. From his ability to create, through language, a world of his own making he derives the *imaginative* model of language; and this provides some further elements of the metalanguage, with words like *story, make up* and *pretend*.

Language in its imaginative function is not necessarily 'about' anything at all: the child's linguistically created environment does not have to be a make-believe copy of the world of experience, occupied by people and things and events. It may be a world of pure sound, made up of rhythmic sequences of rhyming or chiming syllables; or an edifice of words in which semantics has no part, like a house built of playing cards in which face values are irrelevant. Poems, rhymes, riddles and much of the child's own linguistic play reinforce this model of language, and here too the meaning of what is said is not primarily a matter of content. In stories and dramatic games, the imaginative function is, to a large extent, based on content; but the ability to express such content is still, for the child, only one of the interesting facets of language, one which for many purposes is no more than an optional extra.

So we come finally to the representational model. Language is, in addition to all its other guises, a means of communicating about something, of expressing propositions. The child is aware that he can convey a message in language, a message which has specific reference to the processes, persons, objects, abstractions, qualities, states and relations of the real world around him.

This is the only model of language that many adults have; and a very inadequate model it is, from the point of view of the child. There is no need to go so far as to suggest that the transmission of content is, for the child, the least important function of language; we have no way of evaluating the various functions relatively to one another. It is certainly not, however, one of the earliest to come into prominence; and it does not become a dominant function until a much later stage in the development towards maturity. Perhaps it never becomes in any real sense the dominant function; but it does, in later years, tend to become the dominant *model*. It is very easy for the adult, when he attempts to formulate his ideas about the nature of language, to be simply unaware of most of what language means to the child; this is not because he no longer uses language in the same variety of different functions (one or two may have atrophied, but not all), but because only one of these functions, in general, is the subject of conscious attention, so that the corresponding model is the only one to be externalized. But this presents what is, for the child, a quite unrealistic picture of language, since it accounts for only a small fragment of his total awareness of what language is about.

The representational model at least does not conflict with the child's experience. It relates to one significant part of it; rather a small part, at first, but nevertheless real. In this it contrasts sharply with another view of language which we have not mentioned because it plays no part in the child's experience at all, but which might be called the 'ritual' model of language. This is the image of language internalized by those for whom language is a means of showing how well one was brought up; it downgrades language to the level of table-manners. The ritual element in the use of language is probably derived from the interactional, since language in its ritual function also serves to define and delimit a social group; but it has none of the positive aspects of linguistic interaction, those which impinge on the child, and is thus very partial and one-sided. The view of language as manners is a needless complication, in the present context, since this function of language has no counterpart in the child's experience.

Our conception of language, if it is to be adequate for meeting the needs of the child, will need to be exhaustive. It must incorporate all the child's own 'models', to take account of the varied demands on language that he himself makes. The child's understanding of what language it is derived from his own experience of language in situations of use. It thus embodies all of the images we have described: the instrumental, the regulatory, the interactional, the personal, the heuristic, the imaginative and the representational. Each of these is his interpretation of a function of language with which he is familiar.

Varieties of Language

Every normal person possesses language, but the particular forms in which this is manifest depends on a whole range of factors, depending on where he was born, who he is and what he does. A Chinese and a Frenchman both use language to make bets and promises, but the utterances they produce in performing these acts are demonstrably different. A Frenchman promising the same thing to his wife and to his boss will probably do so in a different way, and a Parisian and a Bordelais making the same bet will sound different in certain respects. The manifestations of language appear to be almost infinitely variable, and yet we speak of different bits of language as belonging to the same language, dialect, variety, register or style. Evidently we need, for everyday purposes, to impose some order and classification on this variability. The point is well made by Paul (Section 1, I) when he says that the classification of languages and dialects, like those of orders and genera in zoology, are nothing more than conceptual groupings and distinctions made by the human mind, and that the differences are not matters of kind but of degree.

In what way and to what degree must two forms of speech be different in order to be classified as belonging to two different languages, dialects or registers? The question requires a linguistic answer. But the question itself presupposes that we have already set up the categories language, dialect, register, etc. Clearly, therefore, these categories are at least in part established according to non-linguistic criteria, otherwise we should be in a circularity. Linguistics provides the techniques and categories for describing different languages, dialects and registers but not the criteria for defining them. As Hymes* has said: 'It is clear the status of a form of speech as a dialect or a language or level, cannot be determined from linguistic features alone, nor can the categories be so defined. There is a socio-cultural dimension'.

Ferguson and Gumperz investigate the concepts of social group membership and mutual intelligibility as criteria for classification, whilst

* D. H. Hymes: 'The Ethnography of Speaking' in Joshua A. Fishman (Ed.) *Readings in the Sociology of Language*, The Hague: Mouton, 1968, p. 113.

Crystal and Leech are most concerned with the importance of the social role, status and psychological intentions of the speaker as a means for reducing the infinite variety in the manifestations of language to some sort of order.

Since, then, pupils already possess language, language teachers are not so much *teachers of language* as *teachers of a language*, that is, a new and unfamiliar set of manifestations of what their pupils already possess. It is clearly of importance for language teachers to realize what this means. We learn languages, dialects, varieties, registers in order to enter into certain social relationships for certain purposes with members of other social groups. It is not necessarily the case that this set of social relationships and purposes is identical with those we have within our own social group. Which languages, dialects or registers we acquire will depend on the social group we have in mind, what sort of relationships we propose to have with its members and for what purposes we are gaining these new skills. Anyone setting up a language teaching operation must be able to specify more or less exactly all these factors before he can determine what linguistic forms he will present to the learner in his teaching materials.

10
D. CHRYSTAL and D. DAVY
Stylistic Analysis

Presuppositions

We have outlined [earlier] the methodology we use in describing the linguistic features of any text. In the first instance, the procedures for approaching stylistic analysis are no different from those made use of in any descriptive linguistic exercise: the primary task is to catalogue and classify features within the framework of some general linguistic theory. Our aim is to produce, initially, an inventory of interrelated contrasts. Ultimately, we would expect any descriptively adequate grammar to incorporate, as part of its rules, all stylistically significant information. We are not concerned, as has been pointed out, with the description of everything that goes on within a text, but only with that which can be shown to be of stylistic importance in the sense discussed in Chapter 2. To study everything would produce an undesirable conflation of the notions of stylistics and linguistics. We now have to go a stage further and discuss how we link our linguistic analysis with the stylistic purpose of the exercise. What are the theoretical notions that need to be established in order to bridge the gap between the description of a language, on the one hand, and the description of a variety of that language, on the other?

A first impression of the theoretical problem may be gained in the following way. We have hypothesized that any utterance, spoken or written, displays features which simultaneously identify it from a number of different points of view. Some features may provide information about the speaker's regional background, or his place on a social scale of some kind, for example; other features may reveal aspects of the social situation in which he is speaking, the kind of person to whom he is speaking, the capacity in which he is speaking, and so on; and further features (often the majority in an utterance) will tell us nothing about a situation at all —apart, that is, from the fact that the speaker is using English, as opposed to some other language. The question is, basically, what types of feature

D. Chrystal and D. Davy: Extract from *Investigating English Style*, Chapter 3, Longman, 1969, pp. 64–83.

are there? Into how many categories can these features be classified, and how are the categories to be defined?

Stylistic analysis, in the sense implied by these questions, is something new; and much of the early work which has taken place, while valuable for its stimulus and initiative, is suspect. There are a number of reasons for this. In the first place, the categories which have been set up to account for the features, or sets of features, in the language data are frequently inconsistently used, are incomplete, and usually have no adequate formal basis. The criticism of inconsistency can best be illustrated from the use of the term *register* (which is a fundamental notion in 'Neo-Firthian' stylistics). This term has been applied to varieties of language in an almost indiscriminate manner, as if it could be usefully applied to situationally distinctive pieces of language of any kind. The language of newspaper headlines, church services, sports commentaries, popular songs, advertising and football, amongst others, have all been referred to as registers in one work. We shall however see below that there are very great differences in the nature of the situational variables involved in these uses of English, and that it is inconsistent, unrealistic, and confusing to obscure these differences by grouping everything under the same heading, as well as an unnecessary trivialization of what is a potentially useful concept. The criticism of incompleteness is readily illustrated by the fact that at least one central theoretical variable (*modality* in our sense) has been ignored, and that there are many aspects of the way in which English is used which no one has tried to account for, and which cannot be handled adequately by such categories as *register*, *tenor*, *field*, *mode*, and so on in any of their current senses. And while it is impossible to achieve completeness in the present 'state of the art', the extent to which stylistic theories are at the moment inadequate should at least be admitted and the difficulties outlined. The lack of large-scale formal empirical analysis is well displayed when situational categories such as 'newspaper reporting' are set up, and assumed to have a predictable linguistic identity. It takes only a little analysis of texts to show that many such generalizations are of very little descriptive value. In fact the majority of the situations claimed to be stylistically distinctive have hardly been studied at all from the linguistic point of view, and many of the labels used are vague in the extreme (e.g. 'science', 'literature').

Further, in the published work on the subject, there seem to be many hidden assumptions that can be seriously questioned, for example, that there is a one-for-one correlation between linguistic features and situation, or that the language can be predicted from the situation and the situation from the language with the same degree of certainty. Such assumptions are not valid in our experience; we shall discuss them further below. Finally, we find a great deal of difficulty in understanding the use of such terms as 'restricted language', 'norm' (or 'normal'), 'discourse', 'standard', and 'situation' in the literature. Often a word is used in both an everyday and a specialist sense, without the difference being explicitly recognized.

We cannot but conclude that stylistic theory, at the time of writing, has reached a stage where it would do well to wait for practical analysis to catch up, so that the theoretical categories may be tested against a wide range of data, and more detailed analyses of texts carried out. Consequently, further theorizing in this book is kept to a minimum: we are mainly concerned to establish certain central notions that do not seem to have been sufficiently rigorously defined and verified hitherto.

The main procedural difficulty, which we have already had cause to refer to, arises from the fact that linguistic features do not usually correlate in any neat one-for-one way with the situational variables in an extra-linguistic context. It is of course possible to find examples in most utterances from which predictions can be made with confidence about the situation, or some aspect of the situation—utterances from religious or legal English are particularly clear in this respect. But even here a linguistic feature is frequently ambiguous as to its situational function, indicating more than one variable simultaneously: much of the grammatical idio-syncrasy of written legal and religious English, for example, has a double function, contributing both to *province* and to *status* in the senses described below. Any piece of discourse contains a large number of features which are difficult to relate to specific variables in the original extra-linguistic context, even though they may be felt to have some kind of stylistic value. The majority of linguistic features in English have little or no predictive power, that is, they are ambiguous indications of the situational variables in the extra-linguistic contexts in which they are used. This state of affairs must be recognized by any adequate theory of language variation. And if, working the other way round, one specifies a situation and tries to predict its linguistic features, it is impossible to make reliable predictions about any but a small number of features.

It may, of course, be convenient to posit a one-for-one correlation between a set of linguistic forms and a situation, but while this relation does sometimes genuinely exist, it would be a mistake to assume that it always exists, and to talk rigidly in terms of 'one language—one situation'. It is more meaningful instead to talk of *ranges* of appropriate-ness and acceptability of various uses of language to given situations. Thus, in situation X, feature Y will be highly probable, but one must allow for the possibility of feature Z occurring, other things being equal —for instance, the introduction of informality where on all other occasions one has experienced formality. Situations in which positively only one set of stylistic features is permitted, with no variation allowed (or, to put it another way, where it is possible to state confidently that 'the following features will never occur here . . .'), are far outnumbered by those situations where alternative sets of features are possible, though not usually equiprobable.

It is, then, unreasonable to expect that all situational variables are equally predictable from the language data. The number of constraints influencing the user of language varies from one situation to another: some situations are very clearly predictable, with many constraints; others are vague. Therefore we prefer to see this notion of language-situation predictability as a scale, with linguistic features which are to all intents and purposes totally predictable at one end, features which are entirely unpredictable within the English speech community at the other, and, in between, features showing many different degrees of predictability, some very restricted, some less so. This of course is the interesting area for study. The totally predictable cases, which are those usually cited in the literature on this subject, are relatively uninteresting precisely because of their predictability; they are usually intuitively obvious. It is the area between the extremes which is in need of study.

Another way of making this point, but from a different angle, is to introduce a 'scale of utilization' of the formal linguistic features in English. At one end of the scale there are uses of English where the total range of conceivable linguistic forms might occur (as in literature); at the other end, there are uses where only a very small number of forms ever occur, some linguistic systems available in the rest of the language being completely unused—for example, in the language of knitting patterns, parade-ground commands, heraldic language, and certain kinds of weather-forecasting. For uses of this latter type, the label 'restricted language' has sometimes been used; but it is probably more useful to see these uses as being simply at the 'most restricted' end of a scale of restrictedness, rather than to posit any difference in kind.

Dimensions of situational constraint

For the analyses carried out in this book, the linguistic features of any utterance—apart from their fundamental role of producing intelligible language—were discussed in terms of their correlatability to different kinds of situational function. The linguist, having intuitively noted a particular feature as being stylistically significant in some way, attempts to rationalize the basis of his intuitive response by examining the extra-linguistic context in order to establish any situational facts which might account for restrictions on its use. To take a clear example, the use of 'thou/thee/thy/thine' in Standard English is restricted to those extra-linguistic contexts in which certain religious factors are dominant and obligatory, other factors being relatively random, and usually optional. It is by no means extravagant to conclude that an aspect or aspects of the context exercises some kind of conditioning influence on the feature in question, and the notion of *situation* has been set up to describe the kinds of conditioning influence. Similarly, any other feature which can be shown to display restricted occurrence in a sub-set of extra-linguistic contexts within the English speech community is by definition of importance for stylistic analysis. The stylistician begins by studying what the most significant deviations from random occurrence are, and why.

The entire range of linguistic features in a text functioning in the above way is plotted, and the notion of *situation* is broken down into *dimensions of situational constraint* (which we have so far been referring to rather loosely as 'situational variables'); and the role every feature plays is described in terms of one or more of these dimensions. For example, feature A may be seen to correlate with the geographical area the speaker came from, and is referred to as a *feature of* the dimension of regional variation, or *regional dialect*; feature B is seen to be a result of the kind of social relationship existing between the participants in a conversation, and is referred to as a *feature of* a different dimension (in this case the dimension we shall refer to below as *status*); and so on. Those features which have no situational correlates at all, apart from the stylistically trivial one of *occurring in an English-speaking situation*, are noted for separate discussion (under the heading *common-core* features, cf. below). We would again stress the hypothetical nature of these dimensions. There may be further kinds of constraint which we have overlooked; and further sub-classification of the dimensions will certainly be necessary as more material is analysed. We must remember that no one has yet described the full range of linguistic correlates of any one of these dimensions; nor has there been much experimentation—such as by systematically varying the extra-linguistic factors and examining the accompanying linguistic variation. But it only takes a little analysis to clarify the nature of certain central constraints, and the following is based on the work done here.

Before describing these constraints in detail, we must consider the stylistically neutral, or 'common-core' features which an utterance displays—those linguistic features which the utterance shares in some degree with all other utterances in the speech community, which occur regardless of the situational dimensions outlined below. This is a different kind of descriptive dimension from the others, in that its variability is random in respect of situational constraints. The features of this dimension, taken one at a time, do not discriminate situations of the kind the stylistician is interested in, though he has to be aware of them in order to be able to discount them. Thus most of the segmental phonology of English, and most of the grammatical and lexical patterns are imposed on the language-user as being laws common to the whole community in all situations. For example, the existence of concord between subject and verb is not stylistically significant, nor is the fact that the article comes before the noun, that *man* has the irregular plural *men*, or that *pleasant* is the opposite of *unpleasant*. There is no variety which has no fricative consonants or falling tones, and none which finds it impossible to use colour terms. From the point of view of their form—*not* considering their distribution—such features of English are stylistically neutral, and are, moreover, in the vast majority. Uniquely occurring linguistic features are very much the exception: as we have already mentioned, all varieties of English have much more in common than differentiates them. This is not of course to say that such features as the above cannot be made use of for stylistic purposes at all: as soon as considerations of *frequency* of occurrence and overall distribution are taken into account, then most of the common-core features work in a different way—for example, a text consisting wholly of tone-units with a falling nucleus would certainly be stylistically distinctive. Most of the stylistic statements which we make in this book are in fact of this frequential or distributional type. But the study of constellations of these features is logically dependent on the prior establishment of an inventory, and for this a separate dimension of description is necessary.

All other features of utterance are, by definition, situationally restricted in some way. We shall distinguish eight dimensions in all, grouping these into the three broad types that may be seen in the following list. The reasons for this grouping will be explained below.

A
INDIVIDUALITY
DIALECT
TIME

B
DISCOURSE
a [SIMPLE/COMPLEX] MEDIUM (Speech, Writing)
b [SIMPLE/COMPLEX] PARTICIPATION (Monologue, Dialogue)

C
PROVINCE
STATUS
MODALITY
SINGULARITY

Individuality

In unselfconscious utterance, certain features occur—relatively permanent features of the speech or writing habits—which identify someone as a specific person, distinguish him from other users of the same language, or the same variety of the language. Such idiosyncratic features, not normally altering over quite long periods of time in adults, would be such effects as those constituting a person's voice quality or handwriting, which provide the basis of his recognizability. Also under this heading we might include 'pet' words or phrases with a very high frequency of occurrence. We are of course using 'individuality' in a wide sense, to cover both physical and psychological personal traits which could give rise to phonetic and graphic distinctiveness of any kind. It is also important to note the qualification 'unselfconscious' used above. Obviously, we would not want to deny a speaker the possibility of adopting an alien voice quality or style of handwriting for some purpose (for example, the mimicking of a famous person to make a humorous point), but such usage would have to be described in terms of a very different set of presuppositions. The kind of idiosyncrasy described in this section is also different from the relatively temporary, and usually conscious activity associated with individuality in a literary or other context, which we shall discuss under the heading of singularity.

Dialect

Other features in a person's usage will give an indication of his place of geographical origin (*regional* dialect) or his location on a non-linguistically based social scale (*class* dialect)—what we might refer to as the linguistic correlates of the sociologist's 'primary group'. These too are relatively constant features of language, only altering in humorous situations, or in cases of intense social pressure which cause someone to conform to dialect patterns other than his own. Both types of features are presumably too familiar to need exemplification; they have been centres of linguistic attention for some years. But it should be noted that social dialect features of a wholly predictable type are rare in English: certain tendencies emerge (for example, in choice of vocabulary, or in the use of certain vowels), but there is little which is very systematic.

Time

Another familiar dimension of description covers those features of an utterance which indicate exlusively diachronic information—the temporal provenance of a piece of language. Such information would be of primary importance in any historical study of English, both in the general sense of the language as a whole, and in the particular sense of the development of the language habits of a single human being (linguistic *ontogeny*). Temporal features are the third kind of fairly stable feature in the utterances of an individual.

The relatively permanent features of language which we have just discussed can largely be taken for granted by the stylistician. They are very much background features, which the general or descriptive linguist will be interested in for their own sake, but which are stylistically less interesting because of their insusceptibility to variation in most situations. These features are rarely able to be manipulated by language-users in the way that the remaining groups of features are. One should also note the corollary, that with the dimensions of description so far described there is a powerful mutual predictability between language and situation: if the relevant extra-linguistic factors are known, then certain linguistic features will be readily predictable, and vice versa. Of course these extra-linguistic factors are not the same for all the dimensions: compare, for example, the sense in which the vocal characteristics of a child, as opposed to an adult, can be said to be predictable (on physiological grounds) with the sense in which dialect features are predictable (if one knows the dialect in advance). The point is that within some set of predetermined criteria, there is predictability. And what stylistics is trying to do, in a sense, is to place the other dimensions of situational constraint on a comparably clearly definable footing by trying to specify the relevant extra-linguistic factors precisely. (When one considers the amount of detailed study which traditional dialectology has entered into as a matter of course, it is plain that stylistics, in our sense, has got a lot of work to do before it can ever be as explicit.)

Discourse

We subsume under this heading two kinds of variability in language: the difference between speech and writing, usually referred to under the heading of *medium*, and that between monologue and dialogue, which results from the nature of the *participation* in the language event. This too is not a dimension in precisely the same sense as those shortly to be described, since most of the variability attributable to it could be taken care of by reference to other dimensions, particularly *modality* below. The distinctions that we are seeking to make here are best seen as referring to given, fundamental features of language in use, features which are worth attention not for the descriptive information they are likely to yield but for their value as explanatory clues—by referring to the linguistic differences associated with these distinctions we may be able to explain more adequately the characteristics of certain varieties. This happens, for example, when a specimen of written language shows a number of features that would usually be associated only with informal speech, or when a specimen of spoken language is found to contain constructions typical of writing, or when someone introduces features of dialogue into a monologue; in all cases, the features may be more satisfactorily described by making appropriate reference to distinctions in discourse.

Spoken and written language may be defined by reference to two distinct but overlapping sets of linguistic and non-linguistic characteristics, conveniently summarized by the labels *speech* and *writing*. The distinction is important to maintain for methodological reasons, in addition to the relevance that it has for stylistics. Essentially the distinction is non-linguistic, concerning the primary choice of method or substance with which to communicate—air, or marks on a surface. (We do not discuss here other communicative methods, such as the pictorial, musical, and so on.) But the dichotomy is important for the stylistician, just as it is for the general linguist: speech needs to be handled initially at the phonetic/phonological level, and writing at the graphetic/graphological level. In each case, a different descriptive framework is involved. From the situational point of view, not only are there central functional differences between the two (speech being relatively transient, writing relatively permanent; speech implying personal contact of some kind, writing not —apart from its illustrative function, as on a blackboard in a classroom), there is also the absence of complete formal parallelism between spoken and written varieties of English. No spoken varieties can be written in traditional orthography so as to reflect all contrasts present in speech (consider the range of non-segmental information omitted, for example, or the pressures against writing certain obscene words), and there are many cases of written language which it is impossible to speak without destroying the original graphetic coherence of the text (for example, the punctuationless nature of much written legal language, which has to be broken down into units if it is to be spoken aloud, though these units do not exist in the graphic form). Substantial differences of this kind make the central distinction between speech and writing a very relevant one in linguistics, with clear implications for stylistics.

Under the heading of *participation* in discourse, we distinguish between *monologue* (utterance with no expectation of a response) and *dialogue* (utterance with alternating participants, usually, though not necessarily, two in number). We note this distinction, along with medium, under the same general heading, discourse, for a number of reasons. First, like medium, it operates at a more general level of abstraction than do any of the other situational dimensions put forward in this book. Second, as far as intuitive identification of varieties is concerned, there are clear and central co-occurrences between the categories of medium and those of participation, irrespective of the other dimensions: spoken and written monologue and spoken dialogue are common, as is—perhaps less obviously—written dialogue (used, for example, in filling and in returning forms, in some exchanges of letters, or in some kinds of party game).

Third, there seem to be important functional similarities between medium and participation. In both, there is rarely a real choice as to which category is used in any given extra-linguistic context: one cannot speak to someone out of earshot; one does not use monologue when other people are present, unless for a temporary effect; one does not usually use writing to communicate with someone in the same room; and so on. Again, there are no further possibilities of linguistic contrast within either dimension.

The categories of medium and participation may also function in a 'removed', or 'explanatory' way. This point may be clarified if we consider the case of a category of medium which is being used as a means to an end, instead of as an end in itself; that is, the category is serving as a stopgap in a situation, a temporary device intended to facilitate a transfer to the alternative category at some later stage. We shall refer to this phenomenon as *complex medium*. Thus language which stays within the one category (i.e. spoken to be heard, written to be read) will be formally distinct in certain respects from language which involves a switch (e.g. language which is spoken to be written, as in dictation, or language written to be spoken, as in news broadcasting), and this possibility of systematic difference has to be built in to our theoretical framework. The introduction of phonological criteria into a discussion of written literature (describing the effect of alliteration, assonance, and so on) is a technique which would be covered partly by this dimension. Further sub-classification of complex medium is theoretically possible ('language written to be read aloud as if written', and so on), but it would seem wise not to introduce further complications until the initial distinction has been tested as fully as possible.

The 'explanatory' function of the monologue/dialogue opposition may be seen when it is necessary to account for the presence of dialogue features in an utterance produced by only one person (a common literary device), or for the tendency for monologue to be introduced into a conversation, as when someone tells a joke. Both the joke and the short story may include spoken monologue to be uttered as if dialogue, different accents sometimes being adopted to indicate the change of speaker, and so on; and in drama the relationship between an author and his charac-ters can perhaps be thought of as a function of written monologue which is to be spoken as dialogue (along with all the associated conventions). In these cases, then, we are trying to explain certain features of a variety which would fall as a general rule within one kind of discourse by reference to features which would normally be expected to occur only in another. We shall refer to this as *complex participation*.

The remaining dimensions of constraint all refer to relatively localized or temporary variations in language, and provide the central area of stylistic study.

Province

In this dimension we describe the features of language which identify an utterance with those variables in an extra-linguistic context which are defined with reference to the kind of occupational or professional activity being engaged in. Province features provide no information about the people involved in any situation—about their social status or relationship to each other, for example; they are features which would be found to recur regardless of who the participants were, and which relate to the nature of the task they are engaged in. The occupational role of the language-user, in other words, imposes certain restraints on what may be spoken or written (or, to put it positively, suggests a particular set of linguistic forms which a speaker is at liberty to use). It is these, along with other restraints (of *status* and *modality* in particular) which we shall shortly discuss, which form the stylistic basis of any variety. Clear examples of provinces would be the 'language of' (shorthand for 'distinctive set of linguistic features used in') public worship, advertising, science or law—contexts in which the sociologist would consider 'secondary groups' to be operating. Each of these contexts, it should be noted, has an intuitive coherence and identity which may be defined in non-linguistic terms—though this is not of course to imply that all provinces have comparably clear, readily definable extra-linguistic correlatives.

The situational variables in the contexts referred to may be defined at different levels of generality, depending on the nature of the linguistic features which are being considered. It would be possible, for instance, to speak of 'advertising', as opposed to 'television advertising', as opposed to 'television advertising of washing powders', and so on. Two questions immediately arise: what is the most general level at which a province may be identified, and what is the most specific level? As an example of the kind of problem posed by the first question, we may take the following. Having noticed certain linguistic features of different categories of advertisement, such as public announcements of forthcoming events, newspaper advertisements, magazine advertisements, television advertisements, does one then refer to these as different provinces, or does one go to a more general level and refer to them all as aspects ('sub-provinces') of the one province of advertising, or, at a still more general level, the province of propaganda? Clearly, if this process were continued, all varieties would ultimately fall under the heading of one major province, which might be labelled 'communication', or something of the kind, and the point of the exercise would have been lost.

At the other end of the scale, to examine the second question raised above, it is futile to continue sub-classifying situations when there are insufficient linguistic formal differences to warrant further analysis. 'Washing-powder advertising on television making use of a blue-eyed demonstrator on a Sunday', to continue the example, would not be differentiated, one would hope, because it would not be very difficult to show that there was no significant language difference between this and the language used by other demonstrators of different ocular persuasions on other days of the week. Exactly how much sub-analysis can be justified is something yet to be decided: there is certainly no obvious cut-off point. It is thus essential to view all labels used to refer to different provinces with the greatest suspicion, until further descriptive work has been done —and this applies as much to the labels used throughout this book as elsewhere in literature on stylistics. The concept of province, and the other concepts which we discuss below, must be taken as being simply a basis for investigation, nothing more. The first question to be asked on being given a label such as 'the language of X' is always: What formal features make this use of language unique and correlatable only with this situation? Is the label too broad? Or is it too narrow? How far is there an unclear boundary-area between this and other 'language-of' situations? We shall be looking at a number of these commonly used labels in this way in the course of this book, and finding that many of them are inadequate from a linguistic point of view.

Meanwhile, we should note three further general points about the concept of province. First, province features should not be identified with the subject matter of an utterance, as has sometimes been suggested in connexion with the notion of 'register'. Subject matter, in so far as this is a question of the use of distinctive vocabulary, is but one factor among many which contribute to a province's definition, and in any case has predictive power only in a minority of extremely specialist situations. Knowing the subject matter of an utterance is no guarantee that it is possible to define its situational origin, as consideration of the following chapters shows. In those cases where it is the subject matter (as opposed to the situation) which totally dictates the form, then of course this is not a stylistic matter at all.

Second, we shall be applying the term 'province' to the notion of conversation, but one must remember that conversation is different from all other provinces in that it is the only case where conventional occupational boundaries are irrelevant: whatever conversation is linguistically, it may occur within and between any of the restricted uses of language which one would want to classify as provinces. It is however this very generally which makes it as clear a notion as any of the other provinces, comparable to them in situational distinctiveness; and in view of the fact that conversation may be defined, albeit negatively, with reference to other provinces, it would seem to fall within the terms of the definition given at the beginning of this section.

Lastly, it should be noted that, apart from the distinctions in discourse outlined above, which are fairly fundamental for linguistics as a whole, there is no theoretical ordering between the dimensions, no established priorities, to demand, for example, that province features should always precede status features in description. There is no theoretical hierarchy here. In fact, it is usually easier to begin by looking for province features in any analysis, presumably because province is a more readily established stylistic concept, the relevant variables being easier to specify and label. But one should note that this is a procedural convenience, and not in any sense a theoretical requirement: it does not lead us to develop a 'theory of province', in the same way that some scholars have done with a 'theory of register' (thus to all intents and purposes equating 'register' with 'stylistics'!).

Status

In this dimension we describe the systematic linguistic variations which correspond with variations in the relative social standing of the participants in any act of communication, regardless of their exact locality. The audience may be an individual or a group. It is postulated that status variations occur independently of province variations, although there are some restrictions on co-occurrence. The semantic field which may be subsumed under the label 'status' is of course complex: it involves a whole range of factors related to contacts between people from different positions on a social scale—factors intuitively associated with such notions as formality, informality, respect, politeness, deference, intimacy, kinship relations, business relations, and hierarchic relations in general. A number of areas may be clearly distinguished within the dimension of status in any language, various kinds of formal and informal language being perhaps the most noticeable (though one must be careful to distinguish between formality in a stylistic sense, and the grammatical category of formality which occurs in, say, Japanese, where social status is reflected paradigmatically through many of the forms of the language). Exactly how many categories of status there are awaits elucidation. Joos has postulated five degrees of formality in this connexion (namely 'frozen', 'formal', 'consultative', 'casual', and 'intimate'), but we feel this to be premature. It is likely that a scale of formality exists, but the number of linguistic terms along the scale, and the nature of the polarities, are still matters for speculation. Utterances may be found which seem to fit neatly into the above five slots; but these are far outnumbered by utterances which do not. As with province, therefore, we shall not claim too much for the categories of status which we make use of in our analysis.

Modality

This dimension has not usually been systematically distinguished in stylistic discussion. In it we describe those linguistic features correlatable with the specific purpose of an utterance which has led the user to adopt one feature or set of features rather than another, and ultimately to produce an overall, conventionalized spoken or written format for his language, which may be given a descriptive label. Modality can be described independently of province and status, in that on the whole a choice of some kind exists regardless of a language-user's specific occupational role or relationship to other participants. For example, there would be linguistic differences of modality if, within the province of conversation, in its written form (what might be called 'correspondence', for the sake of convenience), one chose to communicate a message in the shape of a letter, a postcard, a note, a telegram, or a memo; or, within the province of scientific English, if one chose to write up a topic in the form of a lecture, report, essay, monograph, or textbook. In each case there would be linguistic as well as extra-linguistic differences, and it is the overall pattern produced by the former which would be the basis of any decision assigning a text to a particular category of modality. The familiar distinction between 'genres' (traditionally well-recognized divisions in (usually literary) language) could also be seen in terms of modality, though we must remember here that the term 'genre' has never been given a precise, generally agreed definition, and is regularly used to refer simultaneously to varieties operating at different degrees of theoretical abstraction—for example, 'poetry' v. 'prose', as well as 'essay' v. 'short story', which are sub-categories of prose. Most kinds of joke would be describable in terms of modality, and here we can see very clearly the linguistic basis of the format—opening formulae (such as 'Have you heard the one about . . .'), the 'punch line', the various prosodic and paralinguistic accompaniments, and so on. Other examples of modality distinction would be those between types of spoken or written monologue such as anecdote, proclamation, poster, and testimonial.

Modality is clearly partly a question of the suitability of form to subject matter, but it cannot wholly be discussed in these terms, as very often the conventional linguistic format is a result, at least in part, of a tradition whose synchronic relevance has long been lost, as in the form of lettering in many legal documents. We should also like to emphasize the independence of modality as a dimension of stylistic description, particularly in view of the failure to differentiate modality from province hitherto. To think of what is conveniently labelled 'sports commentary' as a province, for example, is to overlook the fact that there are two theoretical variables involved, which should be kept distinct. There *is* a basis for a province here, namely, the business of reporting sports; but commentary is a function of modality (which should be clear when one considers the other linguistic formats a sports reporter could use— newspaper article, retrospective radio report, and so on). Modality differences may both cut across provinces—it is possible to have a commentary about sport or cooking or even a scientific experiment, for example—and also occur within them, some provinces having a very restricted variability (the liturgical English, for example), others having a great deal of flexibility (such as the wide range of modalities which exist in legal or literary English).

Singularity

Once the linguistic features of a text have been described in terms of the above dimensions, features may still be left which cannot be related to anything systematic amongst the community as a whole, or some group of it, but only to the preferences of the individual user. A user may display in his utterance occasional idiosyncratic linguistic features which give a specific effect within the framework of some conventional variety, e.g. when an author introduces a linguistic originality into a poem. Along with idosyncratic deviations from a person's normal linguistic behaviour of any kind in any situation, they may be studied *en bloc* as yet a further possibility of variation, and, if they appear regularly in a person's usage, can be regarded as evidence of authorship. We use *singularity* as a cover-term for these personal, occasional features.

This is thus the only dimension which takes account of linguistic idiosyncrasy: other dimensions are either non-linguistic or non-idio-syncratic. Singularity features are different from the vocal or written reflexes of personality traits mentioned under the heading of individuality above, in that the former are typically short, temporary, and manipulable, usually being deliberately introduced into a situation to make a specific linguistic contrast, whereas the latter are relatively continuous, per-manent, and not able to be manipulated in this way—in short, non-linguistic. It can be difficult to decide which dimension a feature belongs to, cspccially with an unfamiliar speaker; for example, there is the case of the joker who begins by impressing his audience with linguistic ingenuity, such as punning, but who ends up by being a crushing bore, through continual introduction of such devices into his speech. There comes a time when what has been taken as a singularity feature, in our sense, turns out in fact to be an individuality feature: this point is not always easy to detect, however.

We ought also to indicate a procedural difficulty in determining whether a linguistic contrast in a text is a marker of singularity or not, namely, that an intuition of authorship will depend on familiarity—the more one reads of or listens to a person, the more recognizable will be his idio-syncrasies. In the initial study of a text which is largely unfamiliar, there is no way of deciding whether a contrast belongs to province, status, or modality on the one hand, or to singularity on the other. This is only a temporary difficulty, of course, as further analysis of other texts by the same and different authors will in all probability provide sufficient data to suggest the likelier solution; but it is as well to be aware that the difficulty does exist.

We have decided to use the term 'singularity' to avoid the over-general implications of the word 'style', but it should be emphasized that what we are referring to is in no sense new. To talk of studying the 'style' of an author does not usually imply a study of *everything* in the language he has used, but only an attempt to isolate, define, and discuss those linguistic features which are felt to be peculiarly his, which help to distinguish him from other authors—a common use in literary criticism and questions of authorship identification, for example. As far as the student of the language of literature is concerned, styles may well be the most interesting things to study; but we must point out that before he can study these systematically and comprehensively, he must first be able to identify, and thus eliminate, all the variables which are non-idio-syncratic in the language situation—i.e. variables belonging to the other dimensions outlined here—otherwise he will attribute a feature to the style of an author which is in fact a common feature of usage in the language as a whole. This does not happen so much in the study of modern literature, but it is a common mistake to take too much for granted in the study of older literature, where there is no intuitive aware-ness of the everyday norms of the spoken or written language.

Other dimensions

It would be strange if the complexity of language variety could be explained by reference to the above four variables alone, and so we were not suprised to find that, while they accounted for the majority of our data, there remained a number of cases of language use which could not be explained in their terms. For example, there is the kind of language used in talking to babies, which can hardly be called a province in the same sense as above, nor even a sub-province (of conversation); and none of the other dimensions seems relevant. Then there is the case of what is sometimes called the 'fire and brimstone' sermon. In a sermon, a preacher usually conforms to a certain phonological minimum which allows us to identify the variety; but he may introduce a further range of phonological effect into the sermon, such as extra rhythmicality, loudness or pitch width, all of which would be permissible within the province, and which would provide the basis, along with certain grammatical and lexical features, of the 'fire and brimstone' category of sermon. It is important to realize that this is a linguistically conventional type: any preacher wanting to give a sermon which would be recognized as belonging to this category would be forced to use a particular sub-set of linguistic features, and these would not occur in the same way in other contexts. But it is not easy to define the situational variable involved here. It is not province, as the same extra-linguistic factors may underlie the more usual kind of sermon, too; nor is it accountable for by reference to any of the other dimensions.

A stylistic theory should provide further dimensions of description capable of accounting for all such features, but with very little analysis having been done the nature and definitions of the required dimensions are by no means obvious at present. We feel that one potentially relevant dimension might take account of features in terms of whether they reflect a conventional orientation, a generally accepted way of treating some aspect of the communication situation—the subject matter of an utterance, the audience, some feature of expression or of the speaker's situation— within a stylistically restricted context. Such a dimension (which might be called *point of view* or *attitude*, as long as it was not confused with the more general, stylistically unrestricted senses of these terms) might well be able to handle many, though not all, of the above examples. We have not studied a sufficient number of cases, however, to justify setting this up as a separate dimension, consequently we have not given it any theoretical status in the present introductory investigation.

Perhaps causing the most difficult stylistic problem of all are those uses of language which cannot clearly be specified in terms of the above set of dimensions, because the phenomena referred to cut across all these dimensions and require specification with reference to qualitative, non-linguistic criteria. 'Literature' and 'humour' are the two central cases which need to be given separate theoretical status in this way. They are essentially different from other varieties, being fundamentally un-specifiable linguistically, and thus stylistically: it is impossible to list a set of features and predict that the configuration will be called literary or funny. There is a crucial qualitative distinction, which does not occur elsewhere at such a fundamental level, which the linguist, *qua* linguist, is not competent to assess. It is perhaps worth stressing, in view of the tension which has existed in the past between literary critics and linguists, that any decision as to what is of literary value and what is not is not the linguist's to make. His role in relation to literature is to ensure that all relevant linguistic variables prerequisite for understanding are in fact understood before this qualitative assessment is made.

We do not therefore wish to sidetrack ourselves into any discussion of the meaning of 'literature', and related issues. But we do wish to emphasize that there *are* certain factors, which could be considered stylistically distinctive in our sense, in most language normally put under the heading of literature (as defined by a consensus of opinion among those who consider themselves to be literary critics, and who would be considered by others as being so). Such central factors would be the relatively high proportion of singularity features, in the sense described above, the variability of modality (the question of 'genres' again), the high frequency of overt indications of attitude and, most important of all, the possibility of introducing any kind of linguistic convention without its being necessarily inappropriate—features from any other variety can be made use of in a literary context (or a humorous one) for a particular effect. Literature can be mimetic of the whole range of human experience —and this includes linguistic as well as non-linguistic experience. In a poem or novel, one may find pieces of religious or legal English, or any other, which have to be understood in their own right before one can go on to assess their function in terms of the literary work as a whole. Most literary works weld together contrasts which derive from different varieties of language—Eliot's *The Waste Land* and Joyce's *Ulysses* are particularly well-constructed cases in point.

One should also note that literature and humour, more than any other varieties, introduce a large number of descriptive problems which our theory in its present form cannot handle. For example, the above dimensions cannot satisfactorily explain the stylistic differences which exist between such widely varying aspects of literature as oral-formulaic verse, drama involving artificial but conventional vocalizations (such as expression of grief), the use of a chorus, the effect of stereotyped forms such as the limerick or nursery rhyme, and the whole question of introducing such literary effects as bathos. Or, in the case of humour, it is difficult to know how to account for the 'standard' kind of joke, where the familiarity of the linguistic pattern in the narrative is the main source of the effect (such as in the 'shaggy dog', or 'Englishman, Irishman, Scotsman' types, or in the more transient crazes for particular jokes involving outrageous puns or illogicalities). Again, the question is, how does one account for the standardness which is an intrinsic part of the variety and responses to it?

While on the subject of literature, we would point out that our approach in many ways parallels that adopted by textual critics in general. Indeed, some critics (for example, those associated with the methods of *explication de texte*) have markedly similar aims and techniques. The linguist's aim is to ensure that the total range of linguistic features bearing on the interpretation of a text can be made explicit. The normal critical apparatus of editor's notes, biographical allusions, and so on, where of linguistic relevance, is thus subsumed by our approach. This is especially desirable in the case of historical stylistics, where of course one has no direct intuition of the state of the language concerned.

We have not attempted to apply our approach to any literary texts in this book, partly for pedagogical reasons, partly for reasons of space limitation. But in view of the way in which books, articles and theses on stylistics these days tend to concentrate on literature to the exclusion of all else, some further explanation is perhaps necessary. Our omission is not, of course, due to any lack of interest on our part in literary language; indeed, we feel that the application of stylistic techniques to the study of literature is perhaps the most important reason for carrying on this business at all, and ultimately might well provide the most illuminating information. But no introduction to stylistic analysis should begin with literature, as this is potentially the most difficult kind of language to analyse—not only because it allows a greater range and more extreme kinds of deviation from the linguistic norms present in the rest of the language, but also because it presupposes an understanding of the varieties which constitute normal, non-literary language, as we mentioned earlier. One has to be aware of the normal function of the linguistic features constituting these varieties in non-literary English before one can see what use the author is making of them. Which is why the application of stylistic techniques to literature should be the last part of a stylistician's training, not the first. Moreover, in view of the vast range covered by the many different kinds of language which have been gathered together under the heading 'literature'—everything from the most conversation-like of drama to the most esoteric poetry—we feel it would be distorting to select but one or two short extracts for analysis in this book. Clearly, a separate study is needed to cover literary English adequately, and we hope it is not long before such a study is attempted.

Such work, however, will become possible only when stylisticians have appreciated sufficiently the complexities of 'ordinary' language, and have mastered the tools of analysis to the extent of being able to talk reasonably precisely, systematically, and objectively about the phenomena they are observing. So far, there is little evidence that anyone has reached this stage: most stylistic analyses carried out by linguists so far have been severely censured by literary critics for being unhelpful; and few books written by literary critics which purport to discuss an author's language have achieved anything like the degree of precision required to make their observations meaningful to the linguist—or to anyone who concedes the importance of objective, verifiable descriptive information as a critical tool. But it would be premature to condemn the linguistic approach to style before it has had a chance to prove itself: appreciation of the aims of stylistics will only come once an appreciation of the aims of linguistics as a whole has been attained. Meanwhile, we trust that, by restricting our attention to more mundane matters in this book, we can contribute a little towards the clarification of stylistics as a discipline.

We may summarize this discussion by saying that, in any text, the stylistically significant characteristics can be classified into types which correspond to the set of questions outlined below. Putting it crudely, the general question to be asking is, 'Apart from the message being communicated, what other kind of information does the utterance give us?' There are at least thirteen sub-questions here:

Does it tell us which specific person used it? (*Individuality*)

Does it tell us where in the country he is from? (*Regional dialect*)

Does it tell us which social class he belongs to? (*Class dialect*)

Does it tell us during which period of English he spoke or wrote it, or how old he was? (*Time*)

Does it tell us whether he was speaking or writing? (*Discourse medium*)

Does it tell us whether he was speaking or writing as an end in itself, or as a means to a further end? (*Simple v. complex discourse medium*)

Does it tell us whether there was only one participant in the utterance, or whether there was more than one? (*Discourse participation*)

Does it tell us whether the monologue and dialogue are independent, or are to be considered as part of a wider type of discourse? (*Simple v. complex discourse participation*)

Does it tell us which specific occupational activity the user is engaged in? (*Province*)

Does it tell us about the social relationship existing between the user and his interlocutors? (*Status*)

Does it tell us about the purpose he had in mind when conveying the message? (*Modality*)

Does it tell us that the user was being deliberately idiosyncratic? (*Singularity*)

Does it tell us none of these things? (*Common-core*)

Any one text will provide us simultaneously with information about each of these questions. Occasionally it is not possible (as was mentioned earlier) to allocate a linguistic feature or set of features to one dimension rather than another, but this is to be expected in the present stage of study. Ambiguous features in a text can be classified as such for the time being, and given further study at a later stage.

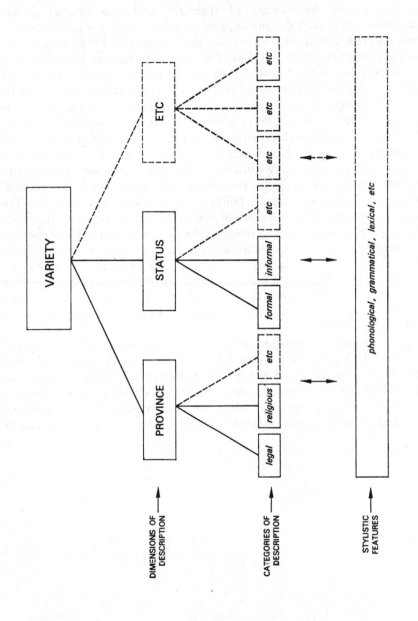

Once the stylistician has become aware of the kind of theoretical variability involved in work of this kind, he has two main tasks to carry out: to specify the number of (formally and functionally) distinct categories within each dimension, and plot the extent to which categories from different dimensions may co-occur. A *variety* will then be seen as a unique configuration of linguistic features, each feature being referable to one or more of the above dimensions of description; the variety displays a stable formal-functional correspondence, which is the basis of the intuitive impression of coherence and predictability that may then be labelled. (One will usually have given it an impressionistic label already, of course, to facilitate discussion. In an ideal world, linguistically based and impressionistically based varieties would coincide: how far they do in fact remains to be seen.) Within each dimension, one may distinguish a number (to be defined) of situational *categories*, such as 'formal', 'informal', 'religious', 'legal'. Different dimensions will have different numbers of categories. A switch in the categories at any one dimension (e.g. legal English becoming religious English, formal English becoming informal English) thus by definition produces a different variety. Some categories are naturally going to be closer together (share more linguistic correlates) than others, such as 'informal' and 'colloquial'; and therefore some varieties will be much closer together than others. But we have not tried to group varieties into more general types here; this is a task which remains to be done.

The categories in turn are defined with reference to sets of linguistic features which correlate with the distinctiveness of a situation, and which operate at some or all of the levels of description. These situationally bound linguistic distinctive features we refer to simply as *stylistic features* (or, if one wishes to get away from the term 'stylistic', *variety-markers*). The diagram on p. 91 may help to interrelate these concepts more clearly.

11 C. A. FERGUSON and J. D. GUMPERZ
Variety, Dialect and Language

First of all, one of the fundamental problems of linguistics is the delimitation of languages as the 'natural' units of linguistic analysis and classification. Put more directly, one of the concerns of linguistics is to find a
consistent, systematic way to answer such questions as: Are these two
particular varieties of human speech *one* language or *two*? Questions of
this kind arise all over the world. Are British English and American
English one language or two? Do all the Arabic dialects constitute one
language or several? Familiar examples from South Asia include: Is
Hindi one language or several? Are Konkani and Marathi two languages
or one? How many Dravidian languages are there? Questions like this
cannot be answered until some kind of definition of language is widely
accepted as valid, or possibly until the concept of language as a unit is
rejected and another formulation of the questions becomes accepted.

Surprisingly little attention is paid to this problem, however, and most
definitions of language which are in vogue among linguists today are more
concerned either with setting off speech behaviour from other human
activity or with setting off linguistic systems from other semiotic systems
than they are with defining the limits of single languages. For example,
linguists frequently define language as 'a system of arbitrary vocal
symbols by means of which a social group co-operates'. This definition
offers no clues whatever for the solution of the problem since two social
groups may use the same language or the same social group may use two
or more languages; and in any case the definition fails to specify 'social
group' either in linguistic or non-linguistic terms. Accordingly, the best
that can be done here is to summarize in a relatively crude, cover-all
definition the uses of the term 'language' in this sense by reputable
linguists.

In order to do this, one additional concept requires definition, the
minimal unit which serves as the 'normal' object of linguistic description.

C. A. Ferguson and J. D. Gumperz: Extract from 'Linguistic Diversity in South Asia',
International Journal of American Linguistics, Vol. 26, No. 3, 1960, pp. 2–13.

A whole language is often too varied to be readily analysed by current descriptive techniques, and descriptive linguists generally restrict their object of study with considerable care. Harris says, 'The universe of discourse for a descriptive linguistic investigation is a single language or dialect'. Bloch uses the term 'idiolect', the 'totality of the possible utterances of one speaker at one time in using the language to interact with one speaker'. These brief definitions, as the authors of them are fully aware, are not completely satisfactory. The idiolect concept for example is a necessary one, since in practice languages are always studied in terms of the speech of single speakers. As a unit of analysis however an idiolect is defined by extra-linguistic criteria, and homogeneity of structure is not a necessary requirement. Thus the speech of two individuals may be so very similar as to cause no difficulty in description while two styles of speech of one individual may be very different, and no one has shown how to delimit styles rigorously in the speech of one person or of many.

At the present state of linguistics it is probably wise to sidestep the issues involved in devising a precise operational definition and to settle for a suggestive description. There is no term in regular use for this concept of the object of descriptive linguistic analysis, but the word 'variety' has been used by several authors in this sense and will be so used here. A VARIETY is *any body of human speech patterns which is sufficiently homogeneous to be analysed by available techniques of synchronic description and which has a sufficiently large repertory of elements and their arrangements or processes with broad enough semantic scope to function in all normal contexts of communication.* With this concept clarified we may now attempt to define a language.

A first approximation to the definition may be in terms of mutual intelligibility. Other considerations aside, two varieties of human speech are said to be the same language if each is readily intelligible to speakers of the other. The difficulties of a definition of this kind are many, however, and are reminiscent of the difficulties of the biologist's use of the possibility of interbreeding as the primary criterion in the definition of the species.

In the first place mutual intelligibility is difficult to determine (or even impossible, as with dead languages). Second, there seems to be little direct correlation between similarity of phonological or grammatical structure on the one hand and mutual intelligibility on the other. This lack of correlation is disturbing because linguists generally regard these structures as fundamental in human speech and often prefer to describe linguistic relationships in these 'internal' terms. Also, we frequently find varieties of speech which do not show high mutual intelligibility but which on totally different grounds we wish to regard as the same language, and vice versa. A well-known example is found in the varieties at the extremes of the German-speaking area which are quite different, with relatively low mutual intelligibility. They are connected, however, by a series of intervening varieties which provide a gradual transition, and linguists generally agree in regarding all as varieties of one language.

On the other hand, certain varieties are regarded as different languages in spite of their high degree of mutual intelligibility. For example, there is a gradual transition between varieties of Dutch and German, but because of the existence of two relatively stabilized, widely-used standard varieties, Dutch (ABN) and German (*Schriftdeutsch*), two speech communities and hence two languages, are usually recognized; any transitional variety is assigned to the language whose standard form is accepted in the community, regardless of the internal linguistic similarities.

Another commonly used criterion for differentiating languages is that of difference in historical development. Two sets of varieties are said to constitute different languages if they differ significantly in their treatment of certain phonological and morphological features of a reconstructed parent variety. In contrast to the problems encountered in the determination of mutual intelligibility, historical relationship is relatively easy to establish by the rigorous and generally accepted methods of historical reconstruction. Grierson used this criterion in classifying speech distribution in what is now called the Hindi regional language area. He grouped the local varieties into five groups, which he calls languages: Bihari, Eastern Hindi, Western Hindi, Rajasthani, and Pahari. Each group is set off from the others by peculiarities of grammar and pronunciation. Modern Hindi-Urdu is part of the Western Hindi group, but its historical relationship to the other local varieties is by no means always very close. Bihari is more directly related to Bengali, the regional language of Bengal; some forms of Rajasthani are usually classed with Gujerati to the south and the Pahari dialects are closest to Nepali, the language of Nepal.

Classifications of the above kind are essential in historical linguistics, and they provide valuable information for students of culture history. They do not, however, present all the facts of language distribution. In spite of the diversity of local speech forms and their relationship to neighbouring regional languages in Grierson's area, Hindi-Urdu is recognized as the language of literature and government throughout. A large proportion of the modern urban population and of the educated speaks it and in other ways regards itself as belonging to a single Hindi-Urdu speech community. Many modern writers thus disregard the historical relationships and refer to all local speech forms as varieties of Hindi. As in the case of the German-Dutch area, the presence of a superposed variety, such as a literary standard, is an important factor in the determination of language boundaries. This factor is irrelevant, however, if the standard language in use in an area is extremely divergent or obviously unrelated to the variety to be classified. All this brings us to our working definition.

A LANGUAGE consists of *all varieties* (whether only a single variety or an indefinitely large number of them) *which share a single superposed variety* (such as a literary standard) *having substantial similarity in phonology and grammar with the included varieties* or *which are either mutually intelligible* or *are connected by a series of mutually intelligible varieties.*

It is evident that, as with the term idiolect, purely linguistic criteria are not currently accepted as sufficient for the delimitation of a language. Rather, a given set of varieties must meet certain minimum linguistic conditions (e.g. structural similarity within the set, structural difference from varieties outside the set) as well as certain sociological conditions (e.g. use of standard, speakers' feeling of belonging to speech community) in order to be regarded as a single language.

When the concepts of 'variety' and 'language' have been explained it is feasible to define the linguistic notion of 'dialect', which is crucial to the present studies. It must be made clear at the outset that two conventional uses of this term are to be disregarded. One is the use of 'dialect' to mean an inferior language of some kind. This use of the term is still widespread in such expressions as 'Mr. A speaks six languages and ten dialects'. 'The inhabitant of that country speaks dozens of languages and innumerable dialects'. Since no linguistic criterion has ever been devised to differentiate superior and inferior languages, linguists prefer to operate without this distinction. The other is the use of 'dialect' to mean any non-standard variety of a language. This use is still current in expressions such as: 'He doesn't speak good German; he speaks only dialect'. 'These children are learning to speak the language without a trace of dialect'. 'This is a dialect word not preserved in the literary language'. Many languages have one variety which is in certain respects dominant, the 'standard' variety, and it is often useful to distinguish between the standard variety and non-standard varieties of a given language, but linguists have found it more useful to leave the word 'dialect' colourless and equally applicable to standard and non-standard varieties. Thus linguists may refer to the 'standard dialect' of a given language, and even if they continue to use the traditional expression 'standard language' they generally regard this as a dialect, often, of course, the most important from some points of view.

In the terminology of linguistics a dialect is, roughly speaking, something between a variety and a language. Sometimes in the analysis of a language an obvious classification of varieties into dialects is clear to the linguist. More often a number of alternative analyses are possible, and any particular classification into dialects runs counter to at least some features which could be used for classification. The elementary concept of dialectology is the isogloss. Any boundary which constitutes the limits of use of a particular linguistic feature is called an isogloss. For example, the word *frappe* is regularly used in the area around Boston to refer to a drink consisting of milk, ice cream, and flavouring beaten together. In most of the United States this drink is called a *milk shake*, a term which in the Boston area refers to a similar drink made without ice cream. The boundary which shows the limits of the use of *frappe* in this sense, and which could be plotted on a map, is called an isogloss. In addition to isoglosses concerned with the occurrence of words in certain meanings (lexical isoglosses), linguists also make use of phonological and grammatical isoglosses.

In classifying dialects linguists generally prefer to place emphasis on isoglosses (*a*) which cut boldly across large areas as opposed to those which are relatively local, or (*b*) which bundle together as opposed to those which are relatively isolated, or (*c*) which correlate with non-linguistic criteria of classification such as differences in material culture, religion, political units, and the like.

Since dialect classification is largely arbitrary it might seem to be of relatively little value or even misleading, but in fact the delimitation of dialects is of great importance, both within linguistics proper and for extra-linguistic fields. In linguistic theory, a dialect may be regarded as the beginning of a linguistic split, as a step in linguistic differentiation. In other words a dialect is a potential new language, and the concept is comparable in validity and significance to that of the 'sub-species' or 'variety' of biology. For the extra-linguistic importance of the dialect we need only note its obvious relevance to the units of other social sciences such as geographical region, social class, or role.

A DIALECT is *any set of one or more varieties of a language which share at least one feature or combination of features setting them apart from other varieties of the language, and which may appropriately be treated as a unit on linguistic or non-linguistic grounds.* Because of the arbitrariness of this concept, linguists using the term 'dialect' for a particular language generally feel under obligation to explain and justify the criteria used for their classification in that language.

Geographical dialects

The extent and nature of dialect differentiation in a language may be described in terms of two major correlates: density of communication and inter-speaker attitudes. It cannot be maintained that these are the only relevant factors since the significance of such matters as the structure of the language (Sapir's 'drift'), interference of other languages, phonetic symbolism, or technological change can be shown, but on the whole these two correlates provide a satisfactory frame of reference for the analysis of dialect diversity.

The assumption with regard to density of communication may be phrased in general terms as follows: *Other things being equal, the more frequently speakers A and B of language X communicate with each other by means of X, the more the varieties of X spoken by them will tend to become identical.* It follows from this that isoglosses will tend to coincide with breaks or lines of weakness in communication. Since such breaks or lines of weakness will often correlate with natural physical boundaries such as mountains or rivers, or with political boundaries, or with economic limits (on the flow of goods and services), it is clear that a large proportion of dialect diversity will be subject to mapping. Possibly because of the effectiveness of cartographic representation of dialect differences, this has been one of the most highly developed fields of work in dialectology. Dialect atlases have been published for many languages, and many special techniques of mapping have been developed. Apart from limited special studies most books in dialectology are either dialect atlases or grammars of non-standard varieties.

Social dialects

The assumption with regards to inter-speaker attitudes may be stated in terms of two processes. First: *any group of speakers of language X which regards itself as a close social unit will tend to express its group solidarity by favouring those linguistic innovations which set it apart from other speakers of X who are not part of the group.* The existence within a speech community of social distinctions such as those of caste, class, professional guild therefore gives rise to differential rates of linguistic change, favouring the creation of new speech differences or the preservation of existing ones. On the other hand: *other things being equal, if two speakers A and B of language X communicate in language X and if A regards B as having more prestige than himself and aspires to equal B's status, then the variety of X spoken by A will tend towards identity with that spoken by B.* It may seem that this is a circular statement since one of the indications of the attitude of prestige is linguistic imitation but it is assumed that prestige relationships may be measured independently of language. As Leach puts it in describing a somewhat different multi-lingual situation: 'For a man to speak one language rather than another is a ritual act, it is a statement about one's personal status: to speak the same language as one's neighbour expresses solidarity with those neighbours, to speak a different language from one's neighbours expresses social distance or even hostility'.

The above two processes create a condition of equilibrium: as old speech differences vanish, new ones arise with the addition of population elements from the outside or through the formation of fresh social distinctions. The total range of speech diversity within a speech community, i.e. the actual language distance between all the varieties found there, is a function of the density of intergroup communication. In societies like our modern American one where social class is fluid and mass communication media are highly developed and shared by most, we would expect the range of variation to be relatively small. Differences would most frequently appear on the level of phonetics or the lexicon but rarely affect the fundamental phonological or morphological structure of the language. In Asia, however, where intergroup communication is severely limited by ritual restrictions we would expect these differences to be much greater.

The parallels between speech variation and social stratification are manifold. This field of investigation has been worked very little by the dialectologist, however, whether because of the difficulty of presenting the data, or the problem of identification of social groupings, or simple historical accident in the development of the science. A handful of valuable studies in this field do exist for various languages and show great promise for the development of sociolinguistic analysis.

Style and superposed varieties

The third kind of variation to be described here is different in nature from the preceding two. Geographical or social dialects tend to be mutually exclusive in the sense that the normal individual is a native speaker of only one dialect, and if he speaks more than one this is a sign of geographical or social transition of some kind on his part. But there are also linguistic variations which regularly coexist in the speech of individuals, with their use reflecting some kind of situational or role differences.

It is part of the nature of language, or of human culture in general, that there should be individual differences in performance and differences in the performance of a given individual in various situations. For example, a speaker normally has 'favourite expressions' (e.g. words, phrases, constructions) which he uses more frequently than other speakers; and any adult speaker normally uses different kinds of speech talking to his young children, participating in a religious ceremony, chatting with old friends, and explaining something to a stranger. To take somewhat different examples, in English the two words *light* and *illumination* have roughly the same meaning, but *light* tends to be used in less formal, less pretentious situations. Or, again, the words *fore, aft, deck, companionway* have meanings very similar to those of *front, back, floor, stairway*, but the first set is generally used either in a maritime setting or to suggest it, or by people who regularly live and work in such a setting.

All languages seem to show variations of this kind. As is the case with social dialects, however, the exact range of these variations and the level of linguistic structure at which they appear vary significantly. In America we find only minor differences in lexicon, syntax, stress and intonation, which do not materially complicate the task of linguistic analysis. Other parts of the world however show more fundamental variations. One of the most extreme situations of this type is that described by Garvin and Riesenberg on Ponape, where different sets of bound morpheme alternants and lexical items were used in social situations calling for honorific and non-honorific speech. Whenever two styles have striking morphological variation (e.g. case endings vs. no case endings) or extensive lexical pairing (e.g. pairs of different words for common items such as 'head', 'go', 'now'), or when both styles in question are regularly used under appropriate circumstances by a large segment of the speech community (e.g. all educated speakers of the language), then special language situations must be recognized which deserve study and which clearly present theoretical and practical problems of quite a different nature. The investigation of stylistic differences of this kind is of interest to the linguist since they constitute a fundamental mechanism of language and their analysis provides an insight into more general aspects of speech dynamics. For other social scientists correlation of style with social situation, personality, and similar factors offers valuable clues to the understanding of non-linguistic human behaviour.

Some styles of speech are sufficiently striking and extensive to require study as more or less autonomous marginal or partial systems within a language, and often enough the styles appropriate to certain occasions are full-fledged varieties of the language existing over and above the primary or 'natural' speech of individuals. There are many kinds of these superposed varieties, the most important being the various types of standard languages.

Very often one variety of a language, e.g. a certain local dialect, becomes widely accepted as standard and is learned by speakers of other varieties in addition to their native variety. Among typical examples of this standard language vs. local dialect situation we may cite important languages of Europe and Asia (e.g. German, Italian, Persian) where many speakers use a local dialect in familiar or 'home' situations but use the standard language in more formal or 'outside' situations. In some speech communities there may even be several layers of superposed varieties of this sort, with national and regional standards in addition to local dialects. To complicate this picture there may also be regionally standardized pronunciations of the national standard as well as various mixed varieties appropriate to certain occasions or used by individuals who have not fully mastered certain levels. This layer phenomenon is fairly frequent in South Asia and has recently been described for Hindi. Another kind of superposed variety is illustrated by the classical-colloquial dichotomy of Arabic, modern Greek, or Swiss German where the standard form of the language is used for written and formal spoken purposes only, the other for ordinary conversation. The spread of a particular standard variety is determined by social and political factors and often has little relation to the actual language distance between the standard and the local dialects. Thus, returning to our German example, we find High German used as a standard by many speakers whose native dialects are much closer to Dutch. Another interesting case in point is that of Southern Nepal where native speakers of Maithili, a dialect related to Bengali, are advocating the adoption of Hindi as a standard language. Other Maithili speakers across the border in Bihar are opposed to Hindi and favour the creation of a new literary standard based on medieval literary Maithili.

Language as a Symbolic System

For either commerce or communication to take place there must be some system of tokens available whose value is known and accepted by both parties to the deal. A language as a symbolic system of communication will only work if the thoughts, ideas, concepts or subjective events which its various items and relations codify are shared by both speaker and hearer. The language system is, of course, something we inherit or acquire from the culture/society in which we grow up; there is virtually nothing the individual can do to change it. The problem with which all the papers in this section are concerned is to establish the nature of the relation between the structure of a language as a symbolic system and the mental functions and cognitive structures of its users. Theories about this relationship are called *theories of linguistic relativity*. The two possible extreme views are, on the one hand, that mental operations are carried out independently of language, i.e. that it is merely a system for 'voicing ideas', or, on the other hand, that mental functions are wholly determined by language, i.e. that it is a 'shaper of ideas'. The latter point of view is known as the 'Whorfian Hypothesis'. Intermediate theoretical positions between these two extremes are, of course, possible, such as those of Carrol and Hockett (quoted by Fishman); these propose that the structure of a language does not determine what can or cannot be thought, but merely make the expression of certain ideas more or less difficult.

It should be noted that the contributors confine themselves to the problem of the relation between cognitive functions and language. But in Section 2 we saw that linguistic communication had other functions besides that of 'expressing thoughts'. Success in communication is not wholly dependant upon the successful communication of cognitive content. No one has suggested that desires, wishes, intentions and emotions are linguistically determined, or that the free expression of them is linguistically constrained.

The significance of the problem of linguistic relativity for language teaching is evident. At one extreme the learning of a new language would involve the acquisition of a more or less completely new conceptual system and mode of thought, if it were possible, and there could be no such thing as adequate translation between many languages. At the other extreme the learning of a new language would involve no more than the learning of a new set of expressions for the same mental functions and concepts already codified in the first language. In other words, we should have to learn little more than a set of rules for automatic translation.

12 B. L. WHORF
Linguistic Relativity

Every normal person in the world, past infancy in years, can and does talk. By virtue of that fact, every person—civilized or uncivilized—carries through life certain naïve but deeply rooted ideas about talking and its relation to thinking. Because of their firm connexion with speech habits that have become unconscious and automatic, these notions tend to be rather intolerant of opposition. They are by no means entirely personal and haphazard; their basis is definitely systematic, so that we are justified in calling them a system of natural logic—a term that seems to me preferable to the term common sense, often used for the same thing.

According to natural logic, the fact that every person has talked fluently since infancy makes every man his own authority on the process by which he formulates and communicates. He has merely to consult a common substratum of logic or reason which he and everyone else are supposed to possess. Natural logic says that talking is merely an incidental process concerned strictly with communication, not with formulation of ideas. Talking, or the use of language, is supposed only to 'express' what is essentially already formulated nonlinguistically. Formulation is an independent process, called thought or thinking, and is supposed to be largely indifferent to the nature of particular languages. Languages have grammars, which are assumed to be merely norms of conventional and social correctness, but the use of language is supposed to be guided not so much by them as by correct, rational, or intelligent *thinking*.

Thought, in this view, does not depend on grammar but on laws of logic or reason which are supposed to be the same for all observers of the universe—to represent a rationale in the universe that can be 'found' independently by all intelligent observers, whether they speak Chinese or Choctaw. In our own culture, the formulations of mathematics and of formal logic have acquired the reputation of dealing with this order of things: i.e. with the realm and laws of pure thought. Natural logic

B. L. Whorf: Extract from 'Science and Linguistics' in *Language, Thought and Reality*, Ed. J. B. Carroll, M.I.T. Press, 1956, pp. 207–19.

holds that different languages are essentially parallel methods for expressing this one-and-the-same rationale of thought and, hence, differ really in but minor ways which may seem important only because they are seen at close range. It holds that mathematics, symbolic logic, philosophy, and so on are systems contrasted with language, which deal directly with this realm of thought, not that they are themselves specialized extensions of language. The attitude of natural logic is well shown in an old quip about a German grammarian who devoted his whole life to the study of the dative case. From the point of view of natural logic, the dative case and grammar in general arc an extremely minor issue. A different attitude is said to have been held by the ancient Arabians:

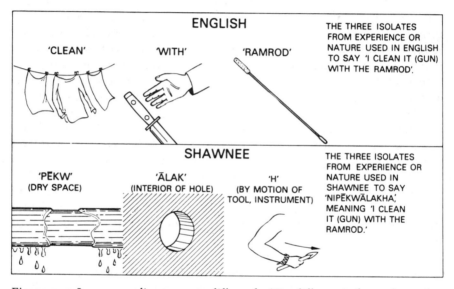

Figure 12.1. Languages dissect nature differently. The different isolates of meaning (thoughts) used by English and Shawnee in reporting the same experience, that of cleaning a gun by running the ramrod through it. The pronouns 'I' and 'it' are not shown by symbols, as they have the same meaning in each language. In Shawnee ni- equals 'I'; -a equals 'it'.

Two princes, so the story goes, quarrelled over the honour of putting on the shoes of the most learned grammarian of the realm; whereupon their father, the caliph, is said to have remarked that it was the glory of his kingdom that great grammarians were honoured even above kings.

The familiar saying that the exception proves the rule contains a good deal of wisdom, though from the standpoint of formal logic it became an absurdity as soon as 'prove' no longer meant 'put on trial'. The old saw began to be profound psychology from the time it ceased to have standing in logic. What it might well suggest to us today is that, if a rule has absolutely no exceptions, it is not recognized as a rule or as anything else; it is then part of the background of experience of which we tend to remain unconscious. Never having experienced anything in contrast to it, we cannot isolate it and formulate it as a rule until we so enlarge our experience and expand our base of reference that we encounter an interruption of its regularity. The situation is somewhat analogous to that of not missing the water till the well runs dry, or not realizing that we need air till we are choking.

For instance, if a race of people had the physiological defect of being able to see only the colour blue, they would hardly be able to formulate the rule that they saw only blue. The term blue would convey no meaning to them, their language would lack colour terms, and their words denoting their various sensations of blue would answer to, and translate, our words 'light, dark, white, black', and so on, not our word 'blue'. In order to formulate the rule or norm of seeing only blue, they would need exceptional moments in which they saw other colours. The phenomenon of gravitation forms a rule without exceptions; needless to say, the untutored person is utterly unaware of any law of gravitation, for it would never enter his head to conceive of a universe in which bodies behaved otherwise than they do at the earth's surface. Like the colour blue with our hypothetical race, the law of gravitation is a part of the untutored individual's background, not something he isolates from that background. The law could not be formulated until bodies that always fell were seen in terms of a wider astronomical world in which bodies moved in orbits or went this way and that.

Similarly, whenever we turn our heads, the image of the scene passes across our retinas exactly as it would if the scene turned around us. But this effect is background, and we do not recognize it; we do not see a room turn around us but are conscious only of having turned our heads in a stationary room. If we observe critically while turning the head or eyes quickly, we shall see, no motion it is true, yet a blurring of the scene between two clear views. Normally we are quite unconscious of this continual blurring but seem to be looking about in an unblurred world. Whenever we walk past a tree or house, its image on the retina changes just as if the tree or house were turning on an axis; yet we do not see trees or houses turn as we travel about at ordinary speeds. Sometimes ill-fitting glasses will reveal queer movements in the scene as we look about, but normally we do not see the relative motion of the environment when we move; our psychic makeup is somehow adjusted to disregard whole realms of phenomena that are so all-pervasive as to be irrelevant to our daily lives and needs.

Natural logic contains two fallacies: First, it does not see that the phenomena of a language are to its own speakers largely of a background character and so are outside the critical consciousness and control of the speaker who is expounding natural logic. Hence, when anyone, as a natural logician, is talking about reason, logic, and the laws of correct thinking, he is apt to be simply marching in step with purely grammatical

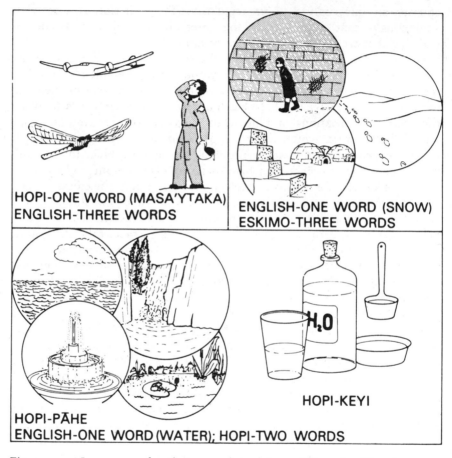

HOPI-ONE WORD (MASA'YTAKA)
ENGLISH-THREE WORDS

ENGLISH-ONE WORD (SNOW)
ESKIMO-THREE WORDS

HOPI-PĀHE
ENGLISH-ONE WORD (WATER); HOPI-TWO WORDS

HOPI-KEYI

Figure 12.2. Languages classify items of experience differently. The class corresponding to one word and one thought in language A may be regarded by language B as two or more classes corresponding to two or more words and thoughts.

facts that have somewhat of a background character in his own language or family of languages but are by no means universal in all languages and in no sense a common substratum of reason. Second, natural logic confuses agreement about subject matter, attained through use of language, with knowledge of the linguistic process by which agreement is attained: i.e. with the province of the despised (and to its notion superfluous) grammarian. Two fluent speakers, of English let us say, quickly reach a point of assent about the subject matter of their speech; they agree what their language refers to. One of them, A, can give directions that will be carried out by the other, B, to A's complete satisfaction. Because they thus understand each other so perfectly, A and B, as natural logicians, suppose they must of course know how it is all done. They think, e.g. that it is simply a matter of choosing words to express thoughts. If you ask A to explain how he got B's agreement so readily, he will simply repeat to you, with more or less elaboration or abbreviation, what he said to B. He has no notion of the process involved. The amazingly complex system of linguistic patterns and classifications, which A and B must have in common before they can adjust to each other at all, is all background to A and B.

These background phenomena are the province of the grammarian— or of the linguist, to give him his more modern name as a scientist. The word linguist in common, and especially newspaper, parlance means something entirely different, namely, a person who can quickly attain agreement about subject matter with different people speaking a number of different languages. Such a person is better termed a polyglot or a multilingual. Scientific linguists have long understood that ability to speak a language fluently does not necessarily confer a linguistic knowledge of it, i.e. understanding of its background phenomena and its systematic processes and structure, any more than ability to play a good game of billiards confers or requires any knowledge of the laws of mechanics that operate upon the billiard table.

The situation here is not unlike that in any other field of science. All real scientists have their eyes primarily on background phenomena that cut very little ice, as such, in our daily lives; and yet their studies have a way of bringing out a close relation between these unsuspected realms of fact and such decidedly foreground activities as transporting goods, preparing food, treating the sick, or growing potatoes, which in time may become very much modified, simply because of pure scientific investigation in no way concerned with these brute matters themselves. Linguistics presents a quite similar case; the background phenomena with which it deals are involved in all our foreground activities of talking and of reaching agreement, in all reasoning and arguing of cases, in all law, arbitration, conciliation, contracts, treaties, public opinion, weighing of scientific theories, formulation of scientific results. Whenever agreement or assent is arrived at in human affairs, and whether or not mathematics or other specialized symbolisms are made part of the procedure, *this agreement is reached by linguistic processes, or else it is not reached.*

As we have seen, an overt knowledge of the linguistic processes by which agreement is attained is not necessary to reaching some sort of agreement, but it is certainly no bar thereto; the more complicated and difficult the matter, the more such knowledge is a distinct aid, till the point may be reached—I suspect the modern world has about arrived at it—when the knowledge becomes not only an aid but a necessity

OBJECTIVE FIELD	SPEAKER (SENDER)	HEARER (RECEIVER)	HANDLING OF TOPIC RUNNING OF THIRD PERSON
SITUATION 1 a.			ENGLISH..'HE IS RUNNING' HOPI........'WARI' (RUNNING, STATEMENT OF FACT)
SITUATION 1 b. OBJECTIVE FIELD BLANK DEVOID OF RUNNING			ENGLISH..'HE RAN' HOPI........'WARI' (RUNNING, STATEMENT OF FACT)
SITUATION 2			ENGLISH..'HE IS RUNNING' HOPI........'WARI' (RUNNING, STATEMENT OF FACT)
SITUATION 3 OBJECTIVE FIELD BLANK			ENGLISH..'HE RAN' HOPI........'ERA WARI' (RUNNING, STATEMENT OF FACT FROM MEMORY)
SITUATION 4 OBJECTIVE FIELD BLANK			ENGLISH..'HE WILL RUN' HOPI........'WARIKNI' (RUNNING, STATEMENT OF EXPECTATION)
SITUATION 5 OBJECTIVE FIELD BLANK			ENGLISH..'HE RUNS' (E.G. ON THE TRACK TEAM) HOPI ....'WARIKNGWE' (RUNNING, STATEMENT OF LAW)

Figure 12.3. Contrast between a 'temporal' language (English) and a 'timeless' language (Hopi). What are to English differences of time are to Hopi differences in the kind of validity.

The situation may be likened to that of navigation. Every boat that sails is in the lap of planetary forces; yet a boy can pilot his small craft around a harbour without benefit of geography, astronomy, mathematics, or international politics. To the captain of an ocean liner, however, some knowledge of all these subjects is essential.

When linguists became able to examine critically and scientifically a large number of languages of widely different patterns, their base of reference was expanded; they experienced an interruption of phenomena hitherto held universal, and a whole new order of significances came into their ken. It was found that the background linguistic system (in other words, the grammar) of each language is not merely a reproducing instrument for voicing ideas but rather is itself the shaper of ideas, the programme and guide for the individual's mental activity, for his analysis of impressions, for his synthesis of his mental stock in trade. Formulation of ideas is not an independent process, strictly rational in the old sense, but is part of a particular grammar, and differs, from slightly to greatly, between different grammars. We dissect nature along lines laid down by our native languages. The categories and types that we isolate from the world of phenomena we do not find there because they stare every observer in the face; on the contrary, the world is presented in a kaleidoscopic flux of impressions which has to be organized by our minds—and this means largely by the linguistic systems in our minds. We cut nature up, organize it into concepts, and ascribe significances as we do, largely because we are parties to an agreement to organize it in this way —an agreement that holds throughout our speech community and is codified in the patterns of our language. The agreement is, of course, an implicit and unstated one, *but its terms are absolutely obligatory*; we cannot talk at all except by subscribing to the organization and classification of data which the agreement decrees.

This fact is very significant for modern science, for it means that no individual is free to describe nature with absolute impartiality but is constrained to certain modes of interpretation even while he thinks himself most free. The person most nearly free in such respects would be a linguist familiar with very many widely different linguistic systems. As yet no linguist is in any such position. We are thus introduced to a new principle of relativity, which holds that all observers are not led by the same physical evidence to the same picture of the universe, unless their linguistic backgrounds are similar, or can in some way be calibrated.

This rather startling conclusion is not so apparent if we compare only our modern European languages, with perhaps Latin and Greek thrown in for good measure. Among these tongues there is a unanimity of major pattern which at first seems to bear out natural logic. But this unanimity exists only because these tongues are all Indo-European dialects cut to the same basic plan, being historically transmitted from what was long ago one speech community; because the modern dialects have long shared in building up a common culture; and because much of this culture, on the more intellectual side, is derived from the linguistic backgrounds of Latin and Greek. Thus this group of languages satisfies the special case of the clause beginning 'unless' in the statement of the linguistic relativity principle at the end of the preceding paragraph. From this condition follows the unanimity of description of the world in the community of modern scientists. But it must be emphasized that 'all modern Indo-European-speaking observers' is not the same thing as 'all observers'. That modern Chinese or Turkish scientists describe the world in the same terms as Western scientists means, of course, only that they have taken over bodily the entire Western system of rationalizations, not that they have corroborated that system from their native posts of observation.

When Semitic, Chinese, Tibetan, or African languages are contrasted with our own, the divergence in analysis of the world becomes more apparent; and, when we bring in the native languages of the Americas, where speech communities for many millenniums have gone their ways independently of each other and of the Old World, the fact that languages dissect nature in many different ways becomes patent. The relativity of all conceptual systems, ours included, and their dependence upon language stand revealed. That American Indians speaking only their native tongues are never called upon to act as scientific observers is in no wise to the point. To exclude the evidence which their languages offer as to what the human mind can do is like expecting botanists to study nothing but food plants and hothouse roses and then tell us what the plant world is like!

Let us consider a few examples. In English we divide most of our words into two classes, which have different grammatical and logical properties. Class 1 we call nouns, e.g. 'house, man'; class 2, verbs, e.g. 'hit, run'. Many words of one class can act secondarily as of the other class, e.g. 'a hit, a run', or 'to man (the boat)', but, on the primary level, the division between the classes is absolute. Our language thus gives us a bipolar division of nature. But nature herself is not thus polarized. If it be said that 'strike, turn, run', are verbs because they denote temporary or short-lasting events, i.e. actions, why then is 'fist' a noun? It also is a temporary event. Why are 'lightning, spark, wave, eddy, pulsation, flame, storm, phase, cycle, spasm, noise, emotion' nouns? They are temporary events. If 'man' and 'house' are nouns because they are long-lasting and stable events, i.e. things, what then are 'keep, adhere, extend, project, continue, persist, grow, dwell', and so on doing among the verbs? If it be objected that 'possess, adhere' are verbs because they are stable relationships rather than stable percepts, why then should 'equilibrium, pressure, current, peace, group, nation, society, tribe, sister', or any kinship term be among the nouns? It will be found that an 'event' to us means 'what our language classes as a verb' or something analogized therefrom. And it will be found that it is not possible to define 'event, thing, object, relationship', and so on, from nature, but that to define them always involves a circuitous return to the grammatical categories of the definer's language.

In the Hopi language, 'lightning, wave, flame, meteor, puff of smoke, pulsation' are verbs—events of necessarily brief duration cannot be anything but verbs. 'Cloud' and 'storm' are at about the lower limit of duration for nouns. Hopi, you see, actually has a classification of events (or linguistic isolates) by duration type, something strange to our modes of thought. On the other hand, in Nootka, a language of Vancouver Island, all words seem to us to be verbs, but really there are no classes 1 and 2; we have, as it were, a monistic view of nature that gives us only one class of word for all kinds of events. 'A house occurs' or 'it houses' is the way of saying 'house', exactly like 'a flame occurs' or 'it burns'. These terms seem to us like verbs because they are inflected for durational and temporal nuances, so that the suffixes of the word for house event make it mean long-lasting house, temporary house, future house, house that used to be, what started out to be a house, and so on.

Hopi has one noun that covers every thing or being that flies, with the exception of birds, which class is denoted by another noun. The former noun may be said to denote the class (FC–B)—flying class minus bird. The Hopi actually call insect, aeroplane, and aviator all by the same word, and feel no difficulty about it. The situation, of course, decides any possible confusion among very disparate members of a broad linguistic class, such as this class (FC–B). This class seems to us too large and inclusive, but so would our class 'snow' to an Eskimo. We have the same word for falling snow, snow on the ground, snow packed hard like ice, slushy snow, wind-driven flying snow—whatever the situation may be. To an Eskimo, this all-inclusive word would be almost unthinkable; he would say that falling snow, slushy snow, and so on, are sensuously and operationally different, different things to contend with; he uses different words for them and for other kinds of snow. The Aztecs go even farther than we in the opposite direction, with 'cold', 'ice' and 'snow' all represented by the same basic word with different terminations; 'ice' is the noun form; 'cold', the adjectival form; and for 'snow', 'ice mist'.

What surprises most is to find that various grand generalizations of the Western world, such as time, velocity, and matter, are not essential to the construction of a consistent picture of the universe. The psychic experiences that we class under these headings are, of course, not destroyed; rather, categories derived from other kinds of experiences take over the rulership of the cosmology and seem to function just as well. Hopi may be called a timeless language. It recognizes psychological time, which is much like Bergson's 'duration', but this 'time' is quite unlike the mathematical time, T, used by our physicists. Among the peculiar properties of Hopi time are that it varies with each observer, does not permit of simultaneity, and has zero dimensions; i.e. it cannot be given a number greater than one. The Hopi do not say, 'I stayed five days', but 'I left on the fifth day'. A word referring to this kind of time, like the word day, can have no plural. The puzzle picture (Fig. 12.3, page 108) will give mental exercise to anyone who would like to figure out how the Hopi verb gets along without tenses. Actually, the only practical use of our tenses, in one-verb sentences, is to distinguish among five typical situations, which are symbolized in the picture. The timeless Hopi verb does not distinguish between the present, past, and future of the event itself but must always indicate what type of validity the *speaker* intends the statement to have: (*a*) report of an event (situations 1, 2, 3 in the picture); (*b*) expectation of an event (situation 4); (*c*) generalization or law about events (situation 5). Situation 1, where the speaker and listener are in contact with the same objective field, is divided by our language into the two conditions, 1*a* and 1*b*, which it calls present and past, respectively. This division is unnecessary for a language which assures one that the statement is a report.

Hopi grammar, by means of its forms called aspects and modes, also makes it easy to distinguish among momentary, continued, and repeated occurrences, and to indicate the actual sequence of reported events. Thus the universe can be described without recourse to a concept of dimensional time. How would a physics constructed along these lines work, with no T (time) in its equations? Perfectly, as far as I can see, though of course it would require different ideology and perhaps different mathematics. Of course V (velocity) would have to go too. The Hopi language has no word really equivalent to our 'speed' or 'rapid'. What translates these terms is usually a word meaning intense or very, accompanying any verb of motion. Here is a clue to the nature of our new physics. We may have to introduce a new term I, intensity. Every thing and event will have an I, whether we regard the thing or event as moving or as just enduring or being. Perhaps the I of an electric charge will turn out to be its voltage, or potential. We shall use clocks to measure some intensities, or, rather, some *relative* intensities, for the absolute intensity of anything will be meaningless. Our old friend acceleration will still be there but doubtless under a new name. We shall perhaps call it V, meaning not velocity but variation. Perhaps all growths and accumulations will be regarded as V's. We should not have the concept of rate in the temporal sense, since, like velocity, rate introduces a mathematical and linguistic time. Of course we know that all measurements are ratios, but the measurements of intensities made by comparison with the standard intensity of a clock or a planet we do not treat as ratios, any more than we so treat a distance made by comparison with a yardstick.

A scientist from another culture that used time and velocity would have great difficulty in getting us to understand these concepts. We should talk about the intensity of a chemical reaction; he would speak of its velocity or its rate, which words we should at first think were simply words for intensity in his language. Likewise, he at first would think that intensity was simply our own word for velocity. At first we should agree, later we should begin to disagree, and it might dawn upon both sides that different systems of rationalization were being used. He would find it very hard to make us understand what he really meant by velocity of a chemical reaction. We should have no words that would fit. He would try to explain it by likening it to a running horse, to the difference between a good horse and a lazy horse. We should try to show him, with a superior laugh, that his analogy also was a matter of different intensities, aside from which there was little similarity between a horse and a chemical reaction in a beaker. We should point out that a running horse is moving relative to the ground, whereas the material in the beaker is at rest.

One significant contribution to science from the linguistic point of view may be the greater development of our sense of perspective. We shall no longer be able to see a few recent dialects of the Indo-European family, and the rationalizing techniques elaborated from their patterns, as the apex of the evolution of the human mind, nor their present wide spread as due to any survival from fitness or to anything but a few events of history—events that could be called fortunate only from the parochial point of view of the favoured parties. They, and our own thought processes with them, can no longer be envisioned as spanning the gamut of reason and knowledge but only as one constellation in a galactic expanse. A fair realization of the incredible degree of diversity of linguistic system that ranges over the globe leaves one with an inescapable feeling that the human spirit is inconceivably old; that the few thousand years of history covered by our written records are no more than the thickness of a pencil mark on the scale that measures our past experience on this planet; that the events of these recent millenniums spell nothing in any evolutionary wise, that the race has taken no sudden spurt, achieved no commanding synthesis during recent millenniums, but has only played a little with a few of the linguistic formulations and views of nature bequeathed from an inexpressibly longer past. Yet neither this feeling nor the sense of precarious dependence of all we know upon linguistic tools which themselves are largely unknown need be discouraging to science but should, rather, foster that humility which accompanies the true scientific spirit, and thus forbid that arrogance of the mind which hinders real scientific curiosity and detachment.

13 J. A. FISHMAN
The Whorfian Hypothesis

When Whorf says that 'there is a precarious dependence of all we know upon linguistic tools which themselves are largely unknown or unnoticed', he hits all of us where it hurts most—at the foundations of our certainty in our scientific findings and in our everyday decisions. When he attacks the view that grammars are 'merely norms of conventional and social correctness' and claims that they are, instead, the cement out of which we fashion experience, we feel that he must either be pointing at an unnoticed and potentially dangerous popular fallacy or tilting at nonexistent windmills. When he says that 'we cut up nature—organize it into concepts—and ascribe significances as we do . . . largely because of the . . . absolutely obligatory . . . patterns of our [own] language', he stirs in us both our ethnocentric group-pride as well as our universalistic anti-ethnocentrism. In short, Whorf (like Freud) impugns our objectivity and rationality. It is not surprising then that recent years have seen many logical as well as not a few experimental efforts to evaluate and re-evaluate both the conceptual and the empirical grounds upon which the Whorfian hypothesis rests.

Level 1. Linguistic codifiability and cultural reflections (The first language-language level)

The weakest level of the Whorfian hypothesis (in the sense of being least pretentious or least novel) is that which provides evidence that languages differ 'in the same ways' as the general cultures or surrounding environments of their speakers differ. Evidence along these lines has long been provided by ethnologists and folklorists, and its fragmentary and belated presentation by Whorfians can hardly be considered as either a serious contribution to the social sciences generally or as a substantiation of higher levels of the Whorfian hypothesis specifically.

J. A. Fishman: Extract from 'A Systematization of the Whorfian Hypothesis' in *Communication and Culture*, ed. A. G. Smith, Holt, Rinehart & Winston, New York 1966, pp. 505–16.

From the point of view of the language data presented at this first level of argumentation, it is not the grammatical structure as such that is under consideration but, rather, the lexical store or the so-called 'semantic structure'. Actually, that which is dealt with at this level might be referred to in present-day terms as contrasts in *codifiability*. Language X has a single term for phenomenon *x*, whereas language Y either has no term at all (and therefore refers to the phenomenon under consideration—if at all —only via a relative circumlocution) or it has three terms, y_1, y_2, and y_3, all within the same area of reference. As a result, it is much *easier* to refer to certain phenomena or to certain nuances of meaning in certain languages than in others. Thus, codifiability is also related to the question of translatability and to 'what gets lost' in translation from one language to another.

Admittedly Whorf's examples are largely drawn from American Indian languages (and contrasted with American English), and the implication is therefore strong that we are not only dealing with groups whose languages differ markedly but whose lives and outlooks also differ greatly. Nevertheless, at *this* level of analysis, Whorf (and others even more frequently than he) does not take pains to relate linguistic factors to non-linguistic ones, but merely presents an enchanting catalogue of codifiability differences. English has separate words for 'pilot', 'fly (n.)', and 'aeroplane', but Hopi has only one. Eskimo has many words for different kinds of 'snow' but English has only two. On the other hand, Aztec has only one basic word for our separate words 'cold', 'ice', and 'snow'. We have one word for 'water', whereas Hopi has two, depending on whether the water is stationary or in motion. English has such words as 'speed' and 'rapid', whereas Hopi has no real equivalents for them and normally renders them by 'very' or 'intense' plus a verb of motion. English has separate terms for 'blue' and 'green' but only one term for all intensities of 'black' short of 'grey'. Navaho, on the contrary, does not have separate highly codeable terms for 'blue' and 'green' but does have two terms for different kinds of 'black'. English has the generic term 'horse' but Arabic has only scores of different terms for different breeds or conditions of horses. The kinship terminology in some languages is certainly vastly different (and in certain respects both more refined and more gross) than it is in English. In all of these cases, it is not difficult to relate the codifiability differences to gross cultural differences. Obviously, Eskimos are more interested in snow, and Arabs in horses, than are most English speakers. Obvious, also, is the fact that these codifiability differences help speakers of certain languages to be more easily aware of certain aspects of their environment and to communicate more easily about them. This, essentially, was the lesson we learned from Bartlett's early work on remembering. In this sense, then, their languages structure their verbal behaviour in a non-trivial way and ostensibly also structure their pre-verbal conceptualizations as well.

Level 2. Linguistic codifiability and behavioural concomitants

At the second level of analysis of the Whorfian hypothesis, we leave behind the limitations of *inference* from codifiability in language to ease of formulation or expression via language. That is to say, we leave behind the *language-language behaviour* level for the level in which *language-nonlanguage behaviour* becomes of paramount interest to us. That this is a necessary direction for our inquiry to take has been recognized by Carroll and Casagrande:

> In order to find evidence to support the linguistic relativity hypothesis it is not sufficient merely to point to differences between languages and to assume that users of these languages have correspondingly different mental experiences. If we are not to be guilty of circular inference, it is necessary to show some correspondence between the presence or absence of a certain linguistic phenomenon and the presence or absence of a certain kind of non-linguistic response.

Note that the above quotation merely refers to '*a certain linguistic phenomenon*' rather than restricting the *type* of linguistic phenomenon that requires attention. The hallmark of the second level is that the 'predictor' variables seem once more to be of the lexical or semantic codifiability type (and in this respect similar to Level 1, discussed above), whereas the 'criterion variables' are of the non-linguistic behaviour type (and in this respect different from, and an advance over, those encountered at Level 1). Thus far, there have been only a very few studies which strike me as operating at this level of analysis. The earliest one by far is that of Lehmann who demonstrated that identifying a different number with each of nine different shades of grey was of substantial help in behaviourally discriminating between these shades of grey. In essence, then, the numbers functioned as verbal labels. The availability (codifiability) of such labels for some *S*s resulted in much better discrimination-identification of the shades of grey than that which obtained in other *S*s who had to perform the same discrimination-identification task without being provided with such labels.

Some exceptionally interesting and sophisticated work with the codifiability concept in the colour area has more recently been reported by Brown and Lenneberg and by Lenneberg alone. These investigators have shown that culturally encoded colours (i.e. colours that can be named with a single word) require a shorter response latency when they need to be named than do colours that are not culturally encoded (i.e. that require a phrase—often an individually formulated phrase—in order to be described). At this point, their evidence pertains to Level 1 that we have previously discussed. In addition, these investigators have gone on to show that the more highly codified colours are more readily recognized or remembered when they must be selected from among many colours after a period of delay subsequent to their original presentation. This finding was replicated among speakers of English and speakers of Zuni, although somewhat different segments of the colour spectrum were highly codeable for the two groups of Ss. The investigators summarize their findings to this point as follows:

> It is suggested that there may be general laws relating codability to cognitive processes. All cultures could conform to these laws although they differ among themselves in the values the variables assume in particular regions of experience.

Going on from this original statement, Lenneberg has further refined its experimental underpinnings by showing that the *learning* of colour-nonsense syllable associations was predictably easier or harder as the learning task involved colour categories that varied in degree from the ones that were most commonly recognized by his English-speaking Ss. He therefore concluded that 'there is good evidence that the shape of word frequency distributions over stimulus continua regulates the ease with which a person learns to use a word correctly'. This conclusion should be as applicable to original language learning as it is to second and to artificial language learning, for it basically pertains not to language usage *per se* but to concept formation as such.

The colour continuum seems to be a particularly fortunate area in which to study codifiability-cognition phenomena precisely because it is a real continuum. As such, no 'objective' breaks occur in it and it is a matter of cultural or sub-cultural consensus as to just which breaks are recognized, just where on the spectrum they are located, and how much of a range they include. The demonstration that these various codifiability considerations influence recognition, recall, and learning has been most fortunately executed. Lenneberg and Brown are also alert to the fact that at this level it is perfectly acceptable to work with intralinguistic designs rather than to necessarily utilize the interlinguistic designs in terms of which the Whorfian hypothesis is most frequently approached. What is easily codifiable, and the specific range and content of easily codeable categories, does depend on the particular language under consideration. It also depends on the particular experiences of subgroups of speakers. As a result, contrasts in rate, ease or accuracy of various cognitive functions should be (and are) demonstrable both intralinguistically and interlinguistically as a function of codeability norms. Intralinguistic codifiability-cognition differentials in various natural population groupings should be of particular interest to students of social stratification.

Brown and Lenneberg have conducted their work with a conscious awareness of the Whorfian hypothesis and how it must be further specified or delimited. On the other hand, there have been other investigators who have also worked in the language-behaviour domain at this level without any particular awareness of the Whorfian hypothesis as such. If the organizational framework here being advanced has been insightfully developed, it should nevertheless be possible to subsume their findings within it. In fact, it may turn out that within the context of the Whorfian hypothesis these other studies will obtain a new coherence and pro-vocativeness.

The only study at this level that is directly inspired by the Whorfian hypothesis while utilizing an *interlinguistic* design is the one which Carroll and Casagrande refer to as 'Experiment I'.

Level 3. Linguistic structure and its cultural concomitants

When we turn our attention from the second to the third and fourth levels of the Whorfian hypothesis, we progress from lexical differences and so-called 'semantic structure' to the more 'formal' and systematized grammatical differences to which linguists have most usually pointed when considering the structure of a language or structural differences between languages. There is some evidence that although Whorf and others may, at times, have reverted to lower levels of presentation and documentation they, nevertheless, did associate linguistic relativity in its most pervasive sense with structural (i.e. grammatical) rather than merely with lexical aspects of language. This is suggested by such formulations as Sapir's that meanings are 'not so much discovered in experience as imposed upon it, because of the tyrannical hold that linguistic *form* has upon our orientation to the world'. Somewhat more forcefully stated is Whorf's claim that 'the world is presented in a kaleidoscopic flux of impressions which has to be organized . . . largely by the linguistic *systems* in our minds'. More forceful still—and there are a large number of possible quotations of this kind—is Whorf's statement that

. . . the background linguistic system (in other words, the grammar) of each language is not merely a reproducing instrument for voicing ideas, but rather is itself the shaper of ideas, the program and guide for the individual's mental activity, for his analysis of impressions, for his synthesis of his mental stock in trade. Formulation of ideas is not an independent process, strictly rational in the old sense, but it is part of a particular grammar and differs, from slightly to greatly, between grammars.

Finally, we may offer in evidence the paraphrasings of the Whorfian hypothesis by two eminent American linguists who have been both interested in and sympathetic to this hypothesis. The first of these says simply that 'It is in the attempt properly to interpret the *grammatical categories* of Hopi that Whorf best illustrates his principle of linguistic relativity'. The other, as part of a more extended and systematic argument, says

> Language as a whole has structure and all of its parts and subdivisions also have structure . . . [if] the rest of cultural behavior has been conditioned by language, then there must be a relationship between the *structure* of language and the *structure* of behaviour.

At the third level of analysis, we once more find ourselves in a realm of rich though ambiguous anthropological and ethnological data. As was the case with Level 1, above, the direct association or chain of reasoning between grammatical structure on the one hand and 'something else' (be it *Weltanschauung* or even some less embracing segment of culture or values) on the other is not explicitly stated. Often, the 'something else' is not stated at all and yet there is the general implication that grammatical oddities of the type presented cannot help but be paralleled by unique ways of looking at or thinking about or reacting to the surrounding environment. Thus, one encounters such evidence as that Chinese has no singular and plural or that it has no relative clauses (which we English speakers *do* have), whereas other languages have more levels of grammatical number (including singular, dual, tri-al, and plural forms—which we English speakers do *not* have). In this vein, the cataloguing of grammatical differences can continue at great length (languages that do recognize gender of nouns and those that do not, languages that have tenses and those that do not, etc.); for both anthropologists, linguists, and a variety of nonspecialists have contributed to the fund of knowledge of phenomena of this type, always with the implication that it is clearly illogical to seriously suggest that linguistic phenomena such as these would have no relationship to life, to thought, and to values.

On the other hand, there are also several investigators that *have* attempted to indicate what the 'something else' might be. In contrasting Hopi with English, Whorf has pointed to such odd grammatical features in Hopi as the absence of tenses, the classification of events by duration categories such that 'events of necessarily brief duration (lightning, wave, flame, meteor, puff of smoke, pulsation) cannot be anything but verbs', the presence of grammatical forms for indicating the type of validity the speaker intends to attribute to his utterance (statement of current fact, statement of fact from memory, statement of expectation, and statement of generalization or law), etc. To Whorf all of these grammatical features seemed congruent with an outlook on life that was 'timeless' and ahistorical in the sense that past, present, and future are seen as a continuity of duration, experience being cumulative and unchanging for countless generations. As a result of the 'timelessness' of Hopi life, it is of greater importance for Hopi speakers to distinguish between the duration of events and their certainty than to indicate when they occurred. A similarly ingenious and sensitive analysis is followed by Hoijer in connexion with the Navaho verb system in which there is no clean separation between actors, their actions, and the objects of these actions. As Hoijer sees it, the Navaho verb links the actor to actions which are defined as pertaining to classes-of-beings. Thus it would appear that people merely 'participate in' or 'get involved in' somehow pre-existing classes of actions rather than serve as the initiators of actions. Hoijer interprets these grammatical characteristics as being consistent with the 'passivity' and 'fatefulness' of Navaho life and mythology in which individuals adjust to a universe that is given. Finally, in Nootka, Whorf finds a connexion between the absence of noun-verb distinctions and 'a monistic view of nature'.

The efforts by Whorf, Hoijer, Glenn and similar scholars merit considerable respect. They must be separated in our evaluation from pseudo-serious efforts to attribute or relate the musicalness of Italians to the light, melodious nature of the Italian language, or the stodginess of Germans to the heavy, lugubrious quality of the German language, or the warm, folksiness of Eastern European Jews to the intimate emotional quality of Yiddish, etc. Superficially, the two approaches may seem similar, but the latter approach does not even have a serious structural analysis of language to recommend it. Nevertheless, the appeal of the Whorfian hypothesis for some lies precisely in the fact that it attempts to apply modern scientific methods and disciplined thought to such 'old chestnuts' as the presumed 'naturalness' that Hebrew (or Greek, or Latin, or Old Church Slavonic) be the language of the Bible, given its 'classic ring' and its 'otherworldly purity'. However, with all of our admiration for those who have had the temerity as well as the ingenuity to attempt a rigorous analysis at this level, we must also recognize the limitations which are built into this approach. As many critics have pointed out, the third level of analysis has not normally sought or supplied independent confirmation of the existence of the 'something else' which their grammatical data is taken to indicate. As a result, the very same grammatical designata that are said to have brought about (or merely to reflect) a given *Weltan-schauung* are also most frequently the only data advanced to prove that such a *Weltanschauung* does indeed exist. Thus, once more, we are back at a language-language level of analysis (language structure ↔ language behaviour-as-indication-of-world-view).

Verbal behaviour may long continue as our major avenue of insight into values and motives. What we must be ever more dissatisfied with, however, are the self-selected lists of grammatical examples and the self-selected enumerations of cultures, cultural values or themes, and the evidence pertaining to the existence of such themes. In attempting to avoid these particular pitfalls, students of the Whorfian hypothesis have increasingly come to express a preference for a study design which investigates the relationship between grammatic structure on the one hand and *individual* non-linguistic behaviour on the other. Although this is both a logical and a very promising solution to many of the above-mentioned problems, there is nevertheless no need to conclude at this point in our knowledge that it is the only one possible.

Level 4. Linguistic structure and its behavioural concomitants

The conceptual and methodological superiority of the fourth level of the Whorfian hypothesis is one thing. The accessibility of this level for study may well be quite another thing. It does seem that this level is in some ways the most demanding of all, for it requires detailed technical training at both the predictor and the criterion ends of the relationship to be investigated. This may be the reason why there currently appears to be only one study which might possibly be said to be an example of work at this level, although in the future we might expect it to elicit greatly increased interest among socio-linguists and social psychologists with technical linguistic training. This is the study by Carroll and Casagrande which they refer to as Experiment II. The grammatic features of interest to Carroll and Casagrande in this study are the particular verb forms required in Navaho verbs for handling materials in accord with the shape or other physical attribute (flexibility, flatness, etc.) of the object being handled. Note that Carroll and Casagrande are concerned here with distinctions in verb *forms* rather than distinctions between mere lexical absence or presence of verbs as such. Presumably it is this fact which permits us to consider Experiment II as a Level 4 study rather than as a Level 2 study. The nonlinguistic data utilized by Carroll and Casagrande are the object-classifying behaviours of their Ss when presented first with a pair of objects which differ from each other in *two* respects (e.g. colour and shape) and then with a third object similar to each member of the original pair in one of the two relevant characteristics. The Ss were asked to indicate 'which member of the (original) pair went best with the (third) object shown him'. If the S's reaction was governed by the requirements of Navaho verbal form, he would have to select a certain one of the original set of objects.

The degree of linguistic relativity

The fascination of the Whorfian hypothesis is in some ways compounded of both delights and horrors. We have already speculated concerning the delights. Let us now mention the horrors. The first is the *horror of helplessness*, since all of us in most walks of life and most of us in all walks of life are helplessly trapped by the language we speak. We cannot escape from it—and, even if we could flee, where would we turn but to some other language with its own blinders and its own vice-like embrace on what we think, what we perceive, and what we say. The second horror is the *horror of hopelessness*—for what hope can there be for mankind?; what hope that one group will ever understand the other?; what hope that one nation will ever fully communicate with the other? This is not the place for a full-dressed philosophical attack on these issues. Let us merely consider them from the point of view of the kinds of evidence supplied by some of the very studies we have mentioned.

The most 'reassuring' facts that derive from Levels 1 and 2, the lexical and semantic codifiability levels of the Whorfian hypothesis, are that the noted non-translatability and the selective codifiability really pertain not so much to all-or-none differences between languages as to differences in relative ease or felicity of equivalent designation. Whenever we argue that there is no English word (or expression) for ——, which means so-and-so (or approximately so-and-so, or a combination of Y and Z) in English, we are partially undercutting our own argument. In the very formulation of our argument that there is 'no English word (or expression) for ——' we have gone on to give an English approximation to it. This approximation may not be a very successful one but if that becomes our concern we can go through the contortions (both intellectual and gesticulational) that are required for an inching up on or a zeroing in on the non-English word or expression that we have in mind. The amount of effort involved may, at times, be quite considerable and even the final approximation may leave us dissatisfied. However, after all is said and done, this is not so different, in terms of both process and outcome, as the communication problems that we face with one another even within our *own* speech community. We can do no better than to quote Hockett's conclusions at this point, in support of what has just been said.

Languages differ not so much as to what *can* be said in them, but rather as to what it is *relatively easy* to say in them. The history of Western logic and science constitutes not so much the story of scholars hemmed in and misled by the nature of their specific languages, as the story of a long and fairly successful struggle *against* inherited linguistic limitations. Where everyday language would not serve, special sub-systems (mathematics, e.g.) were devised. However, even Aristotle's development of syllogistic notation carries within itself aspects of Greek language structure.

The impact of inherited linguistic pattern on activities is, in general, *least* important in the most practical contexts and most important in such 'purely verbal' goings-on as story-telling, religion, and philosophizing. As a result, some types of literature are extremely difficult to translate accurately, let alone appealingly.

Turning now to Levels 3 and 4, where we become concerned with the imbedded structural features of a language, it seems to be important that we realize that Whorf never proposed that *all* aspects of grammatical structure must *inevitably* have direct cognitive effects. Thus, to begin with, we are faced with the task of locating those few grammatical features which might have definable but unconscious functional correlates in our unguarded behaviour.

If we look to Levels 2 and 4, these being the levels in which the behavioural concomitants of linguistic features are experimentally derived, we once more must reach the conclusion that linguistic relativity, where it does exist, is not necessarily an awesomely powerful factor in cognitive functioning. The relationships that have been encountered, though clear-cut enought, seem to be neither very great nor irreversible in magnitude. The very fact that increased infant and early childhood experience with toys and objects requiring primarily a form reaction can result in a *Navaho-like classifying preference* among monolingual English-speaking children also means that other kinds of environmental experiences might very well produce an *English-like classifying preference* among mono-lingual Navaho-speaking children. No one has yet directly studied the success with which behaviours predicted on the basis of linguistic relativity can be counteracted by either (*a*) simply making Ss aware of how their language biases affect their thinking or (*b*) actively training Ss to counteract these biases. It may be, after all, that this is an area in which Ss can, with relatively little effort, learn how to 'fake good'. Furthermore, one might suspect that the impact of language *per se* on cognition and expression ought somehow to be greater and more fundamental than the impact of one or another language feature. Thus the impact of language *determinism* upon cognition ought to be more pervasive and more difficult to counteract than that of language *relativity*.

None of the foregoing should be interpreted as implying that linguistic relativity, wherever it exists, is an unimportant factor in human experience or one that deserves no particular attention except from those who are professionally committed to unravelling the unimportant in painful detail. Quite the contrary; just because it is such a seemingly innocuous factor it is very likely to go unnoticed and, therefore, requires our particular attention in order that we may appropriately provide for it.

Summary and conclusions

The four levels of the Whorfian hypothesis that have been presented here are essentially subsumable under a double dichotomy. As Figure 13.1 reveals, we have essentially been dealing with two factors—one pertaining to characteristics of a given language or languages and the other pertaining to behaviour of the speakers of the language or languages under consideration. The first factor has been dichotomized so as to distinguish between lexical or semantic structure on the one hand (both of these being considered as codeability features) and grammatical structure on the other. The second factor has been dichotomized so as to distinguish between verbal behaviour *per se* (frequently interpreted in terms of cultural themes or *Weltanschauungen*) and individual behavioural data which is other than verbal in nature.

Data of *Language Characteristics*	*Data of* *(Cognitive) Behaviour*	
	Language Data (Cultural Themes)	Non-linguistic Data
Lexical or 'Semantic' characteristics	Level 1	Level 2
Grammatical characteristics	Level 3	Level 4

Figure 13.1. Schematic Systematization of the Whorfian Hypothesis.

In a rough way, we might say that Levels 1 and 3 are concerned with *large group phenomena* whereas Levels 2 and 4 are concerned with *individual behaviour*. Whorf was aware of and interested in both kinds of data, for he held that 'our linguistically determined thought world not only collaborates with our *cultural idols and ideals* but engages even our unconscious *personal reactions* in its patterns and gives them certain typical character(istic)s'.

In general, Whorf is not deeply concerned with 'which was first, the language patterns or the cultural norms?' He is content to conclude that 'in the main they have grown up together, constantly influencing each other'. Nevertheless, he does state that if these two streams are to be separated from each other for the purposes of analysis he considers language to be by far the more impervious, systematic, and rigid of the two. Thus, after a long association between culture and language, innovations in the former will have but minor impact on the latter, 'whereas to inventors and innovators it (i.e. language) legislates with the decree immediate'. Although Whorf is leary of the term correlation it seems most likely that he considered language structure not only as interactingly reflective of 'cultural thought' but as directly formative of 'individual thought'. With proper cautions, the four levels of the Whorfian hypothesis that have been differentiated in this review may be seen as quite consistent with this conclusion.

Some of the characteristics, difficulties, and potentials of further empirical and theoretical study at each of the four differentiated levels have been considered. All levels can make use of both interlinguistic or intralinguistic designs, although Levels 1 and 3 most commonly employ the former—if only for purposes of contrast.

Although evidence favouring the Whorfian hypothesis exists at each level, it seems likely that linguistic relativity, though affecting some of our cognitive behaviour, is nevertheless only a moderately powerful factor and a counteractable one at that. Certainly much experimental evidence has accumulated that points to a large domain of contra-Whorfian universality in connexion with the relationships between *certain* structures of particular languages and *certain* cognitive behaviours of their speakers. The time might, therefore, now be ripe for putting aside attempts at grossly 'proving' or 'disproving' the Whorfian hypothesis and, instead, focusing on attempts to delimit more sharply the types of language structures and the types of non-linguistic behaviours that do or do not show the Whorfian effect as well as the degree and the modifiability of this involvement when it does obtain.

Because of Whorf's central role in making us aware of this phenomenon so that we may now better come to grips with it, both intellectually and practically, none can deny that he richly deserves to be characterized by his own standard for what constitutes a real scientist.

All real scientists have their eyes primarily on background phenomena in our daily lives; and yet their studies have a way of bringing out a close relation between these unsuspected realms . . . and . . . foreground activities.

14 JOHN B. CARROLL
Linguistic Relativity and Language Learning

From ancient times there has been speculation that the total pattern of a particular language exerts an influence on the minds of those who use it, channelling their thoughts in special and distinct ways and perhaps even causing them to experience their world differently from those who speak other languages. Most philosophers of language have been content to make only general observations on this alleged relationship, stopping short of specifying the precise nature of the influence claimed or of offering a theory of how the effect is exerted. The obvious differences among language structures have been assumed to constitute proof that they correspond to different mental structures in language users, but such evidence is patently circular.

The theory that languages have special effects on the mental activities of their users has been called the theory of *linguistic relativity*, because it asserts that mental activity is to at least some degree relative to, and dependent on, the language in which it takes place.

The linguistic relativity theory has received a number of different formulations. Writers have disagreed concerning the strength of the influence exerted by a language system, some believing that it maintains a tight and almost inescapable control over cognitive behaviour, others believing that the strength of the influence is relatively inconsequential and easily avoidable, once it is pointed out. Formulations have differed, too, in the things brought into the correlation. Some writers have stressed the correlations of language structure with what are sometimes called 'cognitive' operations, that is, with mental functions like perceptions, thought, and memory, whereas others seem to stress the correlation of language structure with motivational and emotional aspects of behaviour. Further, some thinkers are concerned chiefly with the relation between language structure and culture, that is, the system of customs, beliefs, and behaviours that are characteristic of a given social group, while

J. B. Carroll: Extract from 'Linguistic Relativity, Contrastive Linguistics and Language Learning', *International Review of Applied Linguistics*, Vol. I, No. 1, 1963, pp. 1–13, 16–19.

others are concerned with relations between language structure and individual personality. Some writers have focused attention on a possible relationship between language structure and national character. Salvador de Madariaga for example, proposed that on account of their languages, Englishmen are men of action, Frenchmen men of thought, and Spaniards men of passion. Such a claim raises the additional question of whether there is such a thing as national character, a question with which we shall avoid dealing, in as much as the linguistic relativity theory even in its most straightforward form raises numerous problems.

If any aspect of the linguistic relativity theory should prove to be correct, however, the possible implications for language teaching would have to be seriously examined.

For example, if we assume the correctness of the extreme form of the theory which asserts that the *Weltanschauung* imposed by one's native language is so dominant and lasting in its effects that one would not be able to acquire the mental outlook implied by another language, it would follow that the acquisition of a second language could be only partial and superficial, and that true bilingualism would be impossible. Further, it would follow that exact translation from one language to another is in principle a contradiction in terms.

If we admit a less strict type of theory in which the learning of a new *Weltanschauung* could go hand in hand with the learning of a second language, we might conclude that the learning of a second language would be facilitated if the student could somehow be helped to acquire the 'mental outlook' associated with the language he is trying to learn. It would also follow that the true bilingual tends to switch from one outlook to another as he switches from one language to another. Nevertheless, completely accurate translation between languages would still be an impossibility.

There are other possible varieties of linguistic relativity, one of which will be supported later on in this paper, but it is also useful, at this point, to consider the alternative to a linguistic relativity theory, namely a theory of linguistic neutrality which would assert that mental operations and other behaviours are independent of the language in which they are carried out. Under this theory, the language teacher could ignore the problem of teaching the mental operations associated with a language, for he would be able to assume that the learner would carry over to the second language the mental operations he already possessed. Indeed, he would assume that the new language would provide merely a new vehicle for expressing the ideas and emotions already expressible in the learner's native language. Under this theory, also, both true bilingualism and accurate translations between languages would be conceived to be attainable.

There are at least three steps which would have to be taken to provide a satisfactory answer to the possible relevance of a linguistic relativity theory in language teaching:

1 The terms and propositions of the theory itself (or of its subvarieties) would have to be carefully defined and stated;

2 Empirical evidence of the correctness of the theory would have to be provided, and

3 The relevance of the theory, if found correct in any respect, to language teaching would have to be explored and demonstrated.

It is the purpose of this article to state where we stand with respect to each of these steps, and to provide tentative conclusions for language teachers.

Theories of linguistic relativity

Over the last 25 years interest in theories of linguistic relativity, at least in the U.S.A., has been generated chiefly as a result of the writings of the American linguist Benjamin Lee Whorf (1897–1941). A widely quoted paragraph by Whorf will serve to introduce the reader to his thinking.

The background linguistic system (in other words, the grammar) of each language is not merely a reproducing instrument for voicing ideas but rather is itself the shaper of ideas, the program and guide for the individual's mental activity, for his analysis of impressions, for his synthesis of his mental stock in trade. Formulation of ideas is not an independent process, strictly rational in the old sense, but is part of a particular grammar and differs, from slightly to greatly, as between different grammars. We dissect nature along lines laid down by our native languages. The categories and types that we isolate from the world of phenomena we do not find there because they stare every observer in the face; on the contrary, the world is presented in a kaleidoscopic flux of impressions which has to be organised by our minds—and this means largely by the linguistic systems in our minds. We cut nature up, organize it into concepts, and ascribe significances as we do, largely because we are parties to an agreement to organize it in this way—an agreement that holds throughout our speech community and is codified in the patterns of our language. The agreement is, of course, an implicit and unstated one, *but its terms are absolutely obligatory;* we cannot talk at all except by subscribing to the organization and classification of data which the agreement decrees.

Nevertheless, this approach can hardly be called new. As Joseph Greenberg writes in a valuable symposium on the linguistic relativity hypothesis which took place at the University of Chicago in 1953:

There is a European tradition, particularly strong in the German-speaking world, which can be traced back at least as far as Herder in the latter part of the eighteenth century, but which first assumed central importance in the writings of Von Humboldt. The influence, direct and indirect, of Von Humboldt on the

Continent has been a profound and continuing one, and may be seen in contemporaries or near-contemporaries such as Ernst Cassirer in philosophy and Johann Leo Weisgerber and Jost Trier in linguistics. A few citations may serve to illustrate the general resemblance of the approaches of these writers to that of Whorf. Thus Cassirer, himself a prominent exponent of this point of view, sums up the position of Von Humboldt in the following words: 'The difference between languages derives, in his view, less from differences in sounds and signs than from differences of world-view'. Weisgerber writes concerning language: 'As an intermediate psychic realm, it is clearly distinct from the area of 'objective meanings', particularly in the sense that it is not a simple reflection of the world of objects, but rather embodies the result of an intellectual remolding of this world'.

A theory cannot be correctly evaluated unless it is precisely stated. Whorf did not provide a clear statement of his linguistic relativity hypothesis in general terms; he provided a number of examples which he thought demonstrated language-thought correspondences, but analysis of these instances shows that they actually exemplify a number of different kinds of language-thought relationships.

A proper statement of a linguistic relativity hypothesis demands the most exacting knowledge of psychological and linguistic theory. One suspects, indeed, that neither psychological nor linguistic theory has progressed to that firm ground which would enable one to formulate the relation between language structure and behaviour. In psychology, there are still remnants of the various schools of thought (behaviourism, *Gestalttheorie*, etc.) which have not yet been thoroughly reconciled, and linguistic theory is currently in ferment due to the efforts of Harris, Chomsky, and others.

Nevertheless, I shall attempt to state a kind of theory; in so doing, I run the risk of exposing either my ignorance or my biases.

The nature and function of language can be understood only by considering it in the broad context of its appearance as a mode of communications between two organisms fully competent to employ it, that is, two organisms who have learned the system of communication called language. This restricts us to the consideration of communication between human beings; communication involving animals cannot employ language in the full sense because the structural aspects of language are not used. Analysis of various kinds of communication situations discloses that persons communicate when they are motivated (by background factors in the situation) to share their perceptions, experiences, desires, or emotions with another person or persons, or to signal comprehension, non-comprehension, agreement, or disagreement with another's communication. Perceptions (of objective reality or of subjectively experienced events like dreams and hallucinations) are necessarily subjective events. In a strict sense, they cannot really be shared, but communication proceeds on the implicit assumption (by all the participants) that the subjective events occurring in the originator of the communication can through the process of communication evoke counterparts in the receiver of the communication which are in some sense similar to those in the sender. If speaker A says to B, 'Bring me a large chair,' B (if he comprehends) can be assumed to experience a feeling of having been ordered to provide A with a specimen (any specimen will do) of a certain class of objects having certain criterial attributes (legs, a configuration suitable for holding the body in a sitting position, etc., etc.) experienced more or less similarly by all members of the speech community using the word 'chair'. Further, the use of the adjective *large* identifies a certain range of objects with respect to size—but probably not to include grotesquely large chairs such as one might find in certain advertising displays of furniture manufacturers. Thus, it can be assumed that A and B would for the most part agree on objects that could be called 'large chairs' and that would fit the requirements of the situation. To take another example: if speaker A says to B, 'I have a headache,' it can be assumed that B recognizes that A is now experiencing a certain kind of subjective feeling which B (whether he himself has ever experienced it) knows is said to be experienced, with certain characteristics, by human beings. (We have difficulty conceiving that babies or animals might have headaches, because infants and animals have no specific way of reporting headaches distinct from other sources of pain or discomfort.)

The basic problem in communicating with language, then, is the selection of language symbols to match subjective events in such a way as to maximize the probability that the subjective events occurring in the receiver of a communication will correspond with those occurring in the originator of the communication, or desired by the originator. It is difficult to state in general how there can be any assurance of correspondence at all, but human beings in their acquisition of language normally acquire considerable skill in detecting whether their communications are understood. When his desires are satisfied, by those to whom he expresses them, or when individuals instructed by him carry out their instructions, the language user knows that he is understood. (The testing of language comprehension can even be elevated into a science, as in the measurement of scholastic achievement through tests and examinations.)

The selection of language symbols to match subjective events may be called *encoding*. Early in language development in the child, encoding may be assumed to be an exclusively automatic process—the child automatically responds to a certain stimulus (internal or external) with a certain language symbol, or a series of them. However, at some stage the child (the language learner) comes to realize on a conscious level that in some cases alternative symbols are possible and that different effects are likely to be obtained by the use of different symbols. For example, the child might realize (in speaking English) that somewhat different effects would be attained by saying 'I'm feeling bad' and 'I'm sick', even though the same subjective event is involved. There is, therefore, some sense in which 'choice' or 'selection' of symbols on the part of the speaker can occur.

Any given language contains a certain set of symbols for encoding subjective events. Indeed, subjective events are the only kinds of things which language symbols can encode. Language symbols may be said to 'stand for' or 'mean' certain objective things or events, but only through the intermediary of a human perceiver. For any given subjective event, the symbols available to a given speaker at a given time will generally be very small in number; they will constitute a sample of the symbols available in his language. Thus, even individuals who speak the same language are unlikely to encode a given type of subjective event in the same way on every occasion, or even on the same occasion.

Languages, too, differ in the sets of symbols they contain for encoding subjective events. Not only are the symbols generally different in their phonemic shapes, but they also assort themselves in different ways with respect to the subjective events they encode. This is revealed in the comparative studies of vocabularies and in studies of comparative grammar. Detailed studies of symbol repertories available in different languages have been made in the field of colour terminology, where it is possible to describe the physical referents with scientific exactitude. It is shown that the speakers of various languages seem to 'cut up' the colour spectrum in different ways. Where one language has a single word for a given range of hues, another language may cut up the same range into several segments, each with its own name. The same sort of thing is found in other spheres of human interest and activity. For example, in kinship systems we find some languages in which there is no separate word for the biological relationship symbolized by the English word *mother*; instead the word ordinarily used for one's biological mother can equally well refer to any of the mother's sisters, or to other female members of her clan. Contrariwise, the English word *brother* is from the point of view of some languages unnecessarily generic for it fails to specify whether the brother is older or younger, or the oldest or the youngest. The problem of translation in such instances is to insure that the range of referents symbolized by an expression in the translation language is approximately the same as the range of referents in the source language; often, recourse must be made to highly involved qualifying phrases.

The phenomena of mandatory classification is often encountered. This occurs whenever it is impossible to make a reference without specifying into which category of a certain classification a referent falls. Among the mandatory categories in English are number and gender. There is little possibility of being indefinite about whether one is talking about one, or more than one, referent. Normally in English one must say *The children got into their bed*, or *The children got into their beds*, depending on the number of beds involved. Lacking this obligatory classification, Mandarin Chinese allows one to say, in effect, 'Child got into bed' without specifying the number of children or the number of beds. It is true that in English there is a dodge whereby one can say 'The children went to bed' without specifying the number of beds, but this dodge is possible only with a very few words (*bed*, *home*, *school*, *market*, and perhaps a few others) and is thus not systematic in the language. The mandatory category of gender occurs in English pronouns, and is often troublesome, as where we must take pains to say *The teacher must prepare his or her lesson well* if we don't wish to have it inferred that teachers are thought to be always males, or females, as the case may be.

Languages apparently differ markedly in the degree to which they allow or compel superordinate classification of concepts. For example, English contains such words as *animal*, *bird*, *insect*, *creature*, whereas some languages contain no such superordinate words, but only words for specific species or subspecies. On the other hand, English fails to contain symbols for certain superordinate concepts recognized by other languages; for example, it has been pointed out that Chinese has a term for the whole class of objects which must be designated in English as either fruits or nuts.

Another possible source of mandatory classification in language is the allocation of concepts to form-classes. In English, three of the major form classes are nouns, verbs, and descriptive adjectives. While it is difficult to arrive at a satisfactory generic meaning of each of these form-classes, Brown has shown that these form classes, respectively, develop in the language of the child from names (1) of concrete objects, (2) of overt physical actions, and (3) of qualities of things accessible to immediate sensory perception. In adult language, items in the noun form-class may therefore be taken to refer to anything that is conceptualized (mentally categorized) as potentially an entity or object of thought, about which a predication could be made. Items found in the verb form-class may be taken to refer to events or states which are conceptualized as potentially taking place or existing at a definite time or over a certain period of time. Items found in the adjectival form-class apparently refer to any quality which can be conceptualized as a dimension or category with respect to which certain items in the noun class may vary. By derivational processes, items found in a given class may be transferred to another class; e.g. *colony* (noun-class) becomes *colonize* (verb-class) or *colonial* (adjective-class); *marry* (verb-class) becomes *marriage* (noun-class) or *marital* (adjective-class); *deep* (adjective-class) becomes *deepen* (verb-class) or *depth* (noun-class). It is hard to find items which resist transfer to other form-classes; the only examples which come immediately to mind are *thing*, in the noun-class, and *have*, in the verb-class, provided one excludes the gerund *having* as a transfer to the noun-class. No example can be found in the adjective class since a noun-class derivative can always be formed by adding some appropriate suffix such as *ness*.

Of more interest is the question of why we conceive items as belonging, in their root forms, in certain form-classes. Why, for example, are the words *fist* and *lightning* found in the noun-class? Whorf pointed out that there is in Hopi (an American Indian language of the American Southwest) no noun counterpart of the English word *lightning*: the concept is found in the verb-class, a fact which suggests that *lightning* is conceived by the Hopis as an active event analogous to *curling*, *hitting*, or *running*. Indeed, according to Whorf, it is almost impossible to define grammatical categories 'from nature'; 'to define them', he writes, 'always involves a circuitous return to the grammatical categories of the definer's language'.

All the cases dealt with thus far may be viewed as instances where the categorizations or encodings provided by one language are not precisely the same as those provided in another language. Is it possible that the categorizations provided by a language add up to a 'world view'? It is difficult, indeed, to see how differential codings of the colour spectrum, obligatory categorizations in terms of number or gender, or form-class allocations could reflect different views of the world. World-views, in fact, would seem to stem from basic attitudes and values attached to things, actions, and ideas rather than from the categorizations provided by linguistic symbols. A world-view might, indeed, be represented by an overall *system* of structure of classifications, but no clear instances of structure in the classification systems of a language have been offered.

Whorf and others have, however, offered instances where they claim that the classification system *itself* implies a world view. Whorf, for example, noted a number of phenomena in Hopi which suggested to him that Hopi is a 'timeless' language, in contrast to English. He found in it

'. . . no words, grammatical forms, constructions or expressions that refer directly to what we call "time", or to past, present, or future, or to enduring or lasting, or to motion as kinematic rather than dynamic . . . Hence the Hopi language contains no reference to "time" either explicit or implicit. . . . I find it gratuitous to assume that Hopi thinking contains any such notion as the supposed intuitively felt flow of "time", or that the intuition of a Hopi gives him this as one of its data.

'Thus, the Hopi language and culture conceals a *metaphysics* such as our so-called naïve view of space and time does, or as the relativity theory does; yet it is a different metaphysics from either . . .'

Whorf goes on to explain that the metaphysics underlying English 'imposes on the universe two grand *cosmic forms*, space and time; static three-dimensional infinite space, and kinetic one-dimensional uniformly and perpetually flowing time . . .' In contrast, the metaphysics of Hopi contains two 'grand cosmic forms' of its own, 'which as a first approximation in terminology we may call *manifested* and *manifesting* (or, *unmanifest*) or, again, *objective* and *subjective*'.

There has never been an adequate critique of Whorf's propositions about the Hopi world-view. Such a critique could be made only after a thorough re-examination of the linguistic data, many of which are not accessible in published form. This, at least, is the assessment made by Greenberg at the above-mentioned symposium. Furthermore, even if it were established that Whorf's linguistic data were correct in all essentials, one would still have to demonstrate that speakers of Hopi actually hold the world-view attributed to them from linguistic facts.

The kind of reasoning employed by Whorf is perhaps better displayed in an article concerning what he called the punctual and segmentative aspects of verbs in Hopi. (*Aspect* is here used as a grammatical term; it refers to a variation in verb form, noted in many languages, dependent upon a classification of different modes of action represented in verbs.) In this article Whorf offered data to show that Hopi speakers must make a broad distinction between events which occur at a point of time (or space) and events which occur as repetitive phenomena, i.e. at many points of time or space. This contrast is signalled by a change in the form of the verb, as illustrated in the following examples:

pi·yi	*it makes a single flap (as a pair of wings)*
pi·ya'yata	*it is flapping wings (repetitively)*
ti·ri	*he gives a sudden start*
tiri'rita	*he is quivering, trembling*
ri''pi	*it gives a flash*
ripi'pita	*it is sparkling*
pa''ci	*it is notched*
paci'cita	*it is serrated*

From such linguistic data, Whorf infers that the Hopi actually have a language 'better equipped to deal with vibratory phenomena than is our latest scientific terminology'. 'This,' he goes on,

is simply because their language establishes a general contrast between two types of experience, which contrast corresponds to a contrast that, as our science has discovered, is all-pervading and fundamental in nature. According to the conceptions of modern physics, the contrast of particle and field of vibrations is more fundamental in the world of nature than such contrasts in space and time, or past present, and future, which are the sort of contrasts that our own language imposes upon us. The Hopi aspect-contrast which we have observed, being obligatory upon their verb forms, practically forces the Hopi to notice and observe vibratory phenomena, and furthermore encourages them to find names for and to classify such phenomena.

While it may be admitted that Hopi appears to have a verbal aspect category not explicitly present in English, the basic concept is one which can easily be conveyed in English (as in the above glosses) and in many other languages. Furthermore, it seems to be a long jump to go from the description of these linguistic data to the inference that the presence of this verbal aspect category in Hopi imposes on the Hopi speaker, or endows him with, the ability to see the world in terms of the physicist's contrast between particle and field of vibrations. This inference, at any rate, is very risky and would need to be validated by some sort of independent check on Hopi world-views. In informal interviews with several educated Hopis I could detect no evidence that Hopi perceptions of the world, at least in this respect, differed from our own, but it could be argued that this evidence was biased because the Hopis whom I interviewed had been educated primarily in English. Indeed, the empirical investigation of Whorf's hypotheses among the Hopis is sharply limited by the fact that these people are now for the most part bilingual in Hopi and English.

As another instance of a hypothesis concerning a relation between a language structure and a world-view, we can cite some of the work of Harry Hoijer, an American anthropological linguist, on Navaho, another Indian language of the American Southwest. Hoijer first points out that Navaho religious practices reflect a belief on the part of the Navaho that they live in a particularly delicate relationship with the physical, social, and supernatural environment. Failures to observe rules of behaviour or ritual will throw this relationship out of gear and result in various unfortunate events either for the individual or the community. The proper relationship between man and nature can be restored only by elaborate ceremonies. Thus, a dominant theme of Navaho culture is that 'Nature is more powerful than man'. Hoijer finds a reflection on this in the Navaho verb system, which exhibits a 'fashion of speaking' in which actors and goals of action are spoken of, 'not as performers of action or as ones upon whom actions are performed, as in English, but as entities linked to actions already defined in part as pertaining especially to classes of beings'. Thus, the form nìńtí which is glossed as *You have lain down* is better understood as *You [belong to, equal one of] a class of animate beings which has moved to rest.*

The somewhat tenuous nature of the relationship postulated by Hoijer will be evident, and admittedly the evidence in support of it is incomplete.

It is indeed possible to take the same data concerning the Navaho language and come to an almost opposite conclusion about the Navaho world-view, namely that it is an excessively physicalistic view in which every event must be described in terms of the kinds of objects involved, the movements which they perform or which they are caused to perform, and the precise space-time extents of these movements. The anthropologists Kluckhohn and Leighton call Navaho a 'fussy' language because it forces its speakers to notice many distinctions which are ignored in most languages. They say, 'Navaho focuses interest upon doing—upon verbs as opposed to nouns or adjectives', English, by implication, being a language which lays stress on nouns and adjectives as opposed to verbs. [Yet we have noted that some writers think of English as reflecting emphasis upon action!] Edward Sapir asserted, 'In many ways the Navaho classifications come closer to a freshly objective view of the nature of events than do those of such languages as English or Latin'. One of the author's favourite examples is the fact that in Navaho a *kiss* is translated in grossly physical terms as 'Two round objects come together'.

There is, therefore, considerable difficulty in establishing a relationship between a world view and the structure of a language. The relationships postulated thus far are only for single languages, sometimes, but not always, in contrast with one other language such as English. More compelling evidence might be obtained, perhaps, by establishing correlations based on a large number of independent languages. At the present time we must draw the conclusion that no satisfactory evidence exists for thinking that languages reflect particular world views. Indeed, the evidence from common knowledge would seem to point in the opposite direction, namely, to the effect that any world-view can be expressed in any language. When we consider the variety of philosophical positions that have been propounded in any one of the major world languages with no apparent difficulties arising from the languages themselves, the notion that language structure predetermined these positions seems like a contradiction.

With all the reference to such out-of-the-way languages as Hopi and Navaho, the reader may have wondered whether world views have been ascribed to English and other well-known Indo-European languages. Whorf himself talked of these languages as 'SAE' languages, that is, 'Standard Average European languages' and ascribed to them a mental outlook which classifies time into past, present, and future, which objectifies units of time, and which forces the description of events into an actor-action-object pattern which does not necessarily correspond with reality. Thus, in English, we have, according to Whorf, three major tenses represented by the forms 'He came, he comes, he will come'.

We can say that a walk 'lasted three hours', thus objectifying units of time that exist only because we choose to observe them. We can say, 'His arrival surprised me,' thus (according to Whorf) making an entity out of an event (his arrival) and ascribing to that entity power to cause a certain emotional state in a person. Whorf implies that these grammatical phenomena reflect a naïve theory of reality which is actually a hindrance to the acquisition of modern physical theories.

It is possible that Whorf was mistaken in his interpretation of these grammatical phenomena of English. For example, with respect to his allegations concerning the implications of the English tense system for a conception of time, we can contrast the views of W. E. Bull who has demonstrated that tense systems should not be identified with systems of time, but solely with dimensions of anteriority, posteriority, retrospection, and anticipation. Bull finds three major classes of tense systems in the languages of the world, differentiated solely by the degree to which they mark the several distinctions found by Bull in a complete tense system such as English. Hopi seems to have a less complete tense system than English, but it is still a tense system, not a time system, any more than English is. With respect to the claim that SAE languages force the description of reality into an actor-action-object frame, perhaps the use of the word 'actor' carries too specific an implication that the subject of a transitive verb is necessarily an independent, 'free-willing' agent. In instance after instance, the subject of a verb is found to be simply an event which is seen to be the source and probably the 'cause' of another event. This, for example, is the case in 'His arrival surprised me.' Strangely enough, one can find a discussion that argues that French is more likely to favour the actor-action-object pattern than English. E. S. Glenn finds that in the proceedings of the United Nations Security Council, the rather impersonal remarks of the chairman in English are almost uniformly translated into French with active constructions. Thus, 'The suggestion of "X" . . . is that . . .' becomes ' "X" propose que . . .'; 'Are there any observations to be made?' becomes 'Quelqu'un a-t-il des observations à formuler?'; and 'a . . . matter . . . to be determined when . . .' becomes 'une question sur laquelle nous pourrons nous prononcer lorsque . . .'. This was not due to the idiosyncrasy of a single translator, and the French constructions were rated as 'plus direct' and 'plus naturel' by native French speakers.

Finally, it may be pointed out that modern physical theory was worked out largely by men whose native languages were 'Standard Average European' languages. To be sure, the theories themselves were worked out largely in the language of mathematics, but it is possible to express them in terms of such languages as English, German, and Russian, for these languages are flexible enough to allow the expression of new concepts. In fact, with a few possible exceptions all languages seem sufficiently flexible to embrace any new science, technology, or philosophy. Whatever its world view may be, the Navaho language has adapted itself to modern medical terminology and thinking, and this has happened despite the fact that certain groups of Navahos have been highly resistant, on principle, to the introduction of modern medical technology.

For practical purposes (or at least for the purposes of applied linguistics) then, we may be well advised to abandon the notion that languages impose world-views on their speakers or that a language tends to reflect a world-view of its own.

A developmental theory of linguistic relativity

Let us turn our attention to a simpler and possibly better established view of the relation between language and mental activity. We must start with an analysis of the early development of concepts and language in the young child.

It is reasonably certain that as a result of his everyday interaction with the environment, the pre-verbal child has acquired a substantial number of what we may call *perceptual invariants*. That is, he has acquired the capacity to recognize certain things, qualities, or events as being in some sense identical or 'invariant' on different occasions or in different presentations. He recognizes his mother's face from day to day, whether seen from the right, left, or the front. He perceives a piece of bread as the same kind of food he had yesterday, even though in a different shape. He notices similarities and differences among these entities in respect to colour, size, shape and number.

Some perceptual invariants represent classifications of experience that are given by laws of nature or by invariant characteristics of the environment. For example, the child undoubtedly arrives very early at some grasp of the fact that things will drop or fall unless supported. Certain perceptual invariants may be 'mistaken' from the point of view of a strict scientific view of the environment, but justified by the correlations and contingencies that can be observed in the environment. For example, children are likely to arrive at a fused concept of size and weight, because most large things are observed to be heavy, and most small things are observed to be light.

The process of learning language can be looked upon partly as a process whereby the child learns to attach labels to the perceptual invariants he has already acquired. In many cases, the labels provided by language will already correspond almost exactly to the perceptual invariants acquired previously by the child. In other cases, they will draw the child's attention to new concepts which he may not have acquired for himself, and in still other cases there may be a mismatch between the preverbal concepts of the child and the categories provided by language. Exactly how the child's preverbal perceptual invariants may be fitted by the categories of the language he is to learn is a highly individual matter which depends on the child and the language involved. Nevertheless, as a hypothetical example, let us suppose that the child has formed a concept or 'perceptual invariant' that puts black puppies and black cats in the same category—a category, let us say, of black objects that move rapidly and that are especially nice to play with. Eventually, of course, the child will learn that the language of his culture has no special word for this class of objects; that is, that the language does not classify objects in this way. Gradually, too, linguistic experience will teach the child that size is not the same as weight, for he will learn that a thing can be called both *big* and *light* or both *small* and *heavy*.

The linguistic labelling of objects and events obviously has important functions in the mental development of the child. Various psychological experiments have shown that children who have learned labels for things are better able to notice and remember those things. Presumably, if there are differences in the logicality or fidelity-to-reality of alternative labelling systems (i.e. different languages), children learning different systems will differ correspondingly in their ability to deal with their environments effectively. For example, a child brought up in a language with relatively few colour words, or who is not taught many colour words, will have less facility in dealing with colour distinctions than a child who learns a large number of colour words and uses them accurately. This, at any rate, is the inference we can draw from some experiments conducted by the psychologists Roger Brown and Eric Lenneberg, who found that college students with good colour vocabularies could identify and remember colours better than those with poor vocabularies. They further showed that recognition and memory were better for those areas of the colour spectrum in which English provides the best organized set of colour labels. All these differences were due to vocabulary factors and not to colour discrimination ability.

A form of linguistic relativity hypothesis that seems to make good psychological sense, then, may be stated as follows:

Insofar as languages differ in the ways they encode objective experience, language users tend to sort out and distinguish experiences differently according to the categories provided by their respective languages. These cognitions will tend to have certain effects on behaviour. The speakers of one language, for example, may tend to ignore differences which are regularly noticed by the speakers of another language. This is not to say that they *always* ignore them, for these differences can indeed be recognized and talked about in any language, but they are differences which are not always salient in their experiences. The effect of any one language category is to lead language users to assume, perhaps mistakenly, that there is uniformity of some sort within the category, whereas the effect of a difference in language categories is to lead language users to assume, again perhaps mistakenly, that there is a real difference between the categories. These effects can be observed even within one language. For example, historians have pointed out that the use of the term 'the Middle Ages' may lead to the false impression that the period between the fall of Rome and the Italian Renaissance was in truth a distinct historical period which had uniform characteristics, throughout its length, which set it apart from other periods. Likewise, educational psychologists have sometimes claimed that 'intelligence' and 'scholastic achievement' *may* not be in truth distinct concepts, for there is some evidence that measurements of intelligence and of scholastic achievement are measurements of the same thing. (The present writer happens not to agree with this claim, but the illustration is still valid.)

Let us now analyse a simple cross-linguistic example. In English, it is possible to report about someone, 'He went to town'. Nothing is said about his mode of travel: he might have walked, run, rode a horse, driven a car, or taken a bus or even a boat or a helicopter. It is well known that in German one would have to specify at least a minimum of information about the mode of travel. Use of the verb *gehen* (as a cognate of *go*, apparently the most direct translation) would imply walking or some other form of self-propelled movement; use of *fahren* would imply going in a vehicle; of *reiten*, going on horseback; etc. Russian, and, it so happens, Navaho, could use an even longer list of verbs to distinguish modes of transportation. Thus, in English, it is possible to focus attention on the mere fact of someone's having departed in the direction of town, even though the speaker of English can be more specific if he wants to: *walked, ran, drove, rode, flew, bicycled, rowed, helicoptered* could be substituted for *went* in the sentence indicated. But it is at the same time as easy for English speakers to ignore questions of the mode of travel as to *fail to notice* such questions. As compared with German speakers, English speakers are sometimes benefited, sometimes disadvantaged by the possible lack of specificity in the meaning of the English term *go*.

Implications for language teaching

Theoretical considerations and experimental evidence converge toward supporting a very limited kind of linguistic relativity hypothesis, namely, the one formulated earlier as a 'developmental hypothesis of linguistic relativity'. This hypothesis relates to the fact that when any two languages are compared, some instances will usually be found in which the codification of a given range of experience differs as between the two languages, one language having a more highly differentiated codification than the other. It is obvious that the native speakers of these languages must learn to pay attention to whatever discriminations are required in their respective languages. The developmental hypothesis of linguistic relativity asserts merely that the process of learning these discriminations requires the speakers of the language with the more highly differentiated referential system for any given range of experience to pay more attention to these aspects of experience, and that this increased amount of attention can have certain effects on behaviour over and above acts of communication.

In general, however, the differences between the referential systems of languages are not systematic. In comparing two languages, one language may be found to be more highly differentiating in one area of experience, but less well differentiated in another area of experience. If we assume that differences in 'world-view' would be indicated only by systematic and broad-ranging differences in the referential systems of languages, we can conclude that differences between languages do not, in all probability, add up to differences in 'world-view' or *Weltanschauung*.

What does all this imply for language teaching? It means that an individual learning a second language must be taught *to observe and codify experience as nearly as possible in the same way as native speakers of that language*.

Relative to the native language of the learner, some phenomena in the second language are convergent, and some are divergent. *Convergent* phenomena occur when the referents of two or more symbols in the native language are represented by a smaller number of symbols in the second language. *Divergent phenomena* occur when the opposite is true, i.e. when the second language contains a larger number of symbols and corresponding semantic distinctions than the first language. The language learner must be apprised of both kinds of phenomena; the divergent ones are probably more critical for him as a speaker, while the convergent ones are more critical for him as a hearer. The English speaker learning German must be trained automatically to report the mode of travel when he encodes his English-bound notion of 'go'; if he has not learned this divergent difference, he is likely to be misunderstood. The native German speaker learning English must be aware of the convergent difference in English, not only so that he may use a form of the verb 'go' when he wishes to be non-specific about the mode of travel, but more importantly, so that he will not misunderstand an English speaker who uses the verb *go* in reference to some mode of travel not covered by *gehen* in German.

The learning of divergent differences is probably more difficult than the learning of convergent differences, since in the former case a selective response must be made, while in the latter case only an interpretative response is necessary. How can learners be trained to be aware of divergent differences and thus properly encode them? The psychological concept of *set* may be of use here. Psychologists have studied its role in determining responses to verbal stimuli, as in a controlled association test. For example, one can establish in a subject, through verbal instructions, a set to give opposites or 'contrast' responses wherever possible: the series of stimuli *white, poor, light,* and *butterfly* will then elicit *black, rich, heavy* or *dark,* and *moth,* respectively. A set to give synonyms would cause the elicitation, let us say, of *snowy, indigent, bright,* and *insect,* to the same series of stimuli. The encoding of meaning can be regarded as a response guided by a particular set. Teaching an English speaker the encoding of a mode of travel in the German equivalent of *to go* involves a particular set to respond in this manner. Inculcation of this set should in theory be facilitated by presenting the learner with a variety of situations in which people 'go' in various modes of travel, and asking him to practice responding, using the proper travel-mode word.

In teaching English to speakers of certain other languages, one of the more difficult learning problems is that of making a proper distinction between the simple tenses and the corresponding 'progressive' tenses. English requires its speakers to notice and report the difference between an action conceived as being performed at a point of time or customarily at different points of time, and an action conceived as being performed over a stretch of time. *He laughed when I came* is to be carefully contrasted with *He was laughing when I came; He sings well* (i.e. every time he sings) is in contrast with *He is singing well* (while I am talking about it, or during this week, etc.). The learner of English must be imbued with the set to notice and report whether an action is conceived in the durative aspect.

Similarly, a person who is learning Spanish must learn to distinguish the occasions on which he should use the verb *ser* from the occasions on which he should use *estar.* Both are translations of the English verb *to be,* but *ser* implies that a certain state or predication is characteristic of something, or relatively permanent, while *estar* implies that it is only temporarily applicable to something. *Ser* would be used to report that a man is an invalid, *estar* to report merely that he is sick. The learner of Spanish must somehow be sensitized to the potential difference in these situations. If he has properly acquired this discrimination, he may be expected even to realize that an expression like *Son las tres* ('it's 3 o'clock') using *ser,* conforms to the pattern because even though the hour of the day seems to be a temporary affair, it remains true that when it is 3 o'clock it can't be any other time; 'Three-o'clockness' is inherently characteristic of a particular time of day.

Thus, the implications of linguistic relativity for language teaching, in so far as we have been able to identify a sense in which it exists, are simple: Through contrastive linguistic studies, it is necessary to identify those instances where there are local or systematic differences between the representational systems of the target and the source languages. Differences may be found in morphology, syntax, or lexicon; and the direction of the differences may be noted as either convergent or divergent with respect to the target language. The structure of these differences is such that whereas in one language a certain range of phenomena or concepts is encoded by one symbol, in the other language the same or an overlapping range of phenomena or concepts is divided into two or more ranges, each with its own symbolization. Thus, one must extend into morphology and syntax the paradigm described by Weinreich for lexical interferences in bilingualism as follows:

> Often two existing semantemes, X and Y, of one language are merged on the model of another language, where the combined content of X and Y is represented by a single sign, Z.

The paradigm can also be extended to include the case where a certain concept represented by a certain symbol in one language appears to have zero representation in another language. For example, there is no word for the concept *too* (as in *too much*) in Amharic, Persian, or Urdu. The concept must be expressed by a periphrasis. For example, in Persian, 'He was too late to catch the train' would be rendered approximately as 'He came that amount late that he didn't catch the train'. Contrastive linguistics must therefore be particularly watchful for apparent 'holes' in the representational system of a language.

The interest here is in *semantic* differences between the referential systems of languages. Contrastive linguistics must study differences in meaning as well as in form. It must study morphological, syntactical, and lexical phenomena at least as much as it studies phonological ones.

Divergent and convergent contrasts having been identified and described, foreign language teachers must develop special teaching techniques and materials to bring these contrasts to the attention of language learners and to allow them to form appropriate habitual sets incorporating them in speaking and hearing behaviour.

According to the present view of linguistic relativity, mental operations are largely independent of the language in which they take place, although they may undergo certain transformations as the individual passes from one language to another. It would seem that true bilingualism is possible for the individual who has learned to manage these transformations. Further, I believe that accurate translation is, in principle, possible (provided the text being translated is free of ambiguities) if the translator is properly aware of differences in linguistic codification and takes account of them in preparing his translation.

The contrasts between languages do not add up to differences in mental outlook or *Weltanschauung*, nor is any world-view inextricably bound with any particular language. Those who may be alarmed about the spread of English, or of any other language, may be assured that there is insufficient evidence for thinking that such a language bears within itself, like a Trojan horse, a particular view of the world. This is not to say that the speakers of a language may not have a particular world view, but if they do have one, it is more likely to have arisen from social and historical factors which have nothing to do with language.

Nevertheless, the differences among languages are interesting and important enough to justify Goethe's assertion, 'Wer kennt nicht eine fremde Sprache, kennt nicht seine eigene'.

Linguistics and the Study of Language

In the preceeding four sections the discussion has been about language, the various ways it could be approached, its function, the variability of its physical manifestation and its relation to culture, personality and human mental functions. There is, as Allen points out, no lack of statements about language in general, but he goes on to suggest that where they are not simply trivial they tend to be *a priori* and experimentally unverifiable. What they lack is some general theoretical basis.

This section is about linguistics. Linguistics is often called 'the study of language'. But many people who would not call themselves linguists also study language; this much is clear from the previous sections. The titles of two of the papers in this section add important qualifications to the word 'study': *linguistic* study and *scientific* study—thereby implying that one can study language or languages in non-linguistic and non-scientific ways. But one must not equate 'linguistic' with 'scientific'. The psychologist would certainly claim to study language scientifically but as one aspect of human behaviour or human cognitive processes. On the other hand much study of language until recent times could properly be called linguistic without achieving the status of a science.

The famous definition of linguistics by de Saussure, quoted by both Allen and Lyons: 'Linguistics has but one proper subject—the language system viewed in its own light and for its own sake' contains two criteria by which linguistics asserts its independance as a discipline. 'In its own light' means that whatever categories are established by a linguistic theory derive exclusively from or relate exclusively to language data and are not part of, or borrowed from, some other general theory, say, of human behaviour or human society. 'For its own sake' means that linguistic theories are not set up to describe or account for, say, human behaviour or human society, in general, but only for language. Lyons explicitly distinguishes linguistics as an independent theoretical study having as its aim the construction of a general theory for the description of languages under the title 'microlinguistics', from the psychological, sociological, neurological and philosophical studies of language, which he calls 'macrolinguistics'. The most recent contributor to this section, Yngve, voices the general dissatisfaction with the narrow approach to linguistics which he calls descriptivism and structuralism. He points out that the study of the structure of language has turned out to be less straightforward than the founders of the study assumed and that it is no longer clear just what is meant by the structure of language. Indeed in a sense the structure of language does not exist. In this he seems to agree with Allen when he says that the structure is imposed on the data by the person who is describing it. If linguistics is to be the study of something which exists, then he suggests that what it should be concerned with is 'states of the mind', that the goal of linguistics should be an understanding of how people use language to communicate.

15 W. S. ALLEN
The Linguistic Study of Languages

Foreword

An inaugural, as I commented in this lecture, is a personal occasion and calls for something other than the reading of just another paper. Its content and style, moreover, are relevant to a particular time and place. In the University of Cambridge in 1957 the subject of General Linguistics was recognized only by the availability of an optional lecture-course and examination-paper in the Faculty of Modern and Medieval Languages. Some awareness of contemporary trends might be inferred from the election to the chair of Comparative Philology of one who, after a student career in Classics at Cambridge, had latterly served under the late J. R. Firth in the Department of Phonetics and Linguistics at the School of Oriental and African Studies in London. But it seemed at the time that if Linguistics were to be recognized in Cambridge as an autonomous discipline, and not a mere appendage of traditional philology, a rather vigorous form of statement would be needed; and if this requirement resulted in some degree of over-simplification, and even over-statement, it may perhaps be excused by the circumstances.

In 1971 the situation is appreciably changed. The subject is officially recognized by the existence of a Department of Linguistics, with staff representing a wide range of interests; there are phonetics and language-teaching laboratories and a linguistic computing centre; and a postgraduate diploma course is attracting an increasing number of students. It will therefore be appreciated that much of what was said in this lecture would now require less emphasis, and could certainly be more subtly expressed.

A few particular points call for some comment in retrospect. On p. 158 I said that 'The linguist is concerned with the actual and not with the possible'. This remark was directed primarily at the 'linguistic' philosophers' sometimes cavalier treatment of natural language. But in 1957 appeared Chomsky's influential work *Syntactic Structures*; and writing after that date one would certainly wish to enter a caveat to this statement, making it clear that one's quarrel was not with the theory of generative grammar, intimately concerned as it is with the potential of language, seeking as it does to account for the speaker's ability to construct an infinity of sentences and to understand those he has never heard before. The

W. S. Allen: Extract from *On the Linguistic Study of Languages*, Inaugural Lecture, Cambridge University Press, 1957. Reprinted in *Five Inaugural Lectures*, ed. P. D. Strevens, Oxford University Press, 1966, pp. 3–26.

stimulus of Chomsky's work has also had the effect of nullifying my criticism of the cut-and-dried 'proceduralism' which characterized some aspects of American linguistics (p. 156), since, regardless of its own merits or failings, it has resulted in a ferment of theoretical discussion which seems likely to continue for some time to come.

Finally there is one statement which appears to have acquired a certain notoriety, namely (p. 153): 'There are no facts in linguistics until the linguist has made them'. To a minority of hearers and readers this seemed an alarming statement, carrying suggestions of cooking the data to suit one's theories. But of course, as was generally recognized, this was not its intention; it was an abbreviated and, I hoped, effective way of saying that one's description will vary according to the conceptual framework that is brought to bear on the data—which are emphatically inviolate; it simply expresses a relativistic view of linguistic theory, and becomes scandalous only if 'language' is substituted for 'linguistics'.

Cambridge, England
June 1971   W.S.A.

Linguistic science in the twentieth century may count amongst its characteristics a critical attitude towards previous linguistic activities, and a growing awareness of its own theoretical foundations. In the words of the Danish theoretician, Louis Hjelmslev, the linguistics of the past— even of the recent past—has concerned itself with 'the physical and physiological, psychological and logical, sociological and historical precipitations of language, not language itself'. For the primary expression of this criticism we are indebted, as in so many points of theory, to the Geneva comparatist and general linguist, Ferdinand de Saussure: the final chapter of his *Cours de Linguistique Générale*, posthumously compiled from his pupils' lecture-notes between 1906 and 1911, ends with these words: 'Linguistics has but one proper subject—the language-system viewed in its own light and for its own sake'.

But it was, as Hjelmslev remarks, 'a long way from plan to execution'; de Saussure neither himself achieved nor lived to see the liberation of linguistics from its traditionally ancillary status. And even today, as we throw off one improper allegiance we are confronted by other diversions of a no less insidious nature.

This state of continued crisis is by no means to be deplored: of a 'crisis' in linguistics we may cheerfully exclaim with Hugo Schuchardt, 'Das ist ein gutes Wort!' But the situation suffices to justify the title of this lecture: the epithet 'linguistic' is necessary in order to differentiate the proper study of language material from the various other studies that threaten to obscure it, and from those related activities of a less *sui generis* character which are conveniently designated in English by the term 'philology'. Whilst the titles as such—'linguistics' and 'philology'—are unimportant, they serve to maintain a basic distinction which has been specifically emphasized by linguists as diverse in outlook as de Saussure and Leonard Bloomfield. But it is well known that the rubric under which linguistics is pursued in several universities of the English-speaking world is that of 'comparative philology'—thereby reflecting a tradition of the nineteenth century. The occupant of a chair thus labelled may in fact handle both the nineteenth- and the twentieth-century disciplines—the former primarily in teaching and the latter in research—but although some degree of cross-fertilization is both inevitable and desirable, the linguistic (or philological) Jekyll is not therefore to be confused with the philological (or linguistic) Hyde.

One school would go so far as to reject even the title of 'linguistics' (in favour of 'glossematics'), on the ground that linguistic studies thus far have failed to perform their true functions. Such an attitude, however, seems ill advised unless one enjoys the full certainty that one's own activities have avoided all the snares that beset one's predecessors, as well as those that are constantly coming into being. It is sufficient if we maintain the opposition of 'philology'/'linguistics' to differentiate the study of language as a means from that of language as an end in itself —regardless of whether its theoretical aims are or are not completely fulfilled in practice.

But it may reasonably be asked of the linguist that he should give a more positive, and not simply oppositive, meaning to the terms 'linguistic' and 'linguistics', by defining his attitude towards certain fundamental matters, such as the nature of his material, his undefined presuppositions, and the method appropriate to his subject.

A difficulty here arises, in that the subject is still in a state of development; linguists are still only working towards agreement on points of basic theory, and there are many matters on which argument is still vigorous. It does in fact seem that unifying trends are gradually prevailing over the fissiparous, but still a linguist's *credo* must be a more or less personal composition, the recital of which is perhaps best suited to a personal occasion.

A recent publication contains a comprehensive statement of the sphere of linguistic studies: 'Linguistics is concerned with language in all its aspects—language in operation, language in drift, language in the nascent state, and language in dissolution'. *Linguista sum, linguistici nihil as me alienum puto!*

But even the adherents of so catholic a creed would probably agree that their primary concern was with 'language in operation'; the less catholic might maintain that 'language in the nascent state' (referring to the process of learning) and 'language in dissolution' (referring to the condition of aphasia) belong rather to the domains of psychology and neurology; and some at least would feel that 'language in drift' (referring to its historical development) is hardly to be grouped with its synchronic, operational aspect. It may, then, be objected that the adoption of so diffuse a definition of linguistics runs the risk of precluding any unified theory, such as would justify its status as a subject, rather than an ill-defined field of activities connected with language.

The reference in the present title to the study of languages rather than of language is not unmotivated. It is intended to emphasize the view that, for all the generality of one's theory, it is to specific languages that it is applied; and it is by its ability to handle the specific language-materials that its validity is to be judged. There is indeed no lack of statements about language in general; and there is a tradition that the linguist should crown his life's work with a definitive volume entitled, with noble simplicity, 'Language'. Whilst the importance of many such works is beyond doubt, their value is in inverse proportion to their fulfilling the promise of their title; their influence on the development of our subject depends upon their dealing in fact with languages and with the principles of linguistics, rather than with the vague generality of 'language'.

General statements about language tend, when they are not simply trivial, either to be *a priori* and experimentally unverifiable, or else founded upon an extrapolation from the writer's own more or less limited experience. On the grammatical side in particular they tend to be expressed in terms of a traditional framework that is presumed to have universal relevance: the linguistic categories established for Greek by Greek philosophers and grammarians were, as is well known, uncritically transferred to Latin; and the Middle Ages saw the elevation of these categories to the universal status which they have done nothing to deserve. In Hjelmslev's words, 'The specific forms of expression peculiar to Greek and Latin had fatal repercussions in European grammar: a single morphological type—a type unique in the world—determined the structure of the theory'.

It is indeed questionable whether any scheme of universal categories can profitably be established. But if we reject this possibility, it does not mean that we have no general theory; the distinction has been summarized by J. R. Firth, who speaks of 'a *general linguistic theory* applicable to *particular linguistic* descriptions, not a theory of universals for general linguistic description'. It is precisely the existence of a theory, or (if we consider our present internal disagreements) the existence of the several theories, that makes linguistics a rather different matter from, for example, the more inductive activity of philology. The broadest outlines of such a theory I shall indicate in considering the question of 'meaning'.

Linguistic categories result from the application of the general theory to the specific languages. And it may happen that we employ the same labels to refer to categories established for different languages. But this is basically a matter of terminology and typographical economy—and it is at our peril that we make any linguistic identification of the homonymous terms. To identify the categories called 'Verb' in analyses of Russian and of Chinese could not be other than misleading—as also, at the phonological level would be an identification of the phonemes /t/ in English and /t/ in Urdu simply because in our analysis we decide to write them both with the same letter. One practical consequence of such false identification may be mentioned; the phonetic confusion of the Urdu and English categories in question was in fact a traditional solecism of the British in India—and phonetic solecisms are no more pardonable in their perpetrators, or less discourteous to their hearers, than the more generally reprehended errors of grammar.

If the linguist is to remain true to his purpose of seeking those modes of statement which are most appropriate to the particular material he is handling, he must be prepared to discard even such general categories as, by their wide attestation, seem likely to reflect universals. But so strong are our traditions that the jettisoning of old prejudices, and the achievement of a conceptual *tabula rasa*, is often a more difficult task than the erection of new frameworks of description. Recent researches on a language of the N.W. Caucasus suggest that in phonological analysis even the traditional trio of Consonant, Vowel and Syllable may not be universally applicable—if one tries to apply it, one is left with the uneasy feeling that the statement is less elegant than the material deserves. A proposed solution shows more affinity to the Arabic writing-system than to the Roman which has moulded so much of our phonological thinking.

It is perhaps obvious that linguistics does not include what Henry Sweet, in an excellent work devoted to it called the 'Practical Study of Languages'. Facility in the *use* of languages is no necessary concern of our discipline. It is of course true that a familiarity with many languages—and the more diverse the better—may do much to reduce the ethnocentrism with which, as native speakers of a language, we are inevitably burdened; for no one who has not had some considerable experience of this kind is likely to surmount the provincialism imposed upon him by the peculiarities of his own tongue, or by the traditional scheme of categories. And actual facility in the use of a foreign language is of course essential in dealing with monoglot informants—who, from some points of view represents a theoretical ideal; but this is an incidental administrative matter, without relevance to linguistic analysis as such.

The phonetic performance of crucial items, on the other hand, is a basic essential of linguistic study. We are handling a facet of social behaviour which is only partially accessible to inspection; we hear the sounds, we can record them and we can analyse them instrumentally in various ways; but the performative side of the activity, the acts of phonation with their delicate and complex muscular movements, are largely invisible to normal observation, and only partially observable by instrumental means (which tend, in any case, to impose artificial conditions and inhibitions upon the speaker). The ability to translate sound heard into terms of sound made—a peculiar exercise of the kinaesthetic faculties—comes only by submission to the discipline of phonetics; and even for the trained phonetician the only check upon his analysis is to put that analysis into reverse—to convert it into utterance in his own mouth—and to observe whether it is accepted as valid by the critical native performer.

A more debatable question is that of the relevance of the historical process to linguistics. We have inherited from the nineteenth century a peculiar obsession with time and with origins. As Marc Bloch has observed in his *Apologie pour l'histoire*, 'The explanation of the nearer by the farther has sometimes dominated our studies to the point of hypnosis'. The historical, genetic study of language owed much to the direct influence of Darwinian biology; much has already been written on the illegitimacy of the analogy, proposed by Schleicher, between languages and living organisms; and there is a growing tendency to deplore the emphasis laid upon diachronic development at the expense of synchronic description.

Certainly in its traditional form the historical study of languages can hardly be considered as a branch of linguistics in the contemporary mode: it is concerned with the causal explanation of individual items—in fact with 'history in reverse'—rather than with the analysis of structure; it is positivist in assuming its facts to reside in the documents which forms its material—its interest, as the late Viggo Brøndal expressed it, is in 'les petits faits vrais', whereas in linguistics, as in other branches of science, the contemporary attitude is anti-positivist.

It is true that recent years have seen the brilliant synthesizing work of André Martinet in structural historical phonology; but here linguistic methods are imposed upon history, rather than the reverse, and time is but one dimension of the matrix in which the material is embedded. This view is confirmed by the experience of Jost Trier, in his work on the less frequented field of structural semantics, which led him to conclude that history conceived in structural terms must be a kind of comparative statics. In fact Martinet's fruitful theory of 'structural asymmetry' suggests the possibility of revising our ideas of linguistic 'explanation'; suppose, for example, that (as in Romance) a shift of velar to palatal articulations is accompanied by the shift of labiovelar to velar: in such a case one may say, in the familiar causal mode, that the delabialization (of e.g. [kʷ] to [k]) is brought about by the palatization (of e.g. [k] to [tʃ])—since it has created a gap in the velar position to which the labiovelar is attracted. But equally one may, with Trubetzkoy, adopt the teleological metaphor and say that the palatization takes place to make way for the delabialization—in fact that y is y not only because it was x but also because it *will be* z. And one may come to the conclusion that either metaphor is better avoided.

These remarks should not be taken to imply that diachronic studies of the traditional type are to be discouraged or belittled: but the climate in which they prosper is historical rather than linguistic. Nor is their preoccupation with documents any criticism in itself: the emphasis in linguistics is admittedly upon spoken material, but one need not deny the legitimacy of analysing written language in its own right—in that case, however, the analyst should be honest, and (unless the written language is otherwise unknown) should not work with one eye upon a spoken language which his documents are presumed to represent; if issues are not to be prejudged, the investigation of the relationship between spoken and written forms must come after the analysis of each. If, on the other hand, one seeks a phonological interpretation of written material (as in the common case of a known dead language), then the first step must be to convert the written sequences into phonetic terms as specific as the evidence will permit, and then to apply to the resulting data the analytical methods appropriate to the study of spoken language. One is otherwise in danger of accepting the elements of the written text as phonological facts—whereas they represent at best an ancient and often inadequate attempt at analysis. There are no facts in linguistics until the linguist has made them; they are ultimately, like all scientific facts, the products of imagination and invention: 'Experience by itself is "silent", and it requires a hypothesis in order to give it a voice. ... Things, events, and facts do not speak, but the scientist does'.*

From this it is clear that the linguist, *qua* linguist, cannot be expected to share the philologist's enthusiasm for the discovery of ancient materials. His interest is in analysis rather than historical explanation; and there still remains a vast body of living material to engage his attention—material intact in all its fullness and complexity, as it proceeds from the mouths of its speakers and functions in it social context; he is therefore less attracted by the shadowy reflections of language which documents provide, particularly in those cases where the meanings and even the forms may be matters of controversy—the interest of such material for cryptanalysis and prehistory is of course another matter. Yet the traditions

* Hutton: *The Language of Modern Physics*, p. 244.

of philology have laid undue stress upon this kind of material; and warnings such as those of Schurchardt have gone too long unheeded:

'The present,' he wrote, 'is more important for science than the past. For its purpose is to comprehend events, and in this it can best succeed if they are present to immediate observation. We can comprehend past events only by reference to the present: we have to "re-present" them to ourselves. As the movements of dunes and glaciers illuminate the pre-history of the earth's surface, so does our everyday speaking and hearing illuminate the prehistory of language'; yet, he continues, we still have an unhealthy respect for the 'dead' languages—with the result that we come to set higher value upon a mutilated Apollo than upon an intact masterpiece.

In a review by J. Z. Young of a recent biography of Darwin, the evolutional discovery is held at least partly responsible for biology being 'still somewhat inexact science' some fifty years after the event. 'Darwin', he points out, 'was the simple naturalist, dissecting patiently, amassing facts over the years, knowing and caring little of philosophy'. Whilst one cannot but respect the Darwinian virtues in general, contemporary linguistics, in growing painfully out of the natural-history stage, can only find them constraining. It is perhaps no paradox to claim that the effects of certain material discoveries may in fact be to hinder the progress of a science, by distracting attention to the *use* of the new material, however fragmentary, and away from the invention of more adequate concepts for the *analysis* of what we already possess.

These remarks are offered with a full realization of the important part played by the so-called 'discovery' of Sanskrit, leading to the vigorous activity of nineteenth-century comparative philology; it was this atmosphere that fostered the interest and material endowments out of which the new linguistics has grown. The linguist is indeed grateful for such stimuli; but he continues to respect the Cartesian distinction of 'science' and 'connaissance', and tenders his loyalty to the former: it is to be noted that Descartes himself classified the study of language together with history and geography as a 'connaissance'—but that he had practical knowledge rather than analysis in mind appears from the provocative remark ascribed to him by Vico, that 'to know Latin is to know no more than Cicero's servant-girl did'.

I have suggested that linguistics is concerned primarily with the living utterance. Such an indication of one's subject-matter carries with it a presupposition—the basic presupposition of our study. We presume that there is a particular mode of human behaviour which it is legitimate to isolate and to label as 'language'; we assume also that this behaviour is such that systematic statements may be made about its various mani-festations. It is probably the most 'systematizable' of all forms of overt behaviour, whence arises the greater rigour of linguistics compared with other special sciences. It follows naturally from this that the linguist tends primarily to be interested in those aspects of the subject which involve the highest degree of systematization—as, for example, phonology and grammar; it follows also that he is little concerned with an itemizing activity such as etymology; in the difficult field of semantics, theories of systematic statement are at an experimental stage. In Western linguistics over the last hundred years, the trend has been from the less to the more systematic studies; but, as a result of the persistence of popular superstition, the earlier, less systematic studies have come to be widely conceived as the prime occupation of the linguist: particularly is this the case with etymology, and particularly with that practice of it which has been termed 'the old curiosity-shop school of linguistics'.

This statement of a positive presupposition may be matched by an emphatic negation—which is, that linguistics assumes *no* categories *in rebus, no* system inherent in the material and awaiting discovery. Linguistics, as I have already suggested, is a creative and not an observational activity: it creates its elements out of the continuum of human speech: it does not observe units unfolding themselves in time, but selects from the continuum such data as are relevant to the characterization of the elements it has established. It is true that some linguists would in fact assume the system to be immanent in the language, and the linguistic analysis to be a process of discovery rather than intention. They might also claim that in any case one's epistemological outlook makes no practical difference. But if a system is supposed to exist in reality, it is presumably a definite, single system; and the assumption of such a system rules out the possibility of alternative analyses. This seems a high price to pay for the satisfaction of presuming to deal in realities. The essential criteria for linguistic statement are generally agreed to comprise simplicity, exhaustiveness, and self-consistency; but it is usual to encounter some conflict between these requirements (more especially the first two), and the proportions of each may then be varied according to the predilections of the linguist and the particular purposes of his statement. We may recall a recently published note of de Saussure's, in which he says: 'This is our profession of faith in linguistics ... that there are no given objects, no things which continue to exist when we pass from one conceptual framework to another'.

There remains the question of method. It is a predominant feature of transatlantic linguistics that method is identified with procedure; and there are important handbooks now in existence which lay down detailed operational techniques for linguistic analysis. In this country the tendency has been to eschew the assembly-line process, and to leave the application of the theory to the genius of the individual craftsman. The stress is upon the prerequisite theory and the resultant statement, and these two are assessed without regard to the intervening processes: so far as method enters into our reckoning, it is to be identified with mode of statement. Such a lack of procedural postulates is not to be taken as a mark of weakness or disorganization: one may even argue that a crystallization of techniques—except for certain specifically organized projects—is liable to result in a fossilization of theory.

One result of the procedural approach is that the labour of analysis may be divided. Thus one worker, say a phonetically trained research student, may be sent into the field to collect and process the material by means of a phonemic technique—in the ambiguous words of a leading American phonetician, 'Phonetics gathers raw material. Phonemics cooks it'. The resulting phonemic statement may then be taken over by another linguist, to provide the material for a morphemic and syntactical analysis of a hierarchically 'higher' order. And there is no doubt that the system works—it produces a means of writing, and a grammatical formulation: and a system of teaching geared to such techniques has shown impressive results. But it suffers from an inherent theoretical weakness, which can have practical repercussions; for any analysis involves a selection from the formless mass of phonic material; and if the phonetician does not know in advance the requirements of the grammarian, he cannot be sure what data most profitably to select or how best to process them; whilst the grammarian cannot be certain that his analysis is the most appropriate to the material, without himself having examined that material phonetically. This vicious circle can be broken by the linguist himself alternating in the roles of phonetician and grammarian, modifying his grammatical analysis as his phonetic investigations proceed, and guiding his phonetic inquiries by the progressive requirements of his grammar. This undoubtedly places a greater burden on the individual linguist, and compels even the most sublime to leave their ivory towers and struggle with the sometimes unpalatable complexities of 'uncooked' speech. The advantage of such an approach is that it leaves the way open for the linguist to decide, if he so wishes, that, for example, the phonemic theory itself is not entirely suitable for his particular grammatical statement, or even that phonological analysis is not a prerequisite to grammar: he may then process the material in terms of some other theory more fitted to his requirements.

If one cannot agree to lay down procedures for analysis, still less can one do so for the personal conduct of one's research in relation to native informants. The linguist is sometimes asked how he elicits his material: how does he guide his informant into the utterances which are crucial to his analysis? how does he effect the initial break-in to previously unknown material? Such matters I should prefer to regard as the individual's private and confidential business—they are irrelevant to his statement and it is the latter to which his activities are directed. It suffices to say that each linguist evolves his own techniques in accordance with his personality, with that of his informant, and with the social and personal relations obtaining between them. Many linguists, however, would probably agree that deception and ambush play an important part in producing the unselfconscious responses that are required; it is usually dangerous for the informant to know in detail what is wanted of him— he may oblige even if the material does not exist. It is true that the linguist's gospel comprises every word that proceeds from his informant's mouth—which cannot, by definition, be wrong: but it is no less true that, as a matter of principle, whatever the informant volunteers *about* his language (as opposed to *in* it) must be assumed to be wrong—he is not after all a linguist (or if he is he will probably be a quite useless informant!); however, it is generally advisable to listen patiently and not to deprive him too sharply of his illusions—the good informant is a rare and valuable phenomenon, and his co-operation must be fostered with care.

My remarks thus far have had the object of delimiting in general the sphere of the linguistic discipline. I have now to mention certain particular trends which threaten to divert linguistic studies into non-linguistic channels.

Recent years have seen a movement in philosophy which has sometimes been known by the confusing title of 'linguistic analysis': its concern has been with the content-analysis of philosophical utterances, and so wide has been its influence that it might almost be said with Seneca, 'Quae philosophia fuit, facta philologia est'.

The method has typically involved the conversion of natural-language statements into presumed 'equivalent' forms such as would reveal their logical affinities. It is at this point that the linguist feels uneasy: for the philosopher thereby begs the whole question of 'equivalence', which, in the linguist's view, itself requires rigorous investigation. The point calls for notice, since similar methods are not entirely unknown even in linguistics: thus, in the famous work of Damourette and Pichon, we find the French negational statement 'non' described as an 'abbreviated [sc. negative] representation of the preceding phrase': a linguist critic of this method has aptly described it as follows:

'One syntactical datum is replaced by something else which is said to "mean" the same thing, but which in fact represents another syntactical datum; then one analyses this second phenomenon, ... and assumes that the first has thereby been analysed'. Similar criticisms may be made of the procedure of 'catalysis' in glossmatics; and in philosophy itself Wittgenstein refers to such cases as when the abrupt command 'Slab!'

is said to be an elliptical expression for 'Bring me a slab'. Why, says Wittgenstein, should one not equally say that 'Bring me a slab' is a lengthened form of 'Slab!'? 'And why', he goes on, 'should I translate the call "Slab!" into a different expression in order to say what someone means by it? Why should I not say "When he says 'Slab!' he means 'Slab!' "?' This is precisely the linguistic point of view: for the linguist, in Wittgenstein's words, every sentence 'is in order as it is'. The linguist is concerned with the actual and not with the possible, with what is said, and not with what, according to the philosopher, might equally well have been said, but, owing to the perversity of natural language, was not.

Whilst the linguist must reject such methods in his own work, it is right that he should be aware of their existence in a neighbouring field. Would that the philosopher were more aware of the methods of linguistics: in a recent work entitled *The Revolution in Philosophy* we do indeed find a recognition that the analysis of natural language-structures may be of interest—but we find also a complete unawareness that such studies are already pursued; the writer concludes by 'venturing the prediction that this little-trodden path will be trodden to some purpose before very long'. As well might one hazard the revolutionary prophecy that steam might soon be harnessed for purposes of locomotion.

Whilst one aspect of philosophy offers some slight embarrassment on the one side, a more dangerous diversion has been created on the other by the concepts and techniques of communication engineering. A number of linguists have in fact accepted the validity of communicational criteria in linguistic studies—thereby perhaps reflecting the traditional body-and-soul metaphor of language as a vehicle for the communication of thought. An alternative view is that these criteria are appropriate to communicational studies, *and no more*. Perhaps the most crucial problem in this respect concerns the concept of 'redundancy'. From the standpoint of message-transmission, it is clearly uneconomical to send the same information twice, or to send it in a more complex form than is essential to its distinctiveness. Thus, in a language which exhibits the common phenomenon generally known as 'vowel-harmony', the presence of a front vowel in the initial syllable of a word might involve fronted varieties of vowel in succeeding syllables; it would therefore be redundant, from the communicational point of view, to transmit the information 'frontness' in respect of other than the first syllable. And if, as in English, all nasal articulations are voiced, it is redundant to transmit voice as well as nasality. All languages abound in such so-called redundancies; as was stated at a Speech Communication Conference at the Massachusetts Institute of Technology in 1950: 'Speech communication is relatively inefficient compared to an ideal sending and receiving system using the same sound spectrum'.

In accordance with such observations there has been a tendency for linguists to describe their material in similar terms. This might be interpreted as arguing a misunderstanding of the true function of linguists. If it is in the nature of language to be of such a character as has been described, it is the function of the linguist to analyse and state it in its own characteristic terms, and not to ascribe to it superfluities which are such only by reference to other and irrelevant criteria. In phonology the analysis in terms of redundancy is largely encouraged by the linearity of roman transcription, which demands the localization of certain features (e.g. 'frontness') in a particular sequential 'segment' or 'letter', when they might more appropriately be considered as properties of a larger unit such as the word. Techniques for non-linear, multidimensional statement are now at an active stage of development.

A further disquieting trend originates within linguistics itself; I refer to the denial, in certain quarters, of the relevance of meaning to linguistic analysis. This attitude is in some ways understandable, since meaning has long been one of the least satisfactory aspects of linguistic studies; it has been dominated by the dualism of content and expression, and sub-servient to changing fashions in psychology—to the theories of Durkheim under de Saussure, and to Weissian behaviourism under Bloomfield. Meaning, as at least one linguist has expressed it, has become 'a dirty word'; but if the name tends to be avoided, there is no doubt that every linguist employs the concept, though some would be unwilling to admit to such improper thoughts. And surely without meaning linguists cannot exist.

It has been remarked that 'linguistics is peculiar among mathematical systems in that it abuts upon reality in two places instead of one'. I should not wish to stress the idea of linguistics as a form of mathematics —although its effective operation certainly demands the use of quasi-algebraic modes of expression, and it is likely that some future develop-ments will require an understanding of statistical techniques. It is certainly a subject not inimical to the mathematical mind—one may mention the name of Grassman, or of our own Joseph Wright, who said, 'Everybody who would be a philologist must have done mathematics or be capable of doing mathematics'; whilst Pānini, the incomparable Indian grammarian, was employing the concept of zero for linguistic purposes many centuries before its appearance in mathematics.

But, reverting to the position of linguistics, it is peculiar amongst sciences in standing astride two streams of phenomena—on one side the phonic material which constitutes speech, and on the other the practical situations in which speech operates. These situations or 'contexts' may be considered as functions of the phonic material which operates within them, or in other words as the 'meanings' of that material.

We could no doubt analyse the material without reference to meaning, but then the theory governing the analysis would have to be determined by some other subject, such as acoustics or physiology. And from either of these standpoints speech would probably not turn out to be particularly interesting material: more interesting noises could be found for acoustic analysis, and more interesting bodily activities for physiological analysis. It is only when we analyse phonic material by reference to its contextual function that those peculiarly systematic statements become possible which are characteristic of linguistics. An analysis which ignored such function, and concerned itself solely with the phonic material, might, for example, define its units in terms of arbitrary vocal intervals and the pauses between them; for linguistics, as Professor Bazell has observed, 'the unit so defined would have the interesting property that nothing whatever profitable could be said about it'—it may be mentioned that the authors of one such study, undertaken for entirely non-linguistic purposes, refrain from giving their unit a linguistic name such as 'sentence', 'phrase', or 'clause', and christen it 'talk-spurt'. The only reason for distinguishing any two sets of phonic data as *linguistically* different is the fact that their functions are different; there is no *a priori* reason why one should consider the difference between the [r] and [l] sounds in English to be such as to justify their allotment to different phonological units; what does justify such an allotment is their consistently distinctive function in regard to the contexts in which they occur. [r] is different from [l] because, *inter alia*, a ram is different from a lamb; and [z] is different from [d] because, *inter alia*, has is not the same as had. We do not recognize phonic differences if they do not have different semantic functions—nor, it may be added, semantic differences if they do not involve phonic differences. This may be made clear if one sets out a general conspectus of theory.

Our material, as we have seen, consists on the one side of *phonic* events, and on the other of *situational* events (which may include, or even entirely consist of, other phonic events than those which are in the focus of present attention). The discipline of *phonetics* provides the tools for the analysis of phonic events and by their means particular data are selected for the establishment of formal categories; according to the kind of criteria involved in the selection, such categories are said to be *phonological* or *grammatical*—phonological if they are based primarily upon similarities or dissimilarities of phonic data and secondarily upon their combinative relations, and grammatical if the converse is the case. The phonetic analysis is not necessarily congruent with that of acoustics ('sibilant', for example, seems to have no clear acoustic correlate), or with that of physiology (thus the 'blade of the tongue' is not an anatomically relevant abstraction). On the other side, *semantics* provides the tools for the analysis of situational events; this analysis likewise is not necessarily congruent with that of logic, psychology, sociology, or even common sense: it is simply such analysis as permits most fruitful phonetic analysis to be made.

The actual procedure is in fact to seek differences in the phonic material and to provide support for them from the situational; the phonetic discipline is consequently more highly organized than the semantic, which remains rather on an *ad hoc* basis. It is possible to imagine a linguistics in which the emphasis would be reversed—in which one noted primarily differences in situations, and supported these by differences in phonic events: two situations would then be different only if they involved differences in phonic events—a ram would be different from a lamb only because [r] differed from [l], and present would be different from past because, *inter alia*, the [z] of has differed from the [d] of had. But the procedure actually adopted is determined by factors of economy; the phonic elements are generally more limited both in extent and inventory than the situational; and whilst phonic events invariably occur within a situational context, many situational events have no phonic ingredients. But it is only by the interlocking roles of the two analyses that our categories are guaranteed their linguistic status.

I conclude by considering a not infrequent criticism of contemporary linguistic method, namely that its results may leave the reader with the feeling 'that we have come by devious and rather tedious ways to something which looks suspiciously like the old grammar'. Whilst such an observation can hardly be extended to phonology, it has perhaps some justification in the grammatical field, so far as it concerns the classical languages and to a lesser extent the Indo-European languages in general. This situation arises because of a certain parallelism between grammatical distinctions and situational distinctions viewed from a commonsense or logical standpoint (I shall not enter into the controversy concerning how far these views in their turn are coloured by the grammatical structure of the viewer's native language.) The traditional grammatical statements have been arrived at largely by non-grammatical, situational criteria, whereas the contemporary method will have formulated its grammatical statements by reference to grammatical criteria. If the two statements to some extent coincide, that is interesting, but it neither justifies the former nor invalidates the latter. It is possible to arrive at the right solution by the wrong means, or without knowing how one arrived there.

The achievements of contemporary linguistics may not yet appear particularly impressive—but at least it is capable of defining its concepts and of stating the criteria upon which its results are based. If its theory seems at times to be in advance of its practice, that is a healthy symptom.

16 JOHN LYONS
The Scientific Study of Language

The title of my inaugural lecture, 'The Scientific Study of Language', is no more than a short and generally-accepted definition of general linguistics. I shall have occasion presently to draw in greater detail some of the more particular implications contained in the term 'scientific'. For the moment, however, it will be sufficient to say that by the *scientific* study of language is meant its investigation by means of empirically verifiable observations and with reference to some general theory of language-structure.

Although no-one denies the importance of studying language, it must be admitted that the methods and principles of modern linguistics have aroused, and continue to arouse, a good deal of hostility. And it would appear to be the linguist's insistence that he is being 'scientific'—at least in aspiration—which provokes this hostility. It is a common assumption, encouraged by our educational system and the traditional attitudes this system reflects, that the study of language belongs wholly and properly to the 'arts'. It is, of course, for purely historical reasons that the study of language has traditionally been associated with, and made subsidiary to, literary criticism and other branches of the 'arts'. Many disciplines suffer, and linguistics perhaps more than most, from the assumption that the division of scholarship into 'arts' and 'sciences', or into 'arts', 'sciences' and 'social sciences', represents something more fundamental than administrative convenience. Whether or not language is properly made the subject of scientific investigation is surely best answered after examining the results so far achieved by those attempting to treat it as such. We should certainly not close our minds in advance to the possibility of establishing the study of language on sound empirical principles. As H. J. Ulldall has said, in discussing this very question: 'Progress in knowledge has been made only when men were willing to criticize preconceived notions so strongly held that they had never been tested'.

John Lyons: Extract from *The Scientific Study of Language*, Inaugural Lecture, Edinburgh University Press, 1965, pp. 4–22.

A more particular reason for the opposition to linguistics lies in the challenge it presents to many current notions about language. Such has been the success of the established 'natural' sciences since the seventeenth century that their practitioner no longer feels the obligation to justify himself to his fellows. It may be pointed out, however, that the main reason why many of us are prepared to accept that the work done by the natural scientist is valuable is not so much that we really understand what he is doing as the fact that we admire and appreciate the practical results of science. We feel, if I may put it like this, that our faith is justified by his works! This is a point I shall come back to, since linguistics also, as it has now been recognized, has important practical, or 'technological', applications. But I wish to stress particularly the importance of theoretical linguistics. And from this point of view the linguist is not in the same happy position as his colleagues in other sciences. The positive side of linguistics, the theories and hypotheses in terms of which the linguist tries to account systematically for what the layman regards as a set of random and unconnected facts, if he considers them at all, is not yet common knowledge. Moreover, the linguist, 'is exposed to a hazard from which many other scientists are shielded: a lay public with relatively easy access to observational data concerning which it has a stock of ready opinion'. So often the linguist first appears before his audience, as did Socrates, as a person who perversely questions this 'ready opinion' and then goes on to demonstrate (if he is allowed to have his say) that many assertions commonly made about language are in need of clarification; that some of them are false, and others tautological or meaningless. No-one likes to be told that he is talking nonsense or platitudes and there are few people who are prepared sincerely to suspend judgement until they have seen and understood the positive content of new doctrine. The linguist may not be forced to drink hemlock or banished from his native city; his books may be ignored or ridiculed rather than banned or publicly burned. Opposition from the academic 'establishment' takes a milder though often no less effective form nowadays! All that the linguist can do to combat it and secure a hearing is to remind his audience that every new science appears first in the role of a destroyer of accepted opinions and attitudes; it is only later that it is seen as something liberating, constructive and enlightening. The linguist must insist, however, that both parts of his science—the destructive, or 'Socratic', part, as well as the constructive part which depends upon it—both parts of linguistics are essential to it, and are educationally valuable.

Although linguistics is not a recognized school-subject, there is a very real sense in which one can say that everyone who comes on from school to university has inevitably done a certain amount of linguistics already by virtue of his having received formal instruction in reading, writing and composition and, what is perhaps more important, by virtue of his belonging to a community in which certain beliefs about language are passed on without question from one generation to the next. Since these beliefs are often erroneous, they should be corrected; and it is the function of linguistics, in what I have called its 'Socratic' mode, to correct them and replace with what now seem truer, or at least more reasonable, beliefs and attitudes about language. And it is mainly upon this 'Socratic' aspect of linguistics that I would base its claim for inclusion as a non-specialized Ordinary Course in the university curriculum: that is to say, as part of a general education.

Nothing is more helpful in acquiring an understanding of the principles of modern linguistics than some knowledge of the history of the subject. Many of the ideas about language which the linguist will question, if he does not abandon them entirely, will seem less obviously self-evident if one knows something of their historical origin. This is true not only of a good deal that is taught formally at school, but also of much that at first sight might appear to be a matter of downright common sense; for, as Bloomfield has remarked of the common-sense way of dealing with linguistic matters, 'like much else that masquerades as common sense it is in fact highly sophisticated, and derives, at no great distance, from the speculations of ancient and medieval philosophers'. As instances of 'common-sense' attitudes to languages which derive from what Bloomfield refers to as 'the speculations of ancient and medieval philosophers' one may cite the commonly-held belief that all languages manifest the same 'parts of speech' (in the form in which this belief is usually held and expressed). The traditional theory of 'the parts of speech', and the standard definitions of classical grammar, reflect ancient and medieval attempts to force together the categories of grammar, logic and metaphysics. Other commonly-held views about language derive not so much from philosophical speculation as from the subordination of grammar to the task of interpreting written texts and especially to that of interpreting works written in Greek and Latin by the classical authors. To this cause may be attributed the view that the written language is in some sense more 'correct', 'nobler' or 'purer', than the spoken language; in particular what might be called 'the classical fallacy'—the idea that languages have a golden period to which they evolve and from which in the course of time they degenerate, unless grammarians, the custodians of correct speech and writing, are successful in arresting this development. This assumption was made by the great Alexandrian grammarians of the Hellenistic period to whom we are mainly indebted for the codification of what we now call traditional grammar. It was taken over by the Romans, together with the framework of grammatical categories developed initially for the description of Greek, and it was embodied in the works of Priscian and Donatus which were used as teaching grammars of Latin throughout the middle ages. With the Renaissance—heralded in this respect by Dante's *De vulgari eloquentia*—interest in the vernacular languages developed enormously, and grammars were written in great numbers. But in all cases it was taken for granted that the grammatical categories established for Greek and Latin were universally valid. In fact the whole classical conception was extended to the modern languages. Languages still meant the language of literature; and literature, when it became the object of academic study in our schools and universities, continued to mean the work of 'the best authors' writing in the accepted genres.

It is true that a more satisfactory academic approach to literature has developed nowadays, and authors are no longer classified by the normative canons of Alexandria and the Renaissance. But the study of grammar in many of the language departments of our schools and universities still tends to be dominated by what I have called the 'classical fallacy'. This fallacy, I should like to think, is less strongly entrenched at Edinburgh than in some other universities of my acquaintance.

I do not wish to give the impression, however, that the history of linguistics is of interest only in so far as it enables us to free ourselves of certain commonly-held misconceptions about language. As an aid to the understanding of the principles and assumptions governing modern linguistics a knowledge of the history of the subject has a positive, as well as a negative contribution to make. Some linguists, including Bloomfield, impressed with the great advances made in the scientific investigation of language in recent years have tended to be unduly iconoclastic in their discussions of the past. If we can see this more clearly now than could Bloomfield and other linguists of his generation, it may only be that linguistics, like other branches of knowledge, advances, partly at least, according to the Hegelian pattern of thesis, antithesis and synthesis.

It is certainly the case that many of the attitudes and ideas of linguists today seem to result from a synthesis of certain traditional ideas with ideas directly opposed to them, their antitheses, expressed by linguists of a previous generation. Many examples could be given to support this point. I shall confine myself to one or two which seem to me particularly important.

I have already said that modern linguistics challenges the 'classical fallacy' that the spoken language is inferior to and in some sense derived from the standard written language. This challenge has frequently been expressed in strong antithetical form, most notably by Bloomfield: 'Writing is not language, but merely a way of recording language by means of visible marks'. Very few linguists nowadays would accept this point of view. They would still maintain, in opposition to the classical view, that there is a sense in which the spoken language is prior to the written; but at the same time they would grant that the written language may have its own grammatical and lexical structure; in short, that the written language has every right to be studied on its own terms. Professor McIntosh expressed this more moderate, 'synthetic', view of the relationship between the written and the spoken language in his article on 'The analysis of written Middle English' published in 1956: it is a view that is now very generally accepted. Moreover, linguists now tend to recognize not only a difference between written and spoken languages, and the legitimacy of studying each, but also a difference between various 'styles' and 'registers' in both spoken and written languages. The late Professor J. R. Firth used to express this fact by saying that we all speak 'many languages' and switch automatically from one to another according to the situation we are in and the social role we are playing at the time. Firth himself put forward this notion in conscious opposition to the thesis of de Saussure, that all members of a given speech-community speak 'une langue une'. In my view, neither de Saussure's thesis nor Firth's antithesis is acceptable as it stands. What is now required is the synthesis which will interpret Firth's 'many languages' as varieties of de Saussure's 'une langue une'. I do not think that this synthesis has yet emerged in any precise form, though much illuminating discussion of the question has taken place in the last few years, particularly among followers of Firth in Britain. Meanwhile, it can be said that linguists are now agreed that the literary language may have its own structure which is to some degree independent of that of the spoken language. The path is now open, and some linguists are making tentative steps along it, to a more fruitful discussion of the use of language in literature, of good and bad style relative to the aims of the author and the effect he is trying to achieve. And it may be mentioned in passing that the current renewal of interest in literature among linguists is only one effect of the reappraisal of the attitude of relativism, or *laissez-faire*, characteristic of so many linguists but a few years ago. 'Leave your language alone!' was the title of a popular book on linguistics published in 1950, it is no longer a rallying-cry of linguists in the mid-sixties. In the last year or so a number of books and articles have been published by linguists which express a much more positive attitude towards the question of standardizing languages. However—and let me stress this point—this does not mean that linguists have now abandoned the distinction between descriptive and prescriptive grammar which they fought to establish a generation ago. This distinction is maintained. But it is now accepted that there might be valid social or political reasons for promoting the wider acceptance of some particular language or dialect in a given community; and also that it is possible and legitimate to evaluate different languages or dialects (*after* they have been described) in terms of such criteria as efficiency and even expressiveness.

A far more important synthesis of traditional and more recent ideas about language is taking place currently in the field of grammatical theory. Undoubtedly, the most significant advance in linguistics in recent years is the development of the principles of generative grammar. Generative grammar takes as its starting-point the fact that the native speaker of any language is able to produce and understand an indefinitely large number of sentences in the language most of which he will never have heard before, and sets out to describe this indefinitely large set of sentences by means of a set of rules which specify precisely what combinations of elements constitute sentences of the language, assigning to each sentence a unique structural description. It is Chomsky who has been principally responsible for the development of this notion of 'generative' grammar. Those of you who heard Professor Chomsky lecture in Edinburgh last November will recall that one of the points he especially emphasized was the similarity between the aims of traditional grammarians and those of present-day generative grammarians; and that he criticized Bloomfield and his followers for misguidedly departing from these traditional aims and restricting the scope of grammatical description to the task of classifying the elements and combinations of elements occurring in particular texts. Chomsky was not of course suggesting that his formulation of the aims of grammatical description is simply a restatement of traditional notions. Although traditional grammar was generative, and to some degree even transformational, in spirit, it was only implicitly so. If we define a generative grammar, in Chomsky's own words, as 'a device (or procedure) which assigns structural descriptions to sentences in a perfectly explicit manner, formulated independently of any particular language', then no traditional grammar came anywhere near satisfying the definition. And the reason is that traditional grammar never set itself the ideal of explicitness, as we now understand this requirement. The ideal of explicitness was introduced only recently into linguistics and was developed, as much by Bloomfield and his followers as by any other group, or 'school', of linguists. Of course, Chomsky's view of what constitutes explicitness in this context has been strongly influenced by work done in the field of symbolic logic and the foundations of mathematics. But this influence is also discernible in the work of certain followers of Bloomfield. In saying this I am not of course trying to diminish either the originality or the magnitude of Chomsky's contribution to linguistics. What I wish to stress is the historical fact that modern generative grammar has not developed, and perhaps could never have developed, directly from traditional grammar. If modern grammatical theory has returned to and revitalized some traditional ideas on language, this is not simply as a result of quietly developing them and drawing out their implications over the years. A period of violent antithesis was necessary and, as I have suggested, has contributed essentially to the present synthesis. If I appear to have emphasized this point unduly, it is because there is a tendency, I think, for those outside the subject to simplify the issues. If linguists now appear to be holding views which they have spent the last thirty years or so condemning—if, for instance, they now say, as many of them will, that there might be such a thing as 'universal grammar' after all—you may be certain that this is not so much a matter of *plus ça change, plus c'est la même chose*, if you just sit tight and wait long enough, but rather *plus cela paraît la même chose, plus cela a en fait changé!* (The present 'encapsulates' the past, to use Collingwood's expression, it does not repeat it.) It is my conviction that any formal instruction in linguistics given in the university should include courses in the history of the subject. I would reject the stultifying proposal that modern linguistics must be 'uninfluenced by previous linguistics insofar as is possible', and would echo instead an aphorism of the great George Saintsbury, Regius Professor of Rhetoric and English Literature in Edinburgh from 1895 to 1915: 'Ancient without Modern is a stumbling block, Modern without Ancient is foolishness utter and irremediable'. The relationship between ancient and modern I would interpret in the changing, 'dialectical' way I have suggested.

The time has now come for me to say something about the different branches of general linguistics and the present state of their development; about their relationship to one another and to disciplines outside linguistics. These questions can be dealt with in terms of three dichotomies: (1) descriptive v. historical and comparative linguistics; (2) 'microlinguistics' v. 'macrolinguistics'; and (3) theoretical v. 'applied' linguistics.

The first of these dichotomies need not occupy us long. Since the publication of de Saussure's *Cours de linguistique générale* in 1915 it has been customary to distinguish between synchronic, or descriptive, linguistics and diachronic, or historical, linguistics; that is to say, between describing languages at particular periods (*états de langue*), without reference to their previous or subsequent development, and giving an account of their attested or postulated historical development from one state to another through time. Since historical linguistics is based upon the comparison of different language-states, it is in a sense part of the wider discipline of comparative linguistics.

It was the principal achievement of nineteenth-century linguistics to demonstrate the fact of linguistic 'evolution' and to group languages into 'families' and 'sub-families' by means of what is referred to as 'the comparative method'. We now give a rather different interpretation to the term 'evolution' from that given to it by certain nineteenth-century scholars; we may understand the terms 'sound-law', 'reconstruction' and 'analogy' somewhat differently; we may recognize more clearly than our predecessors that language-change is not simply a function of time, but also of social and geographical conditions; and we may admit that language can, under certain conditions, 'converge' as well as 'diverge' in the course of time. Most important of all, we now hold that the comparative study of languages is methodologically dependent upon their prior synchronic description. However, none of these modifications is sufficient to invalidate completely either the methods or the earlier conclusions of comparative linguistics.

Comparative linguistics is an explanatory science. It sets out to explain the evident fact that languages change and that different languages are related to one another in different degrees. The changes that languages undergo and the different degrees of relationship between languages are accounted for in terms of hypotheses which, like any other scientific hypotheses are subject to revision as a result of the discovery of new evidence or of the adoption of a new way of looking at, and systematizing, the evidence. The 'Indo-European' hypothesis has been continually modified for both of these reasons. These modifications are to be expected and welcomed. They derive from the fact that comparative linguistics is hypothetical and explanatory; and they do not constitute a reason for denying to comparative linguistics its due place as part of general linguistics, the scientific study of language. Having insisted that the comparative study of languages is a branch of general linguistics I can go on to say that it is, however, a less fundamental part of the subject than the descriptive analysis of languages. Comparative linguistics is less fundamental than descriptive linguistics, since, at least as I understand the relationship between them and have explained it here, comparison presupposes description, but description does not presuppose comparison. Since this is so, it is descriptive linguistics, rather than historical and comparative linguistics, to which we should give the greater emphasis in our teaching of linguistics.

Before passing on to my second dichotomy, I should perhaps mention that I have been employing the term 'comparative linguistics' in the conventional sense in which it is restricted to the comparison of languages with a view to establishing their 'evolutionary' or 'genetic' relationship; that is, the kind of relationship holding between them which is to be explained in terms of their historical development from some common 'ancestral' language. The reason for this restriction in the application of the term 'comparative' is simply that it was the 'evolutionary' study of language which more or less monopolized the interest and energies of linguists in the nineteenth century when the term first became current Nowadays, the comparison of different languages is undertaken by linguists for other purposes as well. The point I have made about the more fundamental status of descriptive linguistics vis-à-vis comparative still holds true under a wider interpretation of the term 'comparative'. Not everything I have said about 'genetic' or 'evolutionary' comparative linguistics is, of course, relevant to other kinds of comparison. Nor am I suggesting that 'evolutionary' comparison takes precedence over the others.

My second and major dichotomy is between 'microlinguistics' and 'macrolinguistics'. I do not very much like these terms and I may be employing them in a somewhat different sense from that in which they have been used by other linguists. Roughly, the distinction I am making is between a narrower and wider conception of what constitutes the subject-matter of linguistics. By the narrower conception I am referring to the view that linguistics is an autonomous science which has as its aim the construction of a general theory for the description of languages—in particular for their synchronic description—without reference to such questions as the learning of languages, the role of language in society, the psychological and neurological aspects of language, the influence of language upon thought and the development of logical and philosophical systems. By 'macrolinguistics' I mean here the study of language in relation to the questions I have just mentioned, as well as to many others. It was de Saussure himself who first insisted upon the restriction of linguistics to the narrower sphere of what I am calling 'microlinguistics'; 'la linguistique a pour unique et véritable objet la langue envisagée en elle-même et pour elle-même'. By 'la langue' de Saussure means, of course, the descriptive system, of elements ('sounds', 'words', etc.) and the relations between them, which the linguist establishes in order to account for the utterances (what de Saussere called 'la parole') of those who are said to 'speak the same language'. We can perhaps best translate the term 'la langue' as the *language-system*. 'Microlinguistics' then, or linguistics proper as understood by most linguists since de Saussure, is the study of language-systems as such.

One may specify the aims of 'microlinguistics' by first invoking the notion of 'acceptability'. 'Acceptable' is a primitive, or prescientific term, which is neutral with respect to a number of different distinctions that are made by linguists, including, for instance, the distinction that is traditionally drawn between 'grammatical' and 'meaningful': it is a more primitive term than either 'grammatical' or 'meaningful' in the sense that, unlike these terms, it does not depend upon any technical definitions or theoretical concepts of linguistics. An acceptable utterance is one that has been, or might be, produced by a native speaker in some appropriate context and is, or would be, accepted by other native speakers as belonging to the language in question. 'Microlinguistics' sets itself the task of specifying for the languages being described what utterances are acceptable.

Since, as I said earlier, the native speaker of a language is able to produce and understand an indefinitely large, and perhaps infinite, number of different utterances, most of which he will never have heard before, it follows that any body of recorded material in a given language, however large that body of material, is but a sample of the language in question. It is one of the tasks of the linguist in collecting the material, his data, to make the sample as representative as possible, and in describing the language to do so by projecting, or 'extrapolating', from the data a very large number of sentences which have not been recorded and yet which would be regarded as acceptable by native speakers. In other words, the description of the language will take the form of a finite set of elements and rules which, on the basis of a finite number of sentences, will account for a much larger, and perhaps infinite, number of sentences, which, in the ideal, are 'all and only the sentences of the language'. Any description of a language which has these properties is a generative description. And I shall take it for granted that the construction of generative descriptions is a necessary aim of modern 'microlinguistics'. Not all linguists would agree with me here perhaps, but one can't be neutral all the time! I shall also take it for granted that the construction of formally different generative systems for the description of different languages is, at least *prima facie*, undesirable; and that it is the construction of a general, generative theory of language-structure in terms of which all languages can be described which is the principal concern of 'microlinguistics'. This assumption is, if you like, the linguist's παράδειγμα ἐν οὐρανῷ, an ideal which haunts and guides him, which provides grounds for his dissatisfaction with particular descriptions and spurs him on to improve and standardize them. It is an assumption that linguists will hold as long as seems reasonable. And it is in the light of this assumption that they are again, and perhaps always have been really, concerned with 'universal grammar'.

Linguists customarily recognize three levels in a language-system and in terms of these account for different kinds or 'layers' of acceptability: the phonological, the grammatical and the semantic level. A certain amount of acceptability (including much of what is popularly referred to as 'accent') can be accounted for at the phonological or even the phonetic level. That is to say, in terms of the 'sounds' which occur in the language and their possible combinations. (I am using the non-technical, though ambiguous term 'sounds' for simplicity.) At the grammatical level of description we recognize units of a 'higher' order than 'sounds' (let us say 'words' for simplicity, although they are not always words) and group them into classes: nouns, verbs, adjectives, etc. Grammar accounts for as much of the acceptability of utterances as can be accounted for in terms of rules which specify the permissible combinations of these word-classes. Modern grammarians, both in their theory and in their practice, differ from traditional grammarians at this point, apart from being more explicit, in at least two ways: first, they set up the word-classes, or 'parts of speech', solely with reference to their general combinatory properties and take no account of the meaning of particular words; second, they make a much finer sub-classification of the 'parts of speech' in terms of their combinatory possibilities than was achieved or thought possible in the past. However, no matter how far the grammatical analysis is taken—and the limits are far from having been reached in the description of any language, although contemporary partial grammars of English have recognized some hundreds of grammatical sub-classes—it will never succeed in accounting for the whole of acceptability. It is at the third level of description, the semantic level, that one accounts for such acceptable and unacceptable combinations of words as can be specified in terms of the meaning of the particular words in question. This view of the matter, it may be pointed out, does not necessarily involve acceptance of the equation: 'synchronic linguistic description minus grammar equals semantics'.

It is with respect to the levels of phonology and grammar that the 'microlinguistic' view has been most strongly, and most successfully, maintained by linguists. Current phonological and grammatical descriptions of languages are undoubtedly freer of vagueness and inconsistencies, and in parts at least are more comprehensive, than those of the past. There is considerable disagreement among linguists about particular theoretical points: I will say nothing about these here. There is also a good deal of controversy about the more general 'goals of linguistic theory', but I think it is fair to say that this controversy is more about widening the scope of phonological and grammatical description than about changing this entirely.

In the more particular approach to linguistic description which, as I said, I am taking for granted—the generative approach—the descriptions of language-systems account for grammatical and phonological acceptability by means of a set of rules which operate in sequence upon certain theoretical intermediate elements introduced for the purpose and 'produce', ultimately, 'strings' of 'words' and 'sounds' together with an associated 'structural analysis' of each 'string'. Looked at from this point of view, the grammar of a language—and let me from now on use the 'term' in a wider sense to include phonology—is a formalized, deductive system which 'generates' sentences as valid 'theorems' of the particular language-system; and the general grammatical theory in terms of which the grammars of particular languages are written determines the form of the rules, the nature of the elements occurring in them, and the conditions for the application of the rules. This conception of the nature of grammatical descriptions and of grammatical theory, for which, as I said earlier, we are of course principally indebted to Chomsky, draws heavily upon formal logic and the foundations of mathematics. Formally different generative systems can be constructed; that is to say, systems which differ as to the nature of the rules or elements that they permit or the more particular constraints that they impose upon the ordering of the application of the rules. Much important work has already been done on the investigation of the relative power and empirical adequacy of systems with different formal properties. This work is very technical; for at this point theoretical grammar, like for instance the theoretical parts of other sciences, merges into applied mathematics. One cannot expect all linguists, still less students of the subject, to become thoroughly conversant with this branch of linguistics; but one can expect, I think, that they should appreciate the general implications of the work being done here and the results so far achieved. Among these results should be mentioned the proof that certain systems with different formal properties which can be set up for a given language may be equivalent in the sense that they will generate the same set of sentences, but non-equivalent in the sense that they will generate these sentences with different associated structural analyses. It thus becomes a question of some interest to decide whether one grammatical description is better than another as the basis for semantic description, in relation to certain wider aims of linguistic theory, or for some particular purpose.

I will not go further into the details of modern grammatical theory. I have deliberately made my stand on what many might consider to be the most arid, 'formalistic' and even 'inhumane' aspects of the subject. I wish therefore to refer briefly to this criticism which is sometimes made of modern grammatical theory.

It is not only laymen, but also certain linguists, who find what they consider to be the excessive 'formalism' of much modern linguistics a stumbling-block. From time to time, books and articles appear which contain pleas for less 'formalism' and more 'realism' in linguistics. To many the word 'realism' has a nice, reassuring sound. To the scientist and the philosopher the word has, of course, quite other connotations. You will recall what Eddington says on this subject in the Gifford Lectures which he delivered in Edinburgh in 1927, on *The Nature of the Physical World*: that 'the word "reality" is generally used *with the intention of evoking sentiment*' and 'loud cheers'; that science has no place for this conception of 'reality'—it has its own 'domestic definition of existence', which 'follows the principle now adopted for all other definitions in science, namely, that a thing must be defined according to the way it is in practice recognized and not according to some ulterior significance that we imagine it to possess'. The fact is that objections to the 'formalism' and 'abstractness' of modern linguistics are usually appealing implicitly to some other ontological framework, which though it may be more vaguely described or different is no less abstract. There is of course legitimate disagreement among linguists about the particular theoretical framework to be used in the description of language. All I wish to suggest is that what is sometimes represented as an argument between 'formalists' and 'realists'—the implication being that the 'realists' have a healthy respect for 'facts', whereas the 'formalists' do not and are moved only by their perverse delight in 'mathematical manipulation'— is an argument in favour of one abstract framework rather than another.

Linguistics is—or perhaps one should say more modestly and more truthfully, sets out to be—a body of scientific theory set up to account for certain data. These data, language-utterances, either result from or are verified by observation. The general theory of language-structure is not, of course, derived simply by induction from the data; it embodies certain assumptions and criteria of relevance taken for granted at the outset (the data, it has been well said—though I cannot now recall by whom, are not 'given' but 'taken'); the theory also embodies such principles as internal consistency and elegance. The data are the evidence for the theory; and the attempt to apply the theory to account for the data may lead to its confirmation, modification or abandonment. Ultimately the gap must be bridged between the system of elements, rules and relation-ships which enter into the theory set up to describe language-systems ('langues') and the observed or observable utterances (instances of 'parole') which are the linguist's data. This, I take it, is assumed by all linguists—by those working at the most general level upon the theoretical foundations of linguistics, as well as by those engaged upon the description of particular languages.

The 'realists' do not observe the 'loud cheers' that the label they have given themselves tend to evoke. If modern linguistics is an abstract subject, this is because it is deliberately, and perhaps at times (as in the present lecture) rather too assertively, scientific; if it is striving towards formaliza-tion, this is because mathematical formalization is the goal of all science. And, if I may quote Eddington again, 'we must follow the path [of science] whether it leads to the hill of vision or the tunnel of obscurity'. It may be that all aspects of language can be brought within the scope of one science. But then linguists are not claiming to deal with 'all aspects of language'—at least, not yet!

If the aims of 'microlinguists' are circumscribed in the way I have outlined the place of semantics immediately comes up for discussion. We are surely interested not merely in the question whether sentences are semantically acceptable, meaningful, but also in *what* meaning they have. And whereas, it might be reasonable to adopt the view that a phonological and grammatical description need do no more than identify elements and specify their combinatory possibilities directly, it would seem to be the case that the meaningfulness, or significance, of at least some combinations of words is a function of what meaning each of them has independently; and also that something of what we call their meaning has to do with their relations with things in the world outside the language-system and with the situations in which particular words and utterances are used. The distinction between 'microlinguistics' and 'macrolinguistics' becomes particularly difficult, and perhaps ultimately impossible, to draw consistently in the case of semantics: and this is no doubt one reason why some linguists have in the past been inclined to exclude the whole of semantics from linguistics proper.

I do not think that linguists have yet produced a satisfactory theory of semantics; nor do I believe that linguistics will ever provide a satisfactory theory of semantics so long as the subject is restricted to the narrower aims of what I have been calling 'microlinguistics'. Semantics is a field where progress depends necessarily upon the collaboration of linguistics and such other disciplines as philosophy, anthropology and sociology. And it is perhaps philosophy that can give the greatest assistance to linguistics in the study of meaning. Philosophers have always been concerned with language and more particularly with meaning, since this is necessarily involved in such questions as the problem of truth and knowledge. And in recent years the dominant 'schools' of philosophy in Britain and elsewhere have been almost exclusively concerned with these questions. As Ryle has said: 'Preoccupation with the theory of meaning could be described as the occupational disease of twentieth-century Anglo-Saxon and Austrian philosophy'. Despite this fact there has been distressingly little collaboration so far between linguists and philosophers, in this country at least, in the discussion of semantic theory.

We have been discussing languages in the deliberately-restricted sense of 'language-systems'. One can of course take a wider view. Everyone agrees that it is by virtue of his possession of language that man differs most strikingly from other animals and is able to engage in discursive reasoning: it is often said that 'homo loquens' would be a more satisfactory classifactory term for man than the traditional label of 'homo sapiens'. Moreover, language is the foundation, or keystone, of social organization; it is an integral part of a community's culture and the principal means whereby the norms of conduct and judgement are maintained and transmitted from generation to generation. It is through our mastery of other languages that we are able, either directly or at second-hand, to enter into and appreciate the experience of individuals living in other ages and other cultures, and so enrich our own life. So much will be readily admitted. One might go further, as some have done, and maintain that language is a conditioning factor in all adult human experience, such that the way in which we think or even perceive the external world is to a considerable degree influenced by the particular native language we happen to speak. This is a controversial question which has been much discussed in recent years. A certain amount of experimental evidence has been cited—though so far, it must be admitted, very little—which would tend to support the hypothesis. It is in any case a widely-held view, and one that has been frequently expressed by those who habitually use more than one language in their normal, everyday life, that the language one is speaking affects not only what one will say in certain situations but even one's moods and emotional reactions; in other words that language affects personality, the 'kind of person' one is. All these questions, and many others, one may refer to 'macrolinguistics' in the sense in which I am using the term. And it is here that one recognizes the links, actual or potential, that linguistics has with such other disciplines as philosophy, psychology, anthropology, sociology, literary criticism, 'the history of ideas', and even with neuro-physiology, animal and human ecology and the study of animal communication-systems.

In recent years a whole host of rather barbarous neologisms have emerged to refer to the work that is being done in the borderline areas between linguistics and other disciplines: 'psycholinguistics', 'ethno-linguistics', 'sociolinguistics', 'neurolinguistics', 'paralinguistics' and so on. I obviously have not the time, and am in any case not competent, to review the work that is being carried out in all these various fields. Much of this research is undoubtedly very tentative; and many of the boundaries will almost certainly have to be redrawn. It must be insisted, however, that what are recognized, at least at present, as border line areas between linguistics and other disciplines are legitimate fields of scientific investigation. In many cases the results achieved even now are encouraging. And where they are not yet encouraging we should not be too ready with the maxim: *Wovon man nicht sprechen kann, darüber muss man schweigen.*

In some instances 'macrolinguistic' research has been inspired directly by the achievements of linguistics in pursuit of its narrower goal of describing language-systems. This is perhaps most notably so in the case of current 'psycholinguistic' work. Let me quote a recent comment of George Miller in this connexion: 'I now believe that mind is something more than a four-letter Anglo-Saxon word—human minds exist and it is our job as psychologists to study them. Moreover, I believe that one of the best ways to study a human mind is by studying the verbal system that

it uses'. It is obvious that generative grammar, and in particular transformational grammar, although set up by linguists for the description of
language-systems without reference to the psychological aspects of
language, has important and suggestive implications for psychological
theories of speech-perception and of the learning and use of language.
These implications have been drawn in recent theoretical and experimental work.

Many of the topics dealt with by modern linguistics, as I have stressed
in the earlier part of this lecture, have been treated by grammarians and
philosophers for centuries. Other questions treated by modern linguistics
and such other disciplines as I have mentioned here have arisen from a
new way of looking at language, or from attempts to relate it to its
cultural 'matrix' and to the psychological and neurological 'mechanism'
which the use of language presupposes. It is surely one of the most
exciting aspects of science that it advances not only by solving the problems with which it starts, but by creating new problems, by charting and
annexing to itself new regions of enquiry, on the way. And we may rejoice
that there is at least one sphere of human activity where 'Parkinson's
law' operates to our entire satisfaction: the field of science expands to
occupy fully the time and energies of scholars engaged in it!

It is impossible for any one person to keep abreast of developments
in all the fields that I have referred to here under the term 'macrolinguistics'. But then it is impossible for anyone to be familiar with more
than a few languages or to control all the evidence that has to be handled,
for instance, in the comparative study of the Indo-European languages.
Linguistics has always relied upon the collaborative work of many
scholars. Exhaustive descriptions of particular languages are required,
as well as work on the general theory, its logical basis and axiomatization.
It is by virtue of the development of the general theory by a variety of
linguists with different, but overlapping, specializations that progress has
been made so far. It is not inconceivable that we shall in time modify our
view of what has seemed to be a desirable restriction of the field of
linguistics proper, to the study of language-systems. And I have already
suggested that in the case of semantics this restriction cannot even now be
maintained. We should obviously be more satisfied with a theory of
language-structure common to those approaching language from many
different points of view—from the point of view of its acquisition, its
pathology, its role in culture, and so on. But no such unified theory yet
exists, and one may be falling victim to the temptations of 'reductionism'
in thinking that it ever will.

17 On Achieving Agreement in Linguistics

VICTOR H. YNGVE

There is in linguistics today a kind of generation gap. The younger generation is not content to accept the values of their parents and they are in some cases in open rebellion. They are not at all clear, however, as to what institutions they would want to erect in place of the existing ones.

The present tacitly accepted values were the hard won gains of a previous revolution fought over a previous generation gap. Mentalism, notionalism and psychologism had been thrown out. Linguistics had been freed from superstitions and set on the road toward becoming a science. Realistic and careful study and description of its data ensued. Linguistics became the study of language, and structure became its major focus.

A number of the most daring revolutionaries have abandoned the old upper middle class suburbs and have established experimental radical action communities. Each of these experimental radical action communities is characterized by much heated discussion, and the mimeograph machines are busy turning out position papers. One of the symptoms of the unrest has been the occasional appearance of graffiti in public places, complete with such four-letter words as taxonomy, performance and Markov.

There seems to be much confusion among the various groups of revolutionaries. They all agree that the older views lack relevance, but there is little agreement as to what really is wrong with the old morality and what kind of values should be afforded any kind of legitimacy in today's world. At this point, most of the disagreement is among the members of the younger generation. Their elders have long since given them up for lost.

In a true science, one does not expect to find the kind of disagreement that exists. One problem is that the study of the structure of language, grounded solidly on data, has turned out in practice to be less straightforward than our fathers appear to have assumed, for it seems to be far

Victor H. Yngve: Extract from *Papers from the Fifth Regional Meeting Chicago Linguistic Society*, April 1969, Department of Linguistics, University of Chicago Press, 1969, pp. 456–62.

from clear just what it means to describe the structure of a language. There is a growing suspicion that the question may not even be properly formulated. What is structure? What are the goals of linguistics? What kinds of insights are we searching for? Linguistics, in practice, seems to be an ill-defined task.

Another problem, probably stemming from this, is that there seems to have grown up a reliance on arbitrary pronouncements on what a grammar must be, or on what the goals of linguistics should be. A large role is often assigned to belief in linguistics and various beliefs or articles of faith are proclaimed by the various groups. Linguistics is often seen in terms of ideologies and isms, an orientation more suited to discussions of divergent religious doctrine or political ideologies and quite different from what one would expect in science. Some of the writings in linguistics have been murky polemics rather than searchlights shining on gleaming gems of truth.

Yet another problem is that the student activists belonging to one or another radical action community often affect the garb, complete with symbolism, of their leaders, who are sometimes too explicitly doctrinaire in their approach, and in their selection of notation and representation. This seems more analogous to the use of such political activities as flag waving, the wearing of uniforms or armbands or buttons. Technical terms in linguistics are sometimes more valued as symbols of allegience than as concise labels for carefully defined and useful scientific concepts.

In an attempt to compare competing representations, a tendency to rely on simplicity and elegance has emerged. The tests of value in linguistics have tended to become aesthetic tests, on a par with the tests of literary or artistic merit. This is surprising for a discipline which aspires to the state of a science. Not that science is unaesthetic. It exhibits a full measure of simplicity and elegance. But the tests for truth in science are quite different.

A number of these new experimental communities would appear to be transitional in nature. In seeing these communities as transitional there is the implication that one can get some conception of a future order. This is correct. The experimentation that is being carried out is helping us, through the revolutionary writings, to get a glimpse of this future order.

There is increasing uneasiness with the most fundamental doctrines of structuralism and descriptivism. There appears to be an increasing necessity to take the language user explicitly into account. Linguists are becoming increasingly interested in certain carefully worked out position papers from linguistic philosophy and from psychology.

It has become more and more clear that linguists must take into account the instrumental use of language. There is a continuing search for relevance. The forms that are used bear some relation to the speaker, and to the purpose that he is trying to serve by using the forms. I see here the seeds of a great and powerful basic agreement among the different camps of dissidents and perhaps here one can discern the shape of things to come. There is a new sense of excitement: one feels it in the air. There must soon be a resolution of the various factional disputes and a new crystal clear set of values and insights will emerge.

I think I see clearly the outlines of this new order. It will be based on a broadened view of our most basic goals in linguistics. We will no longer be satisfied with received doctrine. That is, we will no longer be satisfied merely with trying to describe the structure of language. What we want to know is how people use language to communicate.

As a matter of fact, this has probably actually always been the real goal of linguistics, anyway, that is, how people use language to communicate. But the inhibitions of the older generation have caused them to neglect the study of people as language users. They have tended in public to avert their gaze as if ashamed. But the younger generation has begun to realize that people are beautiful and that there is really nothing wrong in looking at them. They have the suspicion that their elders have always had a secret fascination for the whole subject. But we have somehow got hung up on this language structure business. We have somehow been led to accept a more limited goal, that linguistics is merely the study of the structure of language. This has come to us as received doctrine. Our elders probably set a more limited goal because they couldn't see their way into the broader one, but a more limited goal would seem to be a true hang up. The common thread that lies through all the revolutionary writings is the effort to escape from this hang up. I see that we will escape from it and that a new science will emerge. I have been trying to sketch the outlines of this newly emerging science as best I can in my lectures and in my forthcoming book.

The way to approach how people use language to communicate is, I think, through the concept of mental state or state of mind. One might suspect, in accordance with received taboos, that this is mentalistic, psychologistic and notional, but I would maintain that the state of mind of a language user is based on an ultimate reality on which a genuine science can be based. That ultimate reality is biological, physical and chemical. One can approach the study of mental state through scientific observation and experiment. A rich source of data is available by observation of what the organism, that is, the language user, does. In other words, linguistic behaviour is data to be used in deducing what the organism is doing. The linguists are the ones who have developed the techniques for handling this data. Ultimately, we may obtain chemical or neurological data that will bear on our problem. In the meantime, we will have to be content with less direct linguistic evidence. There may remain a certain indeterminancy in our results, which can be handled by notational means that are specific enough to express what we know without committing us on what we don't know. The fact is, that the concept of mental state can be related to a reality, whereas the concept of the structure of a language cannot. For structure, like beauty, is in the eye of the beholder and this is what much of the arguing has been about.

We're not building castles in the air in any sense of the word. We're trying to find out what really goes on. Some of the problems of linguistics have been related to the playing of games, and some of the problems of psychology as well are also related to the concept of playing games. Given certain rules, what can you do or what can you say? Given a method of analysis and a limited amount of data, or a particular way of obtaining data, what can you say about it? You see, if you're studying behaviour —whether it be linguistic behaviour or other behaviour—and if you try to talk about the structure of the behaviour or the structure of the language, you're talking about something that really doesn't exist. Language exists in a sense: people speak it. But that's a different sense from the sense that brains exist and people exist. If you're asking to describe structure, you're really asking to invent a structure and describe it. And there is a certain air of unreality about this. It's true that one can make observations about language phenomena or language behaviour. It's true that one can put likes together and keep unlikes separate. It's also true that you can build all this up into very nice structures. But this structure is in some sense imposed on the data by the person who is describing it, as long as he doesn't also insist that there be some reality behind the structure such as a biological reality or how some brain mechanism works. But the minute you turn your view rather to how actual living organisms work, then you do have a reality, and you can study the reality and describe it and have some awareness of how much you know about it, how much you don't know about it, how closely your description corresponds to this reality as shown from observations, and so on. And by postulating the concept of the state of the organism we're able to start asking the kind of questions that do have some reality behind them. Behaviour isn't a something in the same sense that a brain is a something. Behaviour is rather a manifestation of the operation of something. And language behaviour can be studied from the point of view that it gives insight into the something that is behind it, that is, the brain. So we're not playing games.

Very much can be done with the concept of mental state, much more than I have time to tell you about, even if I had all day. But permit me to give you one example. Consider the following. Suppose I have a friend in the next room and I want to speak to him for some reason, so I call 'Bill'.

Let us examine this utterance from the point of view of mental state. I have already told you that I wanted to speak to my friend for some reason. The utterance 'Bill' was conditioned in part by my wanting to speak to him, but this is part of my state of mind at the moment. We call it a goal.

Goals are part of state of mind. They can be investigated by observation of goal-directed behaviour such as the uttering of 'Bill' and by a number of other techniques resembling some of the standard informant techniques in linguistics. It turns out that goals are structured in a hierarchical fashion in a way very reminiscent of phrase-structure, and linguists have sharp tools for dealing with such things. I may have a goal to find out what time the concert is, so I choose the subgoal of asking Bill. In order to ask Bill, I must first engage him in conversation so I set of a subgoal to do that. Of the various means at my disposal, I choose to call his name.

One might also think that my choice of this utterance depends on the real life situation of my friend's being in the next room and having the name of Bill. But this is not exactly correct. No. I could be mistaken about his being in the next room. He could have slipped out, unbeknownst to me, to buy a paper, or perhaps it's really someone else and I just think that it is Bill. In such circumstances I would still utter 'Bill' even if he were not there. What really is important for my choice of the utterance 'Bill' is that I think he is there. We have here experimental evidence for this particular aspect of my state of mind. We do not have to be concerned with the real world and its infinite variety. It suffices to be concerned with that aspect of the state of mind of the language user which can be called his current awareness of the real world. And here we need only be concerned with this to the extent that it is relevant to the conditioning of utterances or the conditioning of the understanding of utterances.

The younger generation of linguists has already developed some of the apparatus needed for such a study of the conceptual organization of the human mind. We should recognize it for what it is. It is not heresy, nor is it pornography. It is the striving for an understanding of the beauty of the human mind, and it is the raw material from which we can build a science.

The flavour of the research will be very similar to the flavour that linguistic research already has. But the focus will be different. The focus will be more on the things that condition utterances than on the utterances themselves, and utterances will be viewed more from the point of view of their function in the larger process of communication, which usually has as its object the selective altering or changing of the mental state of the hearer.

The phenomena of ambiguity will be more easily studied. Answers are immediately available as to why it is that when an ambiguous example sentence is read to a class, half the class may take it one way and half may take it the other way, and then it is psychologically difficult for each half to see the other meaning. We may have a reasonable way of handling presuppositions and metaphor.

If we can actually get at the state of mind of the language user in a scientific way, based on solid evidence and experiment, the way is open for the solution of many of the gravest difficulties confronting linguistics at the moment. The task will be a large one, but let me emphasize that it will in no way be an infinite or impossible one. The best-equipped people to undertake this task are those who have had linguistic training.

Thus it seems to me that the shape of the future is that linguists will come to agree on a new goal. They will accept the broad goal that what we want to do is to understand how people use language to communicate. This will lead them into the study of something really in the mind of the language user and from this a new and fruitful science will emerge.

Our new science will be populated initially by brilliant refugees from the older established communities. The theoretical apparatus for handling the concept of state will come to us from information science. And from information science also we will receive the possibility of computer modelling, the possibility of making a working model, and understanding it, of the language user. From psychology, we will receive additional techniques for probing the mind of the informant, who may well become a subject. Other tools will be brought to us from cybernetics, from physiology, and from philosophy. The unification will be achieved through the unification of the goal.

The initial population of immigrants from the older regions will soon fade into the background. The science will be taken over by the new offspring of the mixed parentage. They will be well-educated in the new science and will soon surpass their parents in fluency and in the all-embracing cogency of the insights they will achieve.

The last comfortable suburban value to which we have all tenaciously clung is the very definition as received from our elders of what the goals of our society are. We see crumbling before us the unquestioned position that linguistics is the study of language and that the building of structural descriptions is the proper goal to which we should dedicate our intellectual lives. The search for relevance seeks to relate language to people. The new morality is that what we want to know is how people use language to communicate, and the bringing of people and communication back into our focus will at once humanize and socialize our science and save it from those who would keep it a cold Victorian study of the forms and structure of language.

Linguistics as a Scientific Study

The sometimes sharp disagreements to be observed amongst the views expressed in the papers in this section derive in part from conflicting views about the nature of scientific knowledge and methods, and partly from differing views about the ultimate goals of linguistics. The two extremes, represented by Katz on the one hand and Bloomfield on the other can be somewhat crudely characterized as rationalist and empiricist, proceeding by deductive and inductive methods respectively, and having as their objectives the description of individual languages or sets of language data (corpuses) on the one hand, and characterizing human language as some sort of universal human capacity on the other.

These contrasting approaches and objectives assign different importance to the processes of observation, prediction and verification and imply different attitudes to data and different meanings for the word 'fact'.

For the inductive approach, as exemplified by Joos and Bloomfield, the scientific process starts with observation of a given body of data, i.e. a set of utterances produced by an informant or a group of speakers from the same language community. It assumes *a priori* that this body of data has a structure, that is, that there is a system of categories and relations inherent in the data. These are the linguistic facts and it is the linguist's task to discover them and make generalizations about them, leading to an exhaustive and economical statement about them. We can compare this point of view with that of Allen in Section 5: 'Linguistics assumes *no* categories *in rebus*, *no* systems inherent in the material awaiting discovery' and 'There are no facts in linguistics until the linguist has made them'. The result of this process of analysis and generalization is a linguistic description of that corpus or body of data. A new corpus, i.e. set of utterances in another language is dealt with in the same way. There is, however, no assumption that the elements and systems inherent in the new data will have anything in common with those discovered in the first corpus. There is thus no assumption that languages have anything in common. What is common is the methods of discovery, 'discovery procedures'. It is not surprising that this approach leads to a great emphasis being placed on such procedures. The resultant descriptions are no more than just that, descriptions of a body of utterances. Different linguists following these procedures might arrive at quite different descriptions of the same data. There is no criterion for deciding which description is 'right' or 'better'.

It is only when descriptions are used to predict what further utterances, not included in the corpus, might be made by the informants that we can properly begin to speak of a linguistic theory; in this case a theory about the structure of the language, i.e. a grammar of a language. This is the point made by Hockett: 'The purpose is not simply to account for all the utterances in a corpus—a list would do that. The object is to predict what other utterances might be produced in that language'. Such a description is what Lyons in Section 5 means by a generative description; he suggests that such a description is a necessary aim of modern linguistics. It is not, however, either for Lyons or Hjelmslev a sufficient aim. Hjelmslev voices his criticism when he says that inductive procedures yield concepts which are not general and therefore not generalizable beyond a single language at a single stage.

In contrast to the procedures just described, we have those called deductive, in which the making of a theory is independent of any experience of a specific set of data. The data, in Lyons' words, are what are to be accounted for; they result from or are verified by observation. Data are taken not given. They are not the starting point but the object to which the process is applied. 'The general theory of language structure embodies certain assumptions and criteria of relevance taken for granted from the outset' or, in Hjelmslev's words 'introduces premises of the greatest possible generality which may therefore be able to satisfy the conditions for applications to a large number of empirical data'. 'A linguistic theory must be of use for describing and predicting not only any possible text composed in a certain language but on the basis of the information that it gives about language in general, any possible text composed in any language whatsoever'. Linguistic theories are *applied* to language data. Descriptions are a primary application of linguistic theory. We are here at Firth's 'general linguistic theory applicable to particular linguistic descriptions', quoted by Allen in Section 5. But not a 'theory of universals' for general linguistic description.

Halliday *et al.* appear to stand midway between these two positions. Their starting point is the observation of certain linguistic events about which generalizations are made and hypotheses formed to account for these events. This is the inductive approach. Further observations lead to a construction of a theory, but apparently not just a theory about these events as in Hockett's formulation, but about 'how language works', a general linguistic theory. This part of the formulation suggests the sort of intuitive jump which is characteristic of the deductive approach.

It is at this point that differences in the goals of linguistic theories show themselves. This shift of objective has been characterized by Thorne as 'a shift of the centre of interest from language as organized data to the organizing power capable of producing that data'. Chomsky proposes that linguistic theories are motivated by the problem of accounting for the ability of the speaker to produce and understand an indefinite number of new sentences in his language, which he calls the native speaker's competence. But since Chomsky is concerned with any native speaker and not just the native speaker of a particular language, a linguistic theory of competence must incorporate universal features. Katz is quite explicit: linguistic theory is about the structure of the mechanism underlying any speaker's ability to communicate with others. Linguistics is a branch of cognitive psychology.

18 MARTIN JOOS
Difference and Similarity: Principles of Linguistic Classification

The term *American Linguistics* is current today in two principal senses: first, the registration and analysis of the indigenous languages; and second the American style in linguistic thought. For the first I use the specific 'Amerindian Linguistics' as no worse a name than any other. Finding a good specific name for the American style is a desperate matter; I simply say 'American Linguistics' without argument, because to name any competing term would involve at least equally invidious implications.

The sequence and the ambiguity are historically founded. American Linguistics derives, ultimately and also currently, from the brute necessities of stating what has been found in a particular language. It got its decisive direction when it was decided that an indigenous language could be described better without any pre-existent scheme of what a language must be than with the usual reliance upon Latin as the model. It is usual to name Franz Boas in this connexion; other early contributors are represented in his *Handbook*. From that time to today, the style of American Linguistics continues unbroken, through vast total changes. One transition may be mentioned here; the rest is in these *Readings*.

The abandonment of deduction in favour of induction has never been reversed. At first it left the science stripped of general doctrines about all languages. Favourable at the start, this state of opinion could be, and in many older workers actually was, maintained past its function and could become a hindrance to further development. Once a number of un-prejudiced descriptions had resulted from it, induction could be applied to those new descriptions too, and general doctrines about all languages could emerge again. It should be clear that these would have a better claim to credence than those founded upon Latin or upon a philosophy. But the Boas generation had succeeded in their work by rejecting general doctrine; it would have been strange if they could now have reversed themselves and embraced general doctrines again. Their *leading principle*

M. Joos: Extract from Preface to *Readings in Linguistics*, ed. M. Joos, American Council of Learned Societies, 1957, pp. v–vii.

was that every language has to be explained from the inside out, the explanation being formulated under the logic of that language. Benevolence, of which Boas among others had plenty, was not enough to enable them to adopt new doctrine. A general truth about language, to Boas's way of thinking (or perhaps feeling) would have to be based on nothing less than the biological or indeed even the physiological character of man (he was a physical anthropologist too). Today we can, if we try, base phonemics upon information theory, or upon the theory of games, or a general theory of social interaction, but such theories still lay far in the future. What actually happened consisted principally of the advent of Sapir and Bloomfield.

Both trained in traditional historical linguistics and specifically in Germanics, and always sympathetically attentive to such studies here and abroad; Sapir by instinct what is popularly called 'a psychologist' and possessing unsurpassable empathy and quickness of wit, while Bloomfield was distinguished in disinterested wisdom and love of solid structure, their impacts upon American Linguistics were quite different in essence while both serving similarly to advance linguistic thought beyond the Boas pattern. Sapir stimulated and contributed insights; Bloomfield constructed and simplified. In the long run, then, it had to be Bloomfield that served as the Newton of American Linguistics, while Sapir was its Leibniz.

They valued de Saussure's contribution in equal measure, but used it in ways as different as their different personalities. Sapir gained insights, and stimulation to think out patterns of what very likely goes on inside the skull of *homo loquens*, taking him one at a time. Bloomfield took what he found either solid or well shaped, and shaped the first and made the second firm for use in constructing his model for what plainly goes on between person and person in speech communication. For him there was enough that demanded unambiguous statement in what we all see and hear; why borrow trouble by explaining the invisible?

For me at least (I don't know how many readers share this notion) the English words *statement* and *explanation* have quite different connotations, and I believe that Bloomfield felt the same. If the facts have been fully stated, it is perverse or childish to demand an explanation into the bargain. Explanation could serve only to facilitate filling out a fractional statement into a whole statement; or is explanation something magical? That is, if *explanation* is to have any useful difference in denotation from *statement*, it can only mean 'statement of pattern', while *statement* is reserved for the meaning 'statement ·of what is there and in what spot each item is': the same, but from a different viewpoint. To ascribe any other efficacy to explanation is an obfuscation; and to me that is the difference in connotation: that such obfuscation easily gets attached to *explanation*, but not to *statement*.

Discussion of language (in plain English: talking about talking) resembles keeping a fire in a wooden stove. The stricture applies to the bad connotation of *explanation*, but not at all to *statement*.

Suppose the statement is to be about English, and that the data consist of one hour of overheard conversation. In an obvious sense, a full statement is a stenographic transcription, requiring one hour to read aloud again: net profit, zero. This ·is, then, not only an obvious but a useless sense of *statement*. But the statement must not only be useful; it must cover all the data. Or again, if the statement is half as long as the data, it must cover more than half; if one third as long, it must cover more than one third of the data; and so on down to a fraction too short to be a declarative sentence in English.

If this is not possible, scientific statement is not possible. Either we must pack up and go home right now, or else we must adopt a postulate: *Fractions of the data differing in clock-time* (Bloomfieldian: *successive fractions) can be found which are similar enough to be covered by a single statement shorter than the sum of the fractions.* This postulate can be sharpened. *Similar*, in literary and colloquial usage, implies its contrary: implies that some part is like and that some part is unlike. We subtract the unlike parts from each of the successive fractions and consider the residues. Either these are identical, or else a part of each is still unlike anything in the other, so that another such subtraction is to be performed. Therefore, either (*a*) these subtractions continue, as in peeling an onion, until nothing is left, or (*b*) when 'successive fractions are similar enough to be covered by a single statement shorter than the sum of the fractions', then they contain in each at least one item identical with an item in the other. I call this a *postulate* because ultimately it is based on nothing but (1) common notions (axioms) like onion-peeling, and (2) an act of the will, namely the decision to talk about talking. The decision is indispensable in the most cogent sense, namely that without it this book-page would not be in existence for you to read.

One loop-hole remains to be covered. It has not been shown that this is the only way to do, or that this can't be mixed with another way. Mixture is this, for instance: 'This brick is of a lighter shade than that one, 4 per cent heavier, not so dirty and slightly cracked'. The identical fractions are at least 'brick' and 'cracked [implying that the other brick is not]', for an object of discourse is either a brick or not and is either cracked or not. Other items here are not of that sort, for instance '4 per cent heavier' and 'slightly'; these are *gradual* items, in the sense that '4' is one of infinitely many possibilities such as 3, 3·14159265, 4¼, etc., and that the probability of a randomly chosen English witness agreeing with the 'slightly' label is a continuous variable. Statements can't be made with graduals alone: each of them has to have a substratum, such as 'brick' for '4 per cent heavier'. But statements *can* be made with nothing but identicals, e.g. 'It takes three trees to make a row'. With more space, I could undertake to show that there are only two kinds of factual statements, those made with nothing but identicals, and those in which both identicals and graduals are employed. It would follow that a homogeneous statement must be one that employs only identicals.

Now homogeneity implies simplicity, or what is called *elegance* among mathematicians: we prefer to have a language-discussion style that employs only identicals if possible, rather than one that employs identicals and graduals both. We need another postulate. We got our first postulate without reference to any particular data; and that is always possible in beginning to set up postulates for a particular one of all the sciences that there may be. But then a second postulate will involve not only an act of will; it must involve a choice among possible postulates. Such a choice is made by reacting profitably to facts; that's what Bloomfield was referring to with his 'every descriptive or historical fact becomes the subject of a new postulate'. The reaction is not a logical act but an organic one; otherwise the result would be a theorem and not a postulate.

Now certain experiences together may persuade us that a language-discussion style employing only identicals can be set up in at least one way; namely by assigning a certain ancillary role to meaning. (Other choices could no doubt be made, resulting in quite different types of 'Postulate 2', some of them relating to the role of meaning and others perhaps not; I speak only of the choice actually made.) If we are persuaded that social correlates (earlier, later, and simultaneous non-speech acts) change stepwise, never smoothly, when utterances are altered, then we will adopt a second postulate more or less like this: *Statement* can and must be made to cover all the *socially relevant* data by mentioning *nothing but identical fractions*.

I don't know how Bloomfield verbalized his way of arriving at his first two *Postulates*, which together are equivalent to mine. His verbalization has remained unpublished; his rule here was *Don't invite your guests into the kitchen!* But he also had *Man kann sich den Leser nie zu dumm vorstellen*. That is the one I follow when I can find the space. My readers will, I hope, forgive the slur for the sake of the reanalysis of Bloomfield's two fundamental postulates which determined that his *linguistics* would be *a way of stating*, not *a certain set of statements*.

The first says that linguistic science is possible. The second defines a direction for it to take. That is the direction which we call Descriptive Linguistics, one principal factor in the American style (not the only one). And this is the 'transition' mentioned before; from then on we find ourselves in the contemporary period of American Linguistics.

Progress in these three decades has been swift: they parallel the history of mathematics from the *Principia* of Newton to about 1850, or the history of chemistry from Dalton's formulation of the atomic theory to the late nineteenth century. And in linguistics North America in these three decades has played pretty much the same role as France did in those two centuries of mathematics and Germany in those two generations of chemistry.

Just above, I hinted that *the descriptive habit* is not the only factor in American Linguistics. Other traits need mention to colour the picture at least, if not to define it. I would place foremost the *inductive habit* already alluded to. Induction is of course the only possibility in discovering the facts of one language at a time. The specifically American habit I have in mind is the habit of using *the inductive tone of voice* in arguing pure theory also. This is worth considering in some detail.

When a contribution to theory is advanced by an American, the steps are apt to be more or less these: (1) a warning is given concerning what the theoretical points will be; this step is facultative. (2) a collection of data *from a single language* is presented. (3) a way of 'handling' the data is proposed, which means a way of 'stating' them in my terminology above, with consideration of as many alternative ways as may be known to the writer or occur to him at the moment; the treatment of alternatives constitutes due warning that this is a *theoretical* paper (in case step 1 was omitted), whereas it is almost *de rigueur* to avoid mention of alternatives in describing a single language, which latter habit has caused outsiders to consider the descriptivists arrogant. (4) the *theoretical implications* of the chosen description are stated. (5) [this step may be placed before the fourth mentioned] other languages are drawn upon for data lying around loose or not well covered by current practice; thus Bloomfield's remark 'we are obliged to predict' which he used to characterize linguistics as a science, is now used to classify *general theory* as a science also—this gives the theoretical paper, American style, a familiar air to the American reader accustomed to reading descriptions of particular languages, wherefore both kinds of paper are read with a similarity of appreciation which, for all I know, may be unique as well as characteristic of the American scene. (6) the aforesaid theoretical implications get their formal statement *as a contribution to* theory; this last step, like the first, is facultative.

Omission of the first step is preferred: readers might, if any theoretical point is stated before its data, feel that the case has been prejudiced. And the last is very likely to be omitted, for a similarly very American set of reasons: the formal statement *is felt to assign to theory an emphasis that properly belongs to facts and the stating thereof*, or is felt to encroach on the reader's right of opinion. The second step is mandatory. It must not be mixed with the fifth; failure to maintain the segregation is frequently condemned as a confusion and falls under suspicion of having vitiated the whole argument: see the Boas generation's 'leading principle' for the origin of this attitude. The third step is not just mandatory; it is *essential*: otherwise the paper is not Descriptive. The fourth step is apt to be veiled, or fragmented and dispersed throughout the paper; my readers may test their comprehension of the American style by formulating a suitable reason or two. Altogether, then, there is ample reason why both Americans and (for example) Europeans are likely on each side to consider the other side both irresponsible and arrogant. We may request the Europeans to try to regard the American style as a tradition *comme une autre*; but the Americans can't be expected to reciprocate: they are having too much fun to be bothered, and *few of them are aware that either side has a tradition.*

19 LEONARD BLOOMFIELD
Objectivity in Linguistics

Language and handling activity

The difference between utterance of speech and all other events is naturally paramount in the study of language. The human acts which are observable under ordinary conditions are thus divided into *language*, the vocal utterance of the conventional type, and *handling activities*, a somewhat narrow name to cover all other normally observable acts, including not only manipulation but also mimicry, gesture, locomotion, acts of observation, etc. The linguist studies sequences in which language mediates between non-linguistic events.

Language creates and exemplifies a twofold value of some human actions. In its *biophysical* aspect language consists of sound-producing movements and of the resultant sound waves and of the vibration of the hearer's eardrums. The *biosocial* aspect of language consists in the fact that the persons in a community have been trained to produce these sounds in certain situations and to respond to them by appropriate actions. The biosocial function of language arises from a uniform, traditional, and arbitrary training of the persons in a certain group. They have been trained to utter conventional sounds as a secondary response to situations and to respond to these slight sounds, in a kind of trigger effect, with all sorts of actions.

In their turn, on a tertiary level of response, handling actions may be subjected biosocially to language: specific handling actions are conventionalized as a response to specific forms of speech, and these handling actions or their products serve as stimuli to call forth these same forms of speech. These substitutes for speech occur scantily in simple communities but play a great part in our civilization. Apart from speculations about a prehuman or semihuman antiquity, in man as we see him, all handling actions which bear elaborate communicative value owe this value to their biosocial subjection to language.

L. Bloomfield: Extract from 'Linguistic Aspects of Science', Section I § 7, 8 and 9, *International Encyclopaedia of Unified Science*, Vol. I, No. 4, University of Chicago Press, 1939, pp. 8–13.

The most familiar example of this is the art of writing: permanent visible marks are produced conventionally as responses to speech and serve as stimuli for the production of speech. For this it is necessary, of course, that the marks be conventionally associated with features of language. These features may be of various kinds: Chinese characters and our numerical digits represent words; the letters of the alphabet represent single typical speech-sounds. The biophysical aspect of writing consists in the materials used for producing the marks, in the shape of the marks, and in the movements by which one makes them. Once we have established the communal habit or convention which attaches them biosocially to speech-forms, the biophysical features may vary within the convention. Thus, the variety of paper, pencil, or ink; the shape, always within our convention, of the letters—script, printed, Roman or italic, small or capital, etc.—and the movements of the writer's hand or the kind of printing press are all indifferent so far as the verbal message is concerned,

The biophysical features of substitutes for language are important enough on their own level. Systems of writing may differ as to the time and labour required for making the marks and as to their legibility. The permanence of the materials is sometimes important. Mechanical devices like the typewriter and the printing press may yield great advantages.

More important for our discussion are the conventions which associate the written marks with forms of language. The alphabet, which associates, in principle, each mark with a typical sound of speech, makes reading and writing relatively easy, since it requires only a few dozen different characters; for the same reason it lends itself easily to mechanical transmission and reproduction. The system of writing, best exemplified in Chinese, where a character is assigned to a word of the language, is much harder to use and to mechanize. On the other hand, a piece of writing can be read in various languages, provided that these agree in structure and that minor divergences are bridged by means of supplementary conventions. Moreover, word-writing has the value of compactness and easy survey. These advantages appear very clearly in the case of our numeral digits. Here, by confining a system of word-writing to a very limited domain of speech-forms, we make it readable, with the aid of supplementary conventions, in any language. Thus, a graph like 71 is read in English as 'seventy-one', in German as 'one and seventy', in French as 'sixty-eleven', in Danish as 'one and half-four-times' (sc., 'twenty'), etc.

Our numeral digits illustrate the advantage of a well-arranged written symbolism. Simple discourses which move entirely in this domain can be carried out by means of a calculating machine. Short of this extreme case, we may cite cable codes, where the written forms are revised in the direction of brevity; or, again, systems of notation such as are used in symbolic logic, where a stock of symbols is so devised as to yield extremely simple rules of discourse. The construction of a calculating machine or the rules of arrangement and substitution in a system of logistics require great care and present great interest: it is decidedly advantageous to study them for their own sake and without reference to the linguistic end points of the sequences in which they operate. Nevertheless, if they are to operate, they must be so planned that, starting with speech-forms, they yield speech-forms in the end. No serious use would be made of a calculating machine, or of a code, or of a system of logistics, which failed to deliver a linguistically significant end result. By way of contrast, the reader may find it not without value to consider such non-linguistic systems as musical notation, say for the piano, or, again, the moves of a game of chess. Persons unaccustomed to the consideration of language are prone to the error of overlooking the linguistic character of notational or mechanical subsidiaries of language and viewing them as 'independent' systems; at the same time they may resort to the metaphor of calling these systems 'languages'. This metaphor is dangerous, since it may lead to the notion that such systems can liberate us from uncertainties or difficulties which inhere in the working of language.

Some students of language, among them the present writer, believe that widespread and deep-seated errors in supposedly scientific views of human behaviour rest upon misconceptions of this sort—upon failure to distinguish between linguistic and non-linguistic events, upon confusion of the biophysical and the biosocial aspects of language and its sub-sidiaries, and, above all, upon a habit of ignoring the linguistic parts of a sequence and then calling upon metaphysical entities to bridge the gap. Several phases of this error will here demand our attention.

Apriorism

In the prescientific view of these matters, a term such as 'reasoning' covers, on the one hand, observations which cost no great labour and, on the other hand, utterances of speech which are not recognized for what they are. Thus there arises the notion that knowledge may be obtained by a process of 'reasoning *a priori*'. Everyday observations, generally human or systematized by tribal tradition, are viewed as innate data of reason, and the ensuing deductions are clothed in a mystic validity. If the deductions are correctly made, the '*a priori*' procedure differs from an ordinary act of science only in that the basic observations are unsystematic and remain untested.

In scientific procedure we mean by *deduction* the purely verbal part of an act of science which leads from the report of observation and the hypotheses to a prediction. If we replace the report of observation by arbitrarily invented postulates, the discourse makes no pretence to validity in the sphere of handling actions. Deductive discourse of this kind is produced in logic, mathematics, or the methodology of science. It is made to fit some type of observational data, or else it exists for its own sake, in readiness for the emergence of observational data to which it may be applied. Until modern times, Euclidean geometry was viewed as an *a priori* system: the underlying everyday observations about the spatial character of objects were viewed as inborn and unquestionable truths. Today the same system, apart from the correction of flaws, is treated as a purely verbal discourse of deduction from postulates. It is especially useful because these postulates, by virtue of their historic origin, are such as to make the discourse applicable to the placing of objects, as this placing is observed in the first approximation that is customary in everyday handling. We have learned, however, that astronomical magnitudes make sensible the error in these postulates, and they accordingly demand a different discourse, based upon other postulates which, in turn, will be chosen so as to fit the new observations. One employs postulates which fit the observed data within the margin of error. The postulates are chosen so as to yield a simple calculation; the discrepancies are set aside to await more accurate measurements, which, in their turn, will make possible a more closely approximative discourse.

Mentalism

In the common sense of many peoples, perhaps of all, language is largely ignored, and its effects are explained as owing to non-physical factors, the action of a 'mind', 'will', or the like. These terms, as well as the many others connected with them, yield service in daily life, in art, and in religion; that they have no place in science is the contention of many scientists. Mentalistic terms do not figure in the procedure of physics, biology, or linguistics, but many students of these subjects employ them in the theoretical parts of their discourse.

An individual may base himself upon a purely practical, an artistic, a religious, or a scientific acceptance of the universe, and that aspect which he takes as basic will transcend and include the others. The choice, at the present state of our knowledge, can be made only by an act of faith, and with this the issue of mentalism should not be confounded.

It is the belief of the present writer that the scientific description of the universe, whatever this description may be worth, requires none of the mentalistic terms, because the gaps which these terms are intended to bridge exist only so long as language is left out of account: If language is taken into account, then we can distinguish science from other phases of human activity by agreeing that science shall deal only with events that are accessible in their time and place to any and all observers (strict *behaviourism*) or only with events that are placed in co-ordinates of time and space (*mechanism*), or that science shall employ only such initial statements and predictions as lead to definite handling operations (*operationalism*), or only terms such as are derivable by rigid definition from a set of everyday terms concerning physical happenings (*physicalism*). These several formulations, independently reached by different scientists, all lead to the same delimitation, and this delimitation does not restrict the subject matter of science but rather characterizes its method. It is clear even now, with science still in a very elementary stage, that, under the method thus characterized, science can account in its own way for human behaviour—provided, always, that language be considered as a factor and not replaced by the extra-scientific terms of mentalism.

20 CHARLES F. HOCKETT
Linguistic Prediction

Linguistics—specifically, descriptive or structural linguistics—can be regarded as a game or as a science. As a game, the necessary equipment is a body of utterances from some language or dialect, or, indeed, a body of pseudo-utterances coined by a nimble mind for the purposes (as Nida, who does not take linguistics to be a game, makes up Papawapam problems for the training of his students). The rules of the game are any rules you prefer, with one limitation. The object of the game is to compare and analyse the utterances of the corpus and arrive at a redescription of them as composed of smaller recurrent (or occasionally non-recurrent) parts. The limitation on rules—that is, the one rule that all devotees of the game agree on pretty well—is that all the utterances of the corpus must be taken into account; as a matter of fact, even on this some players like to hedge, as when it is considered desirable to remove recent loan-words before describing phonology.

As a game, it matters not a whit what relation there may exist between the 'structure' produced by the player as he manipulates his toy, and anything that a native speaker of the language might say, either in or about his language, save for those very utterances of his which comprise the corpus.

No one can quarrel with games as games. In this particular case, extensive experimentation with the game, as a game, can be of use over and above its entertainment value, precisely as the proliferation of pure mathematics, which is in essence a game, is of tremendously great value for the 'practical' application of mathematics in physics, biology, and perhaps someday in social science. This practical value, however, is not susceptible of being described unless we stand away from game-linguistics and consider the science of the same name, as a science.

The task of the structural linguist, as a scientist, is essentially one of classification. The purpose, however, is not simply to account for all the

C. F. Hockett: Extract from 'A Note on "Structure"', *Linguistics* 14, 269–71, 1948. Reprinted in *Readings in Linguistics*, ed. M. Joos, University of Chicago Press, 1957, pp. 279–80.

utterances which comprise his corpus at a given time; a simple alpha-
betical list would do that. Rather, the analysis of the linguistic *scientist*
is to be of such a nature that the linguist can account also for utterances
which are *not* in his corpus at a given time. That is, as a result of his
examination he must be able to predict what *other* utterances the speakers
of the language might produce, and, ideally, the circumstances under which
those other utterances might be produced.*

The analytical process thus parallels what goes on in the nervous
system of a language learner, particularly, perhaps, that of a child learning
his first language. The child hears, and eventually produces, various whole
utterances. Sooner or later, the child produces utterances he has not
previously heard from someone else. At first these newly coined utterances
may be rejected by those about him; but by a process of trial and error,
supplemented by the constant acquisition of new whole utterances from
those who already speak the language, the child eventually reaches the
point of no longer making 'mistakes'. *Lapses* there may still be—that is,
utterances which the speaker himself, sometimes, follows by remarks of
the general nature of 'Oh, I meant to say such-and-such', or else by simple
partial repetition with the lapse eliminated. But by the time the child has
achieved linguistic adulthood, his speech no longer contains *errors*; for
he has become an authority on the language, a person whose ways of
speaking *determine* what is and what is not an error.

The child's coining of an utterance he has not heard is, of course, a
kind of prediction: 'If I make such-and-such noises, those about me will
react in a certain way'. (We do not imply that any such 'thought' passes
through the 'mind' of the child.) The parallel between this and the process
of analysis performed by the linguist is close. When the child is just
beginning, his coinage of utterances is often ineffective; when the linguist's
corpus is small, his predictions are inaccurate. As the child continues to
learn, or as the corpus grows and analysis is modified, prediction becomes
more and more accurate. In theory, at least, with a large enough corpus
there would no longer be any discernible discrepancy between utterances
the linguist predicted and those sooner or later observed.

The essential difference between the process in the child and the procedure of the linguist is this: the linguist has to make his analysis overtly,
in communicable form, in the shape of a set of statements which can be
understood by any properly trained person, who in turn can predict
utterances not yet observed with the same degree of accuracy as can the
original analyst. The child's 'analysis' consists, on the other hand, of a
mass of varying synaptic potentials in his central nervous system. The

* Attempts to include prediction of the circumstances (except in terms of preceding
utterances) constitute semantic analysis. Structural analysis can be scientific without
being semantic. [Author's footnote.]

child in time comes to *behave* the language; the linguist must come to *state* it.

The player of linguistics as a game has no criterion by which to judge the relative merits of one analysis versus another. This gives him a freedom for experimentation which is valuable—but not for any reason, as we have said, stable within the economy of the game as a game. The worker in linguistics as a science (and he may be wrapped in the same skin as the game addict) has such a criterion: accuracy of prediction beyond one's corpus, and communicability of the basis for such prediction to others.

The structure of a language may be regarded as the end-product of a game; in this sense structure is created by the person who plays the game. But every speaker of a language plays just such a game, the end-product being a state of affairs in his nervous system rather than a set of statements. The linguistic scientist must regard the structure of the language as consisting precisely of this state of affairs. His purpose in analysing a language is not to create structure, but to determine the structure actually created by the speakers of the language. For the scientist, then, 'linguistic structure' refers to something existing quite independently of the activities of the analyst: a language is what it is, it has the structure it has, whether studied and analysed by a linguist or not.

There is no reason why we should not use the term 'structure' in both of the senses just given. They can be kept apart when necessary; in most linguistic discussions one is apt to be referring to both senses at the same time anyway. What does need to be avoided is useless argument as to whether linguistic structure is 'objective' or 'subjective', or the like; the purpose of this note is to help ward off such time-wasting discussion.

21 The Aim of Linguistic Theory

L. HJELMSLEV

It is the aim of linguistic theory to test, on what seems a particularly inviting object, the thesis that a process has an underlying system—a fluctuation an underlying constancy. Voices raised beforehand against such an attempt in the field of the humanities, pleading that we cannot subject to scientific analysis man's spiritual life and the phenomena it implies without killing that life and consequently allowing our object to escape consideration, are merely aprioristic, and cannot restrain science from the attempt. If the attempt fails—not in particular performances, but in principle—then these objections are valid, and humanistic phenomena can be treated only subjectively and aesthetically. If, however, the attempt succeeds—so that the principle shows itself practicable—then these voices will become silent of their own accord, and it would then remain to perform corresponding experiments in the other fields of the humanities.

Linguistic theory and empiricism

A theory will attain its simplest form by building on no other premises than those necessarily required by its object. Moreover, in order to conform to its purpose, a theory must be capable of yielding, in all its applications, results that agree with so-called (actual or presumed) empirical data.

At this point, every theory is faced with a methodological requirement, whose purport will have to be investigated by epistemology. Such an investigation may, we think, be omitted here. We believe that the requirement we have vaguely formulated above, the requirement of so-called empiricism, will be satisfied by the principle that follows. By this principle, which we set above all others, our theory is at once clearly distinguishable from all previous undertakings of linguistic philosophy:

The description shall be free of contradiction (self-consistent), exhaustive, and as simple as possible. The requirement of freedom from

L. Hjelmslev: Extract from *Prolegomena to a Theory of Language*, Sections 2–6, (trans. F. J. Whitfield), University of Wisconsin Press, 1943, pp. 10–19.

contradiction takes precedence over the requirement of exhaustive description. The requirement of exhaustive description takes precedence over the requirement of simplicity.

We venture to call this principle the *empirical principle*. But we are willing to abandon the name if epistemological investigation shows it to be inappropriate. From our point of view this is merely a question of terminology, which does not affect the maintenance of the principle.

Linguistic theory and induction

The assertion of our so-called empirical principle is not the same as an assertion of inductivism, understood as the requirement of a gradual ascent from something particular to something general, or from something more limited to something less limited. Here again we are in the realm of terms that require epistemological analysis and refinement, this time terms which we ourself shall later have occasion to apply more precisely than we can here. And here again, both now and later, a terminological reckoning remains to be made with epistemology. For the time being we are interested in clarifying our position as opposed to that of previous linguistics. In its typical form this linguistics ascends, in its formation of concepts, from the individual sounds to the phonemes (classes of sounds), from the individual phonemes to the categories of phonemes, from the various individual meanings to the general or basic meanings, and from these to the categories of meanings. In linguistics, we usually call this method of procedure *inductive*. It may be defined briefly as a progression from component to class, not from class to component. It is a synthetic, not an analytic, movement, a generalizing, not a specifying, method.

Experience alone is sufficient to demonstrate the obvious shortcomings of this method. It inevitably leads to the abstraction of concepts which are then hypostatized as real. This realism (in the mediaeval sense of the word) fails to yield a useful basis of comparison, since the concepts thus obtained are not general and are therefore not generalizable beyond a single language in an individual stage. All our inherited terminology suffers from this unsuccessful realism. The class concepts of grammar that are obtained by induction, such as 'genitive', 'perfect', 'subjunctive', 'passive', etc., afford striking examples of this fact. None of them, as used till now, is susceptible of general definition: genitive, perfect, subjunctive, and passive are quite different things in one language, Latin for example, from what they are in another, say Greek. The same is true, without any exception, of the remaining concepts of conventional linguistics. In this field, therefore, induction leads from fluctuation, not to constancy, but to accident. It therefore finally comes in conflict with our empirical principle: it cannot ensure a self-consistent and simple description.

If we start from the supposed empirical data, these very data will impose the opposite procedure. If the linguistic investigator is given anything (we put this in conditional form for epistemological reasons), it is the as yet unanalysed *text* in its undivided and absolute integrity. Our only possible procedure, if we wish to order a system to the process of that text, will be an analysis, in which the text is regarded as a class analysed into components, then these components as classes analysed into components, and so on until the analysis is exhausted. This procedure may therefore be defined briefly as a progression from class to component, not from component to class, as an analytic and specifying, not a synthetic and generalizing, movement, as the opposite of induction in the sense established in linguistics. In recent linguistics, where the contrast has been actualized, this method of procedure or an approximation thereto has been designated by the word *deduction*. This usage disturbs epistemologists, but we retain it here since we believe we shall later be able to demonstrate that the terminological opposition on this point is not insuperable.

Linguistic theory and reality

With the terminology that we have chosen, we have been able to designate the method of linguistic theory as necessarily empirical and necessarily deductive, and we have thus been able to cast light from one direction on the primitive and immediate question of the relation of linguistic theory to the so-called empirical data. But we still have to cast light on the same question from another direction. That is to say, we must investigate to see whether the possible influences between the theory and its object (or objects) are reciprocal or unidirectional. To formulate the problem in a simplified, tendentious, and deliberately naïve form—does the object determine and affect the theory, or does the theory determine and affect its object?

Here too, we must set aside the purely epistemological problem in its entire scope and restrict our attention to that aspect of it which directly concerns us. It is clear that the frequently misused and disparaged word *theory* can be taken in different senses. *Theory* can mean, among other things, a system of hypotheses. If the word is taken in this—now frequent —sense, it is clear that the influence between theory and object is unidirectional: the object determines and affects the theory, not vice versa. Hypotheses can be shown to be true or false by a process of verification. But it may have already been apparent that we are using the word *theory* in another sense. In this connexion, two factors are of equal importance:

1 A theory, in our sense, is in itself independent of any experience. In itself, it says nothing at all about the possibility of its application and relation to empirical data. It includes no existence postulate. It constitutes what has been called a purely deductive system, in the sense that it may be used alone to compute the possibilities that follow from its premises.

2 A theory introduces certain premises concerning which the theoretician knows from preceding experience that they fulfil the conditions for application to certain empirical data. These premises are of the greatest possible generality and may therefore be able to satisfy the conditions for application to a large number of empirical data.

The first of these factors we shall call the *arbitrariness* of a theory; the second we shall call its *appropriateness*. It seems necessary to consider both these factors in the preparation of a theory, but it follows from what has been said that the empirical data can never strengthen or weaken the theory itself, but only its applicability.

A theory permits us to deduce theorems, which must all have the form of implications (in the logical sense) or must be susceptible of transposition into such a conditional form. Such a theorem asserts only that if a condition is fulfilled the truth of a given proposition follows. In the application of the theory it will become manifest whether the condition is fulfilled in any given instance.

On the basis of a theory and its theorems we may construct hypotheses (including the so-called laws), the fate of which, contrary to that of the theory itself, depends exclusively on verification.

No mention has been made here of axioms or postulates. We leave it to epistemology to decide whether the basic premises explicitly introduced by our linguistic theory need any further axiomatic foundation. In any event, they are traced back so far and they are all of so general a nature that none would seem to be specific to linguistic theory as opposed to other theories. This is done because our aim is precisely to make clear our premises as far back as we can without going beyond what seems directly appropriate to linguistic theory. We are thereby forced in some degree to invade the domain of epistemology, as has appeared in the preceding sections. Our procedure here is based on the conviction that it is impossible to elaborate the theory of a particular science without an active collaboration with epistemology.

Linguistic theory, then, sovereignly defines its object by an arbitrary and appropriate strategy of premises. The theory consists of a calculation from the fewest and most general possible premises, of which none that is specific to the theory seems to be of axiomatic nature. The calculation permits the prediction of possibilities, but says nothing about their realization. Thus, if linguistic theory, taken in this sense, is set in relation to the concept of reality, the answer to our question, whether the object determines and affects the theory or vice versa, is 'both ... and': by virtue of its arbitrary nature the theory is *arealistic*; by virtue of its appropriateness it is *realistic* (with the word *realism* taken here in the modern, and not, as before, in the mediaeval sense).

The aim of linguistic theory

A theory, then, in our sense of the word, may be said to aim at providing a procedural method by means of which objects of a premised nature can be described self-consistently and exhaustively. Such a self-consistent and exhaustive description leads to what is usually called a knowledge or comprehension of the object in question. In a sense, then, we may also say, without risk of being misleading or obscure, that the aim of a theory is to indicate a method of procedure for knowing or comprehending a given object. But at the same time a theory is not only meant to provide us with the means of knowing one definite object. It must be so organized as to enable us to know all conceivable objects of the same premised nature as the one under consideration. A theory must be general in the sense that it must provide us with tools for comprehending not only a given object or the objects hitherto experienced, but all conceivable objects of a certain premised nature. By means of a theory we arm ourselves to meet not only the eventualities previously presented to us, but any eventuality.

The objects of interest to linguistic theory are texts. The aim of linguistic theory is to provide a procedural method by means of which a given text can be comprehended through a self-consistent and exhaustive description. But linguistic theory must also indicate how any other text of the same premised nature can be understood in the same way, and it does this by furnishing us with tools that can be used on any such text.

For example, we require of linguistic theory that it enable us to describe self-consistently and exhaustively not only a given Danish text, but also all other given Danish texts, and not only all given, but also all conceivable or possible Danish texts, including texts that will not exist until tomorrow or later, so long as they are texts of the same kind, i.e. texts of the same premised nature as those heretofore considered. Linguistic theory satisfies this requirement by building on the Danish texts that have existed up to now; and since these alone are of enormous number and extent, it must be content with building on a selection from them. But by using the tools of linguistic theory, we can draw from this selection of texts a fund of knowledge to be used again on other texts. This knowledge concerns, not merely or essentially the *processes* or *texts* from which it is abstracted, but the *system* or *language* on which all texts of the same premised nature are constructed, and with the help of which we can construct new texts. With the linguistic information we have thus obtained, we shall be able to construct any conceivable or theoretically possible texts in the same language.

But linguistic theory must be of use for describing and predicting not only any possible text composed in a certain language, but, on the basis of the information that it gives about language in general, any possible text composed in any language whatsoever. The linguistic theoretician must of course attempt to satisfy this requirement likewise, by starting with a certain selection of texts in different languages. Obviously, it would be humanly impossible to work through all existing texts, and, moreover, the labour would be futile since the theory must also cover texts as yet unrealized. Hence the linguistic theoretician, like any other theoretician, must take the precaution to foresee all conceivable possibilities—even such possibilities as he himself has not experienced or seen realized—and to admit them into his theory so that it will be applicable even to texts and languages that have not appeared in his practice, or to languages that have perhaps never been realized, and some of which will probably never be realized. Only thus can he produce a linguistic theory of ensured applicability.

It is therefore necessary to ensure the applicability of the theory, and any application necessarily presupposes the theory. But it is of the greatest importance not to confuse the theory with its applications or with the practical method (procedure) of application. The theory will lead to a procedure, but no (practical) 'discovery procedure' will be set forth in the present book, which does not, strictly speaking, even offer the theory in systematic form, but only its prolegomena.

By virtue of its appropriateness the work of linguistic theory is empirical, and by virtue of its arbitrariness it is calculative. From certain experiences, which must necessarily be limited even though they should be as varied as possible, the linguistic theoretician sets up a calculation of all the conceivable possibilities within certain frames. These frames he constructs arbitrarily: he discovers certain properties present in all those objects that people agree to call languages, in order then to generalize those properties and establish them by definition. From that moment the linguistic theoretician has—arbitrarily, but appropriately—himself decreed to which objects his theory can and cannot be applied. He then sets up, for all objects of the nature premised in the definition, a general calculus, in which all conceivable cases are foreseen. This calculus, which is deduced from the established definition independently of all experience, provides the tools for describing or comprehending a given text and the language on which it is constructed. Linguistic theory cannot be verified (confirmed or invalidated) by reference to such existing texts and languages. It can be judged only with reference to the self-consistency and exhaustiveness of its calculus.

If, through this general calculation, linguistic theory ends by constructing several possible methods of procedure, all of which can provide a self-consistent and exhaustive description of any given text and thereby of any language whatsoever, then, among those possible methods of procedure, that one shall be chosen that results in the simplest possible description. If several methods yield equally simple descriptions, that one is to be chosen that leads to the result through the simplest procedure. This principle, which is deduced from our so-called empirical principle, we call the *simplicity principle*.

It is by reference to this principle, and only by reference to it, that we can attach any meaning to an assertion that one self-consistent and exhaustive solution is correct and another incorrect. That solution is considered the correct one which complies in the highest degree with the simplicity principle.

We may then judge linguistic theory and its applications by testing whether the solution it produces, while satisfying the requirements ·of self-consistency and exhaustive description, is also the simplest possible.

It is, then, by its own 'empirical principle' and by it alone that linguistic theory must be tested. Consequently, it is possible to imagine several linguistic theories, in the sense of 'approximations to the ideal set up and formulated in the "empirical principle" '. One of these must necessarily be the definitive one, and any concretely developed linguistic theory hopes to be precisely that definitive one. But it follows that linguistic theory as a discipline is not defined by its concrete shape, and it is both possible and desirable for linguistic theory to progress by providing new concrete developments that yield an ever closer approximation to the basic principle.

In the prolegomena to the theory, it is in the realistic side of the theory that we shall be interested—in the best way of meeting the requirement of applicability. This will be studied by an investigation of each feature that may be said to be constitutive in the structure of any language, and by an investigation of the logical consequences of fixing those features with the aid of definitions.

22 M. A. K. HALLIDAY, P. D. STREVENS and A. McINTOSH
The Relation between Observation and Theory

We should here briefly examine the claim of the linguistic sciences to be sciences. 'Claim' is perhaps misleading, since the reason for using the term is not that science is an 'O.K. word' nowadays, but that the subjects have certain specific characteristics to which the term is appropriate. What we have to do is rather to state in what sense the linguistic sciences are scientific. With phonetics there is no problem; it is, as we have seen, closely related to established natural sciences, and is scientific in the same sense that they are. More specifically, articulatory phonetics is related to human physiology, while acoustic phonetics, the study of sound waves, is linked to physics: phonetics thus has a place in both the physical and biological sciences. In the study of the perception of speech, it is linked again with physiology and also with psychology.

Linguistics on the other hand is concerned with patterns of relationship between events. These events are pieces of socially determined human activity; the link here is with the social sciences, psychology, sociology and social anthropology. The patterning of these events is, as we have seen, both internal and external. The internal patterning is what is known as linguistic 'form'; the study of the form of language follows the general principles governing the study of systematically related properties and events, being in essence logical and potentially statistical. The external patterning is what we here call 'context'; this is the patterned relation between linguistic events and non-linguistic phenomena. The study of context, best known under the name 'semantics', is difficult to classify; 'semantics' has usually implied a specifically conceptual approach and one which has tended to be somewhat separate from other linguistic studies. The approach through language and 'situation', which owes much to anthropology, is still at an early stage of development.

There is a warning to be made here. If we say that linguistics is partly a 'logical' study, this is not to be taken to imply that there is any relation

M. A. K. Halliday, P. D. Strevens and A. McIntosh: Extract from *The Linguistic Sciences and Language Teaching*, Chapter I, Section 5, Longman, 1964, pp. 12–14.

between logic and *language*, that propositional or predicate logic can be used to explain the relations between linguistic items. This assumption was held for many years, but it is not a fruitful one. What we do imply is a relation between logic and *linguistics*: that a symbolic or 'scientific logic' may be considered to underlie the *theoretical* validity of the categories used to describe language, and the consistency of their relations to each other within the total framework of categories.

So when we classify the linguistic sciences according to which other sciences they resemble, they turn out to be a mixture. The mixture includes components of natural science, social science, and logic and mathematics. That the mixture itself is unique hardly needs pointing out, since language is a unique phenomenon.

If, however, we talk about 'the linguistic sciences' it is not so much because they are like this or that other science in particular, but because they share something which is common to all sciences: their methods fall within what could be called general scientific method. What we understand by this is as follows. Behind any statements made about languages in linguistics and phonetics lies a chain of abstraction. First, certain events, linguistic events, are observed. They are found to display partial likeness: so, second, generalizations are made about them. Third, on the basis of these generalizations hypotheses are formulated to account for the events. These are tested by further observations, and out of them, fourth, is constructed a theory of how language works. From this theory are derived methods for making statements about linguistic events. These statements link the theory to the events it is set up to account for, and they can now be evaluated by reference both to the theory and to the events: the best statements are those which make maximum use of the theory to account most fully for the facts.

The chain is thus 'observation—generalization—hypothesis—theory—descriptive statement'. This is not of course a process carried out by each linguist, or even carried out in successive steps at all. It is a model of the relation between observation, theory and description, a relation which results from developments taking place over many years. Any particular theory will be judged by its effectiveness; while in use it controls and gives meaning to the descriptive statements made. A theory of this kind can take the form of a set of categories of a high order of abstraction; the nature and status of each category is explicitly formulated, and so are the interrelations among them. The categories and their interrelations can then be examined to see whether they are valid, consistent and complete.

We are not concerned with the label 'scientific' as a status symbol. If a subject which uses such methods is scientific, then linguistics and phonetics are sciences. If we require 'experiment' and 'prediction', as used in the natural sciences, as prerequisites of a scientific discipline, linguistics (though not phonetics) is, with other social sciences, largely excluded. There is a sense in which all theories predict, linguistic theory included: they predict that all events falling within their field of observation will be accounted for by the theory. The relation between this and the prediction of the natural sciences is complex and, since we are not trying to prove anything, irrelevant. What the linguistic sciences do is to use theory to account for language, how it works and how it persists. The reason for discussing why they are called 'sciences' is to show in what respects they are like other subjects that are called 'sciences'.

Until recently linguists were more concerned to state the uniqueness of their subject than to claim for it relationships with other subjects. This attitude was understandable: linguistics had been able to advance only after the success of a long struggle to disentangle it from other subjects. It had to set up its own categories for talking about language, instead of adopting ready-made ones from elsewhere. Once linguists learnt to do this our understanding of language was immeasurably increased; and it is not surprising that for a time they were a little sensitive on this point and inclined vigorously to proclaim the autonomy of linguistic science. This claim can now be regarded as beyond dispute, and we can turn our attention to the much more interesting question of the ways in which the linguistic sciences are *not* unique. They are not unique in the way they use theory. They are unique in what theory they use and in what they use it for.

23 NOAM CHOMSKY
A Theory of Competence

Generative grammars as theories of linguistic competence

Linguistic theory is concerned primarily with an ideal speaker-listener, in a completely homogeneous speech-community, who knows its language perfectly and is unaffected by such grammatically irrelevant conditions as memory limitations, distractions, shifts of attention and interest, and errors (random or characteristic) in applying his knowledge of the language in actual performance. This seems to me to have been the position of the founders of modern general linguistics, and no cogent reason for modifying it has been offered. To study actual linguistic performance, we must consider the interaction of a variety of factors, of which the underlying competence of the speaker-hearer is only one. In this respect, study of language is no different from empirical investigation of other complex phenomena.

We thus make a fundamental distinction between *competence* (the speaker-hearer's knowledge of his language) and *performance* (the actual use of language in concrete situations). Only under the idealization set forth in the preceding paragraph is performance a direct reflection of competence. In actual fact, it obviously should not directly reflect competence. A record of natural speech will show numerous false starts, deviations from rules, changes of plan in mid-course, and so on. The problem for the linguist, as well as for the child learning the language, is to determine from the data of performance the underlying system of rules that has been mastered by the speaker-hearer and that he puts to use in actual performance. Hence, in the technical sense, linguistic theory is mentalistic, since it is concerned with discovering a mental reality underlying actual behaviour. Observed use of language or hypothesized dispositions to respond, habits, and so on, may provide evidence as to the nature of this mental reality, but surely cannot constitute the actual subject matter of linguistics, if this is to be a serious discipline. The

A. N. Chomsky: Extract from 'Methodological Preliminaries' in *Aspects of the Theory of Syntax*, Chapter I, § 1, 4 and 5, M.I.T. Press, 1965, pp. 3–10, 18–30.

distinction I am noting here is related to the *langue-parole* distinction of Saussure; but it is necessary to reject his concept of *langue* as merely a systematic inventory of items and to return rather to the Humboldtian conception of underlying competence as a system of generative processes.

A grammar of language purports to be a description of the ideal speaker-hearer's intrinsic competence. If the grammar is, furthermore, perfectly explicit—in other words, if it does not rely on the intelligence of the understanding reader but rather provides an explicit analysis of his contribution—we may (somewhat redundantly) call it a *generative grammar*.

A fully adequate grammar must assign to each of an infinite range of sentences a structural description indicating how this sentence is understood by the ideal speaker-hearer. This is the traditional problem of descriptive linguistics, and traditional grammars give a wealth of information concerning structural descriptions of sentences. However, valuable as they obviously are, traditional grammars are deficient in that they leave unexpressed many of the basic regularities of the language with which they are concerned. This fact is particularly clear on the level of syntax, where no traditional or structuralist grammar goes beyond classification of particular examples to the stage of formulation of generative rules on any significant scale. An analysis of the best existing grammars will quickly reveal that this is a defect of principle, not just a matter of empirical detail or logical preciseness. Nevertheless, it seems obvious that the attempt to explore this largely uncharted territory can most profitably begin with a study of the kind of structural information presented by traditional grammars and the kind of linguistic processes that have been exhibited, however informally, in these grammars.

The limitations of traditional and structuralist grammars should be clearly appreciated. Although such grammars may contain full and explicit lists of exceptions and irregularities, they provide only examples and hints concerning the regular and productive syntactic process. Traditional linguistic theory was not unaware of this fact. For example, James Beattie (1788) remarks that

Languages, therefore, resemble men in this respect, that, though each has peculiarities, whereby it is distinguished from every other, yet all have certain qualities in common. The peculiarities of individual tongues are explained in their respective grammars and dictionaries. Those things, that all languages have in common, or that are necessary to every language, are treated of in a science, which some have called *Universal* or *Philosophical* grammar.

Somewhat earlier, Du Marsais defines universal and particular grammar in the following way (1729):

Il y a dans la grammaire des observations qui conviennent à toutes les langues; ces observations forment ce qu'on appelle la grammaire générale: telles sont les remarques que l'on a faites sur les sons articulés, sur les lettres qui sont les signes de ces sons; sur la nature des mots, et sur les différentes manières dont ils doivent être ou arrangés ou terminés pour faire un sens. Outre ces observations générales, il y en a qui ne sont propres qu'à une langue particulière; et c'est ce qui forme les grammaires particulières de chaque langue.

Within traditional linguistic theory, furthermore, it was clearly understood that one of the qualities that all languages have in common is their 'creative' aspect. Thus an essential property of language is that it provides the means for expressing indefinitely many thoughts and for reacting appropriately in an indefinite range of new situations. The grammar of a particular language, then, is to be supplemented by a universal grammar that accommodates the creative aspect of language use and expresses the deep-seated regularities which, being universal, are omitted from the grammar itself. Therefore it is quite proper for a grammar to discuss only exceptions and irregularities in any detail. It is only when supplemented by a universal grammar that the grammar of a language provides a full account of the speaker-hearer's competence.

Modern linguistics, however, has not explicitly recognized the necessity for supplementing a 'particular grammar' of a language by a universal grammar if it is to achieve descriptive adequacy. It has, in fact, characteristically rejected the study of universal grammar as misguided; and, as noted before, it has not attempted to deal with the creative aspect of language use. It thus suggests no way to overcome the fundamental descriptive inadequacy of structuralist grammars.

Another reason for the failure of traditional grammars, particular or universal, to attempt a precise statement of regular processes of sentence formation and sentence interpretation lay in the widely held belief that there is a 'natural order of thoughts' that is mirrored by the order of words. Hence, the rules of sentence formation do not really belong to grammar but to some other subject in which the 'order of thoughts' is studied. Thus in the *Grammaire générale et raisonnée* (Lancelot *et al.*, 1660) it is asserted that, aside from figurative speech, the sequence of words follows an 'ordre naturel', which conforms 'à l'expression naturelle de nos pensées'. Consequently, few grammatical rules need be formulated beyond the rules of ellipsis, inversion, and so on, which determine the figurative use of language. The same view appears in many forms and variants. To mention just one additional example, in an interesting essay devoted largely to the question of how the simultaneous and sequential array of ideas is reflected in the order of words, Diderot concludes that French is unique among languages in the degree to which the order of words corresponds to the natural order of thoughts and ideas. Thus 'quel que soit l'ordre des termes dans une langue ancienne ou moderne, l'esprit de l'écrivain a suivi l'ordre didactique de la syntaxe française'; 'Nous disons les choses en français, comme l'esprit est forcé de les considérer en quelque langue qu'on écrive'. With admirable consistency he goes on to conclude that 'notre langue *pédestre* a sur les autres l'avantage de l'utile sur l'agréable'; thus French is appropriate for the sciences, whereas Greek, Latin, Italian, and English 'sont plus avantageuses pour les lettres'. Moreover,

le bons sens choisirait la langue française; mais . . . l'imagination et les passions donneront la préférence aux langues anciennes et à celles de nos voisins . . . il faut parler français dans la société et dans les écoles de philosophie; et grec, latin, anglais, dans les chaires et sur les théâtres; . . . notre langue sera celle de la vérité, si jamais elle revient sur la terre; et . . . la grecque, la latine et les autres seront les langues de la fable et du mensonge. Le français est fait pour instruire, éclairer et convaincre; le grec, le latin, l'italien, l'anglais, pour persuader, émouvoir et tromper: parlez grec, latin, italien au peuple; mais parlez français au sage.

In any event, insofar as the order of words is determined by factors independent of language, it is not necessary to describe it in a particular or universal grammar, and we therefore have principled grounds for excluding an explicit formulation of syntactic processes from grammar. It is worth noting that this naïve view of language structure persists to modern times in various forms, for example, in Saussure's image of a sequence of expressions corresponding to an amorphous sequence of concepts or in the common characterization of language use as merely a matter of use of words and phrases.

Returning to the main theme, by a generative grammar I mean simply a system of rules that in some explicit and well-defined way assigns structural descriptions to sentences. Obviously, every speaker of a language has mastered and internalized a generative grammar that expresses his knowledge of his language. This is not to say that he is aware of the rules of the grammar or even that he can become aware of them, or that his statements about his intuitive knowledge of the language are necessarily accurate. Any interesting generative grammar will be dealing, for the most part, with mental processes that are far beyond the level of actual or even potential consciousness; furthermore, it is quite apparent that a speaker's reports and viewpoints about his behaviour and his competence may be in error. Thus a generative grammar attempts to specify what the speaker actually knows, not what he may report about his knowledge. Similarly, a theory of visual perception would attempt to account for what a person actually sees and the mechanisms that determine this rather than his statements about what he sees and why, though these statements may provide useful, in fact, compelling evidence for such a theory.

To avoid what has been a continuing misunderstanding, it is perhaps worth while to reiterate that a generative grammar is not a model for a speaker or a hearer. It attempts to characterize in the most neutral possible terms the knowledge of the language that provides the basis for actual use of language by a speaker-hearer. When we speak of a grammar as generating a sentence with a certain structural description, we mean simply that the grammar assigns this structural description to the sentence. When we say that a sentence has a certain derivation with respect to a particular generative grammar, we say nothing about how the speaker or hearer might proceed, in some practical or efficient way, to construct such a derivation. These questions belong to the theory of language use—the theory of performance. No doubt, a reasonable model of language use will incorporate, as a basic component, the generative grammar that expresses the speaker-hearer's knowledge of the language; but this generative grammar does not, in itself, prescribe the character or functioning of a perceptual model or a model of speech production.

Confusion over this matter has been sufficiently persistent to suggest that a terminological change might be in order. Nevertheless, I think that the term 'generative grammar' is completely appropriate, and have therefore continued to use it. The term 'generate' is familiar in the sense intended here in logic, particularly in Post's theory of combinatorial systems. Furthermore, 'generative' seems to be the most appropriate translation for Humboldt's term *erzeugen*, which he frequently uses, it seems, in essentially the sense here intended. Since this use of the term 'generate' is well established both in logic and in the tradition of linguistic theory, I can see no reason for a revision of terminology.

Justification of grammars

Before entering directly into an investigation of the syntactic component of a generative grammar, it is important to give some thought to several methodological questions of justification and adequacy.

There is, first of all, the question of how one is to obtain information about the speaker-hearer's competence, about his knowledge of the language. Like most facts of interest and importance, this is neither presented for direct observation nor extractable from data by inductive procedures of any known sort. Clearly, the actual data of linguistic performance will provide much evidence for determining the correctness of hypotheses about underlying linguistic structure, along with introspective reports (by the native speaker, or the linguist who has learned the language). This is the position that is universally adopted in practice, although there are methodological discussions that seem to imply a reluctance to use observed performance or introspective reports as evidence for some underlying reality.

In brief, it is unfortunately the case that no adequate formalizable techniques are known for obtaining reliable information concerning the facts of linguistic structure (nor is this particularly surprising). There are, in other words, very few reliable experimental or data-processing procedures for obtaining significant information concerning the linguistic intuition of the native speaker. It is important to bear in mind that when an operational procedure is proposed, it must be tested for adequacy (exactly as a theory of linguistic intuition—a grammar—must be tested for adequacy) by measuring it against the standard provided by the tacit knowledge that it attempts to specify and describe. Thus a proposed operational test for, say, segmentation into words, must meet the empirical condition of conforming, in a mass of crucial and clear cases, to the linguistic intuition of the native speaker concerning such elements. Otherwise, it is without value. The same, obviously, is true in the case of any proposed operational procedure or any proposed grammatical description. If operational procedures were available that met this test, we might be justified in relying on their results in unclear and difficult cases. This remains a hope for the future rather than a present reality, however. This is the objective situation of present-day linguistic work; allusions to presumably well-known 'procedures of elicitation' or 'objective methods' simply obscure the actual situation in which linguistic work must, for the present, proceed. Furthermore, there is no reason to expect that reliable operational criteria for the deeper and more important theoretical notions of linguistics (such a 'grammaticalness' and 'paraphrase') will ever be forthcoming.

Even though few reliable operational procedures have been developed, the theoretical (that is, grammatical) investigation of the knowledge of the native speaker can proceed perfectly well. The critical problem for grammatical theory today is not a paucity of evidence but rather the inadequacy of present theories of language to account for masses of evidence that are hardly open to serious question. The problem for the grammarian is to construct a description and, where possible, an explanation for the enormous mass of unquestionable data concerning the linguistic intuition of the native speaker (often, himself); the problem for one concerned with operational procedures is to develop tests that give the correct results and make relevant distinctions. Neither the study of grammar nor the attempt to develop useful tests is hampered by lack of evidence with which to check results, for the present. We may hope that these efforts will converge, but they must obviously converge on the tacit knowledge of the native speaker if they are to be of any significance.

One may ask whether the necessity for present-day linguistics to give such priority to introspective evidence and to the linguistic intuition of the native speaker excludes it from the domain of science. The answer to this essentially terminological question seems to have no bearing at all on any serious issue. At most, it determines how we shall denote the kind of research that can be effectively carried out in the present state of our technique and understanding. However, this terminological question actually does relate to a different issue of some interest, namely the question whether the important feature of the successful sciences has been their search for insight or their concern for objectivity. The social and behavioural sciences provide ample evidence that objectivity can be pursued with little consequent gain in insight and understanding. On the other hand, a good case can be made for the view that the natural sciences have, by and large, sought objectivity primarily insofar as it is a tool for gaining insight (for providing phenomena that can suggest or test deeper explanatory hypotheses).

In any event, at a given stage of investigation, one whose concern is for insight and understanding (rather than for objectivity as a goal in itself) must ask whether or to what extent a wider range and more exact description of phenomena is relevant to solving the problems that he faces. In linguistics, it seems to me that sharpening of the data by more objective tests is a matter of small importance for the problems at hand. One who disagrees with this estimate of the present situation in linguistics can justify his belief in the current importance of more objective operational tests by showing how they can lead to new and deeper understanding of linguistic structure. Perhaps the day will come when the kinds of data that we now can obtain in abundance will be insufficient to resolve deeper questions concerning the structure of language. However, many questions that can realistically and significantly be formulated today do not demand evidence of a kind that is unavailable or unattainable without significant improvements in objectivity of experimental technique.

Although there is no way to avoid the traditional assumption that the speaker-hearer's linguistic intuition is the ultimate standard that determines the accuracy of any proposed grammar, linguistic theory, or operational test, it must be emphasized, once again, that this tacit knowledge may very well not be immediately available to the user of the language. To eliminate what has seemed to some an air of paradox in this remark, let me illustrate with a few examples.

If a sentence such as 'flying planes can be dangerous' is presented in an appropriately constructed context, the listener will interpret it immediately in a unique way, and will fail to detect the ambiguity. In fact, he may reject the second interpretation, when this is pointed out to him, as forced or unnatural (independently of which interpretation he originally selected under contextual pressure). Nevertheless, his intuitive knowledge of the language is clearly such that both of the interpretations (corresponding to 'flying planes are dangerous' and 'flying planes is dangerous') are assigned to the sentence by the grammar he has internalized in some form.

In the case just mentioned, the ambiguity may be fairly transparent. But consider such a sentence as

I had a book stolen.

Fewer hearers may be aware of the fact that their internalized grammar in fact provides at least three structural descriptions for this sentence. Nevertheless, this fact can be brought to consciousness by consideration of slight elaborations of the sentence for example: (i) 'I had a book stolen from my car when I stupidly left the window open,' that is, 'someone stole a book from my car'; (ii) 'I had a book stolen from his library by a professional thief who I hired to do the job,' that is, 'I had someone steal a book'; (iii) 'I almost had a book stolen, but they caught me leaving the library with it,' that is, 'I had almost succeeded in stealing a book'. In bringing to consciousness the triple ambiguity of the sentence in this way, we present no new information to the hearer and teach him nothing new about his language but simply arrange matters in such a way that his linguistic intuition, previously obscured, becomes evident to him.

In short, we must be careful not to overlook the fact that surface similarities may hide underlying distinctions of a fundamental nature, and that it may be necessary to guide and draw out the speaker's intuition in perhaps fairly subtle ways before we can determine what is the actual character of his knowledge of his language or of anything else. Neither point is new (the former is a commonplace of traditional linguistic theory and analytic philosophy; the latter is as old as Plato's *Meno*); both are too often overlooked.

A grammar can be regarded as a theory of a language; it is *descriptively adequate* to the extent that it correctly describes the intrinsic competence of the idealized native speaker. The structural descriptions assigned to sentences by the grammar, the distinctions that it makes between well-formed and deviant, and so on, must, for descriptive adequacy, correspond to the linguistic intuition of the native speaker (whether or not he may be immediately aware of this) in a substantial and significant class of crucial cases.

A linguistic theory must contain a definition of 'grammar', that is, a specification of the class of potential grammars. We may, correspondingly, say that *a linguistic theory is descriptively adequate* if it makes a descriptively adequate grammar available for each natural language.

Although even descriptive adequacy on a large scale is by no means easy to approach, it is crucial for the productive development of linguistic theory that much higher goals than this be pursued. To facilitate the clear formulation of deeper questions, it is useful to consider the abstract problem of constructing an 'acquisition model' for language, that is, a theory of language learning or grammar construction. Clearly, a child who has learned a language has developed an internal representation of a system of rules that determine how sentences are to be formed, used, and understood. Using the term 'grammar' with a systematic ambiguity (to refer, first, to the native speaker's internally represented 'theory of his language' and, second, to the linguist's account of this), we can say that the child has developed and internally represented a generative grammar, in the sense described. He has done this on the basis of observation of what we may call *primary linguistic data*. This must include examples of linguistic performance that are taken to be well-formed sentences, and may include also examples designated as non-sentences, and no doubt much other information of the sort that is required for language learning, whatever this may be. On the basis of such data, the child constructs a grammar—that is, a theory of the language of which the well-formed sentences of the primary linguistic data constitute a small sample. To learn a language, then, the child must have a method for devising an appropriate grammar, given primary linguistic data. As a precondition for language learning, he must possess, first, a linguistic theory that specifies the form of the grammar of a possible human language, and, second, a strategy for selecting a grammar of the appropriate form that is compatible with the primary linguistic data. As a long-range task for general linguistics, we might set the problem of developing an account of this innate linguistic theory that provides the basis for language learning. (Note that we are again using the term 'theory'—in this case 'theory of language' rather than 'theory of a particular language'—with a systematic ambiguity, to refer both to the child's innate predisposition to learn a language of a certain type and to the linguist's account of this.)

To the extent that a linguistic theory succeeds in selecting a descriptively adequate grammar on the basis of primary linguistic data, we can say that it meets the condition of *explanatory adequacy*. That is, to this extent, it offers an explanation for the intuition of the native speaker on the basis of an empirical hypothesis concerning the innate predisposition of the child to develop a certain kind of theory to deal with the evidence presented to him. Any such hypothesis can be falsified (all too easily, in actual fact) by showing that it fails to provide a descriptively adequate grammar for primary linguistic data from some other language— evidently the child is not predisposed to learn one language rather than another. It is supported when it does provide an adequate explanation for some aspect of linguistic structure, an account of the way in which such knowledge might have been obtained.

Clearly, it would be utopian to expect to achieve explanatory adequacy on a large scale in the present state of linguistics. Nevertheless, considerations of explanatory adequacy are often critical for advancing linguistic theory. Gross coverage of a large mass of data can often be attained by conflicting theories; for precisely this reason it is not, in itself, an achievement of any particular theoretical interest, or importance. As in any other field, the important problem in linguistics is to discover a complex of data that differentiates between conflicting conceptions of linguistic structure in that one of these conflicting theories can describe these data only by *ad hoc* means whereas the other can explain it on the basis of some empirical assumption about the form of language. Such small-scale studies of explanatory adequacy have, in fact, provided most of the evidence that has any serious bearing on the nature of linguistic structure. Thus whether we are comparing radically different theories of grammar or trying to determine the correctness of some particular aspect of one such theory, it is questions of explanatory adequacy that must, quite often, bear the burden of justification. This remark is in no way inconsistent with the fact that explanatory adequacy on a large scale is out of reach, for the present. It simply brings out the highly tentative character of any attempt to justify an empirical claim about linguistic structure.

To summarize briefly, there are two respects in which one can speak of 'justifying a generative grammar'. On one level (that of descriptive adequacy), the grammar is justified to the extent that it correctly describes its object, namely the linguistic intuition—the tacit competence—of the native speaker. In this sense, the grammar is justified on *external* grounds, on grounds of correspondence to linguistic fact. On a much deeper and hence much more rarely attainable level (that of explanatory adequacy), a grammar is justified to the extent that it is a *principled* descriptively adequate system, in that the linguistic theory with which it is associated selects this grammar over others, given primary linguistic data with which all are compatible. In this sense, the grammar is justified on *internal* grounds, on grounds of its relation to a linguistic theory that constitutes an explanatory hypothesis about the form of language as such. The problem of internal justification—of explanatory adequacy—is essentially the problem of constructing a theory of language acquisition, an account of the specific innate abilities that make this achievement possible.

Formal and substantive universals

A theory of linguistic structure that aims for explanatory adequacy incorporates an account of linguistic universals, and it attributes tacit knowledge of these universals to the child. It proposes, then, that the child approaches the data with·the presumption that they are drawn from a language of a certain antecedently well-defined type, his problem being to determine which of the (humanly) possible languages is that of the community in which he is placed. Language learning would be impossible unless this were the case. The important question is: What are the initial assumptions concerning the nature of language that the child brings to language learning, and how detailed and specific is the innate schema (the general definition of 'grammar') that gradually becomes more explicit and differentiated as the child learns the language? For the present we cannot come at all close to making a hypothesis about innate schemata that is rich, detailed, and specific enough to account for the fact of language acquisition. Consequently, the main task of linguistic theory must be to develop an account of linguistic universals that, on the one hand, will not be falsified by the actual diversity of languages and, on the other, will be sufficiently rich and explicit to account for the rapidity and uniformity of language learning, and the remarkable complexity and range of the generative grammars that are the product of language learning.

The study of linguistic universals is the study of the properties of any generative grammar for a natural language. Particular assumptions about linguistic universals may pertain to either the syntactic, semantic, or phonological component, or to interrelations among the three components.

It is useful to classify linguistic universals as *formal* or *substantive*. A theory of substantive universals claims that items of a particular kind in any language must be drawn from a fixed class of items. For example, Jakobson's theory of distinctive features can be interpreted as making an assertion about substantive universals with respect to the phonological component of a generative grammar. It asserts that each output of this component consists of elements that are characterized in terms of some small number of fixed, universal, phonetic features (perhaps on the order of fifteen or twenty), each of which has a substantive acoustic-articulatory characterization independent of any particular language. Traditional universal grammar was also a theory of substantive universals, in this sense. It not only put forth interesting views as to the nature of universal phonetics, but also advanced the position that certain fixed syntactic categories (Noun, Verb, etc.), can be found in the syntactic representations of the sentences of any language, and that these provide the general underlying syntactic structure of each language. A theory of substantive semantic universals might hold for example, that certain designative functions must be carried out in a specified way in each language. Thus it might assert that each language will contain terms that designate persons or lexical items referring to certain specific kinds of objects, feelings, behaviour, and so on.

It is also possible, however, to search for universal properties of a more abstract sort. Consider a claim that the grammar of every language meets certain specified formal conditions. The truth of this hypothesis would not in itself imply that any particular rule must appear in all or even in any two grammars. The property of having a grammar meeting a certain abstract condition might be called a *formal* linguistic universal, if shown to be a general property of natural languages. Recent attempts to specify the abstract conditions that a generative grammar must meet have produced a variety of proposals concerning formal universals, in this sense. For example, consider the proposal that the syntactic component of a grammar must contain transformational rules (these being operations of a highly special kind) mapping semantically interpreted deep structures into phonetically interpreted surface structures, or the proposal that the phonological component of a grammar consists of a sequence of rules, a subset of which may apply cyclically to successively more dominant constituents of the surface structure (a transformational cycle, in the sense of much recent work on phonology). Such proposals make claims of a quite different sort from the claim that certain substantive phonetic elements are available for phonetic representation in all languages, or that certain specific categories must be central to the syntax of all languages, or that certain semantic features or categories provide a universal framework for semantic description. Substantive universals such as these concern the vocabulary for the description of language; formal universals involve rather the character of the rules that appear in grammars and the ways in which they can be interconnected.

On the semantic level, too, it is possible to search for what might be called formal universals, in essentially the sense just described. Consider, for example, the assumption that proper names, in any language, must designate objects meeting a condition of spatiotemporal contiguity, and that the same is true of other terms designating objects; or the condition that the colour words of any language must subdivide the colour spectrum into continuous segments; or the condition that artifacts are defined in terms of certain human goals, needs, and functions instead of solely in terms of physical qualities. Formal constraints of this sort on a system of concepts may severely limit the choice (by the child, or the linguist) of a descriptive grammar, given primary linguistic data.

The existence of deep-seated formal universals, in the sense suggested by such examples as these, implies that all languages are cut to the same pattern, but does not imply that there is any point by point correspondence between particular languages. It does not, for example, imply that there must be some reasonable procedure for translating between languages.

In general, there is no doubt that a theory of language, regarded as a hypothesis about the innate 'language-forming capacity' of humans, should concern itself with both substantive and formal universals. But whereas substantive universals have been the traditional concern of general linguistic theory, investigations of the abstract conditions that must be satisfied by any generative grammar have been undertaken only quite recently. They seem to offer extremely rich and varied possibilities for study in all aspects of grammar.

24 JERROLD J. KATZ
Mentalism in Linguistics

Linguists who conceive of their science as a discipline which collects utterances and classifies their parts often pride themselves on their freedom from mentalism. But freedom from mentalism is an inherent feature of the taxonomic conception of linguistics, for, according to this conception, a linguist starts his investigation with observable physical events and at no stage imports anything else.

We may expand on this inherent freedom from mentalistic commitment as follows. Utterances are stretches of physical sound. Since the primary data for a taxonomic linguistic investigation is a set of utterances elicited from informants or obtained from texts, the linguist begins with observable physical events, sounds or inscriptions. At the first stage of classification—the cataloguing of phonemes on the basis of these stretches of sound or some grouping of them—the linguist erects classes of significant sounds. At the next stage he forms classes of sequences of phonemes, thus producing a catalogue of the morphemes of the language. Finally he classifies sequences of morphemes as sentential constituents of various types. Even if at some point the linguist should also consider an aspect of the speaker himself (such as his intuitive judgements about well-formedness) or an aspect of the speaker's environment (such as what he is referring to), such consideration is restricted to just those aspects that are capable of being observed by anyone who cares to carry out the same investigation. Therefore, on the taxonomic conception of linguistics, there is nowhere from the beginning to the end of a linguistic investigation, any appeal to mental capacities or mental processes. Alternatively, the taxonomic conception is a very narrow form of reductionism, which holds that every linguistic construction, at any level, reduces ultimately, by purely classificational procedures, to physical segments of utterances.

This philosophy of linguistics is never explicitly defended in current literature, because the linguists who hold it generally assume that Bloomfield long ago conclusively refuted mentalism. Hence a taxonomic linguist

J. J. Katz: Extract from 'Mentalism in Linguistics', *Language* 40, 1964, pp. 124–8.

considers it unnecessary to put forth arguments of his own against this doctrine. When he criticizes other linguists for subscribing to a mentalistic philosophy of linguistics or for adoping a mentalistic theory of linguistic structure, he relies on Bloomfield's critique of mentalism for support.

But when we look at Bloomfield's critique of mentalism and compare the doctrine he criticized with the doctrines that modern taxonomic linguists criticize for being mentalistic, we find, curiously enough, that the most influential of the latter turn out not to be the kind of doctrine that Bloomfield attacked. Bloomfield criticized, not mentalism in the contemporary sense of this term, but a highly theologized conception of mentalism, which very few who regard themselves as mentalists would have any desire to call their own. Typical of Bloomfield's criticism of mentalism is this:

> The *mentalistic* theory . . . supposes that the variability of human conduct is due to the interference of some non-physical factor, a *spirit* or *will* or *mind* . . . that is present in every human being. This spirit, according to the mentalistic view is entirely different from material things and accordingly follows some other kind of causation or perhaps none at all.

Here and in similar statements, Bloomfield makes it clear that he is criticizing mentalism because it renders prediction and explanation of linguistic behaviour in terms of causal laws completely impossible. Since Bloomfield's critique applies only to a theologized version of mentalism, it follows that taxonomic linguists are not justified in appealing to Bloomfield's 'refutation' to support their criticism of a version of mentalism according to which mental capacities and processes are subject to causal laws. Indeed, such a version of mentalism is wholly compatible with the doctrine Bloomfield called 'mechanism'.

There is, however, another feature of Bloomfield's discussion of mentalism which, though it can hardly be construed as a refutation of anything, does provide the taxonomic linguist with some basis in Bloomfield's work for his polemic against a nontheological version of mentalism. This feature is Bloomfield's endorsement of the empiricist viewpoint on scientific methodology. In this vein, he writes,

> . . . we can distinguish science from other phases of human activity by agreeing that science shall deal only with events that are accessible in their time and place to any and all observers (strict *behaviorism*) or only with events that are placed in coordinates of time and space (*mechanism*), or that science shall employ only such initial statements and predictions as lead to definite handling operations (*operationalism*), or only terms such as are derivable by rigid definition (*physicalism*).

The charge against mentalism made by those who cite Bloomfield in support of their dismissal of mentalism, then, is that mentalistic theories deal with events that do not meet the methodological demands of behaviourism, mechanism, operationalism, and physicalism. They believe the charge to be justified because they believe that a theory of linguistic structure which deals with such events is based on bad scientific methodology.

It is extremely important to note that Bloomfield goes on to say,

... These several formulations [behaviorism, mechanism, operationalism, and physicalism], independently reached by different scientists, all lead to the same delimitation, and this delimitation does not restrict the subject matter of science but rather characterizes its method.

Bloomfield is here at pains to stress that the empiricist viewpoint on scientific methodology does not restrict the range or kind of phenomena that a scientist can describe and explain. The present paper denies just this claim. Against it, I argue two points. First, the taxonomic linguist's criticism of mentalistic theories for being based on bad scientific methodology fails through the inadequacy of the empiricist viewpoint on which it depends. That is, I shall argue that the empiricist viewpoint does not deserve to be the standard by which any conception of linguistics or any other science is judged. Second, a mentalistic theory is better than a taxonomic one because the delimitation imposed by the empiricist viewpoint, and accepted by taxonomic linguists, so severely restricts the character of a taxonomic theory that the range and kind of linguistic phenomena for which such a theory can account is considerably narrower than the range and kind that a mentalistic theory can handle. If these two points are both established, there should be an end to the criticizing of linguistic theories for being mentalistic; and, more significantly, there should be an end to taxonomic theories themselves.

One may formulate the controversy between taxonomic linguistics and mentalistic linguistics in terms of the following opposition. The linguist who adopts a causal conception of mentalism is contending that purely linguistic theories cannot succeed in predicting and explaining the facts of linguistic performance without making reference to the mental events, capacities, and processes of speakers, i.e. that linguistic theories must contain concepts which enable linguists to formulate the principles of mental operation that underlie speech. On the other hand, the linguist who adopts the taxonomic conception of linguistics is contending that purely linguistic theories can succeed in predicting and explaining the facts of linguistic performance.

It might appear that there is no way to settle this controversy short of some abstruse examination of the philosophical principles underlying the taxonomic and mentalistic positions, but this is false. The dispute can be settled simply by determining whether a taxonomic or a mentalistic theory is, in principle, better able to account for what is known about the general facts of linguistic phenomena. This determination can be made by showing that a mentalistic theory accounts for everything that a taxonomic theory accounts for, and, in addition and with no extension of the theory, for many things that the taxonomic theory must fail to account for. This is the spirit of Chomsky's criticisms of theories of grammar constructed within the taxonomic framework. Unfortunately, Chomsky's arguments are often not taken in this way but are taken rather as trying to establish a new kind of taxonomic system.

The basic point of Chomsky's criticisms is that the failure of a taxonomic theory to handle the full range of facts about linguistic structure is due to the failure of such theories to concern themselves with mental capacities, events, and processes. The point which has been missed by those who interpret his arguments as trying to establish a new kind of taxonomic system is that only by introducing mentalistic concepts into our theories do we provide ourselves with the conceptual machinery which makes it possible to account for the full range of linguistic facts.

The general form of Chomsky's criticism of taxonomic linguistics is summarized as follows. The best kind of theory is one which systematizes the widest range of facts; hence a mentalistic theory is better than a taxonomic one because the former can handle any fact that the latter can handle, whereas the latter is unable to handle many kinds of facts that the former handles easily and naturally. The difference in the facts that these theories can handle is a direct function of the difference in the conceptual machinery they contain.

If it is to be shown that mentalism thus succeeds where taxonomic linguistics fails, it will be necessary to clarify certain features of the mentalist conception of linguistic theories. In particular, it must be made clear just what a mentalist means when he says that reference to mental states is a necessary aspect of any adequate linguistic theory, and just what status he intends mentalistic concepts to have. Unless his meaning is clarified, it will remain unclear whether it is the reference to mental states that is responsible for the margin of explanatory power by which mentalistic theories excel taxonomic theories. Unless the status of his concepts is clarified, it will remain open for the taxonomic linguist to claim that, although the mentalist says that his reference to mental states is a reference to things or events within the causal realm, the actual way in which this reference is made gives no clue how mental states might stand as causal antecedents of physical events like vocalization and speech sounds. These matters must be clarified in such a way that those who construe Chomsky's arguments as seeking to establish a new kind of taxonomic system cannot claim that the machinery in Chomsky's theories which produce the margin of explanatory power by which they are more empirically successful have no psychological reality but are merely new kinds of data-cataloguing devices.

First, how can mental events like those referred to in mentalistic linguistic theories be links in the causal chain that contains also vocalizations and sound waves? To explain how speakers are able to communicate in their language, the mentalist hypothesizes that, underlying a speaker's ability to communicate, there is a highly complex mechanism which is essentially the same as that underlying the linguistic ability of other speakers. He thus views the process of linguistic communication as one in which such mechanisms operate to encode and decode verbal messages. The aim of theory construction in linguistics is taken to be the formulation of a theory that reveals the structure of this mechanism and explains the facts of linguistic communication by showing them to be behavioural consequences of the operation of a mechanism with just the structure that the formulated theory attributes to it.

The step of hypothesizing such a mechanism in the process of theory construction in linguistics is no different from hypothetical postulation in theory construction in any other branch of science where some component of the system about which we wish to gain understanding is inaccessible to observation. The linguist can no more look into the head of a fluent speaker than a physicist can directly observe photons or a biologist directly inspect the evolutionary events that produced the human species. The linguist, like the physicist and biologist, can only achieve scientific understanding by constructing a model of the system which contains a hypothesis about the structure of the components of the system that are not observable. If the logical consequences of the model match the observable behaviour of the system and would not do so without the hypothesis, the scientist may say that this hypothesis accounts for the behaviour of the system in terms of the behaviour of the unobservable but causally efficient component. If the model is the simplest one which enables the scientist to derive all the known facts and predict previously unknown ones as effects of the hypothesized component, he can assert that his model correctly pictures the structure of the system and its unobservable components. In this way, a linguist can assert that his theory correctly represents the structure of the mechanism underlying the speaker's ability to communicate with other speakers.

Linguistics and Language Teaching

Linguists and language teachers have different preoccupations: the first with the structure of language and its description and perhaps more generally with the nature of cognitive processes, the other with the practical task of creating the conditions in which a performance ability in a language may be learned.

What we are concerned with in this section is the connexion between these two preoccupations, if any. Common sense would suggest that anyone engaged in a practical task in which language is central should know something of it. A physics teacher must know physics, a history teacher, history. But in the case of a language teacher *knowledge* is an ambiguous term. No one would nowadays question the necessity of the teacher knowing how to perform in the language he is teaching, i.e. he must possess an internalized grammar of the language (Chomsky). The question here is the degree to which he must also have an explicit knowledge about the language as well. If teaching means a principled (systematic) organizing of the conditions in which learning takes place then it is difficult to see how this could be done without some explicit knowledge about the language also. If this were not so, as Corder points out, any native speaker of a language could teach it as well as a qualified language teacher.

The problem then is not whether a teacher should know about language but what he should know. This is where the question of the relevance of linguistics to language teaching arises. Theoretical linguistics, as we have seen in previous sections, has important but strictly limited aims, and even these are, as Chomsky and Mackey point out, a matter of disagreement at the present time. The problem then is one of determining which theories are relevant and which not. This is the central question discussed by Halliday, Rosenbaum and Mackey—the question of validity. But, as Rosenbaum and Halliday are careful to make clear, validity has in this context two meanings; '*evaluation* in the light of the goals recognized for the theory', a matter internal to linguistics, and the *value*, or usefulness of a theory for certain aims external to linguistics, its applicability or appropriateness. The relation between these two is evident. No theory can be of value to language teaching unless it is valid linguistically (Saporta), but it does not follow that a valid linguistic theory is necessarily of value to language teaching. Rosenbaum and Saporta put up a case for the validity of a particular linguistic theory but Rosenbaum suggests that its usefulness is 'entirely dependent on the ingenuity and imagination of linguists, teachers and educators *competent in both areas*' (editors' italics). The sort of person Rosenbaum has in mind appears to be what is now coming to be called an 'applied linguist'. A similar notion lies behind the suggestion made by Mackey that some training in practical linguistics for the language teacher could put him in the position to evaluate each linguistic contribution and its applicability to language teaching. Chomsky also insists that it is the language teacher 'who must validate or refute any specific proposals' for the application of linguistics, although he does not specify how the teacher is to do this without a knowledge of linguistics; on the other hand, Halliday suggests that the linguist is 'not unaware of the needs of the consumer' but does not specify how the linguist achieves this awareness without training in, and experience of, language teaching.

Almost all the contributors speak of the 'language teacher' as if one and the same person performed all the variety of functions which are involved in a language teaching operation. This is a dangerous over-simplification. Language teaching is not a simple face-to-face interaction between a single teacher and a body of learners in a classroom. If teaching is an activity concerned with the creation of the best conditions for learning, one, at least, of those conditions is the provision of appropriate linguistic data in a form and sequence which can be most readily made use of by the learner. This means samples of the language to be learned with descriptive comments, explanations, and co-ordinate non-linguistic data where appropriate. In other words, teaching requires texts, written or spoken. The teacher may supply some of these, but in most teaching situations most of the linguistic data is supplied from outside the class-room. The classroom teacher is in such cases a mediator; he operates, in the modern jargon, 'at the interface' between the data and the learner.

It is, therefore, important when considering the relevance of linguistics to language teaching to make a distinction between its relevance to the classroom teacher and its relevance to those who prepare the teaching materials. This is a distinction which is too rarely made and the failure to make it leads to a lot of unnecessary misunderstanding and confusion, some of it exemplified in the articles in this section.

A truer picture of the normal language teaching situation is that it is an interaction between the classroom teacher, the author of the teaching materials and the learner. The question of the relevance of linguistic knowledge to language teaching is, then, one of determining how such knowledge should be distributed between the interacting parties.

Both Corder and Saporta agree that the principal value of linguistics lies in its application to the preparation of teaching materials, the making of pedagogic grammars. These they see as the central concern of the applied linguist. Corder, however, goes further. He maintains that no teacher can use these materials adequately without some knowledge of linguistics, a language for talking about language.

25 NOAM CHOMSKY
The Utility of Linguistic Theory to the Language Teacher

I should like to make it clear from the outset that I am participating in this conference not as an expert on any aspect of the teaching of languages, but rather as someone whose primary concern is with the structure of language and, more generally, the nature of cognitive process. Furthermore, I am, frankly, rather sceptical about the significance, for the teaching of languages, of such insights and understanding as have been attained in linguistics and psychology. Surely the teacher of language would do well to keep informed of progress and discussion in these fields, and the efforts of linguists and psychologists to approach the problems of language teaching from a principled point of view are extremely worthwhile, from an intellectual as well as a social point of view. Still, it is difficult to believe that either linguistics or psychology has achieved a level of theoretical understanding that might enable it to support a 'technology' of language teaching. Both fields have made significant progress in recent decades, and, furthermore, both draw on centuries of careful thought and study. These disciplines are, at present, in a state of flux and agitation. What seemed to be well-established doctrine a few years ago may now be the subject of extensive debate. Although it would be difficult to document this generalization, it seems to me that there has been a significant decline, over the past ten or fifteen years, in the degree of confidence in the scope and security of foundations in both psychology and linguistics. I personally feel that this decline in confidence is both healthy and realistic. But it should serve as a warning to teachers that suggestions from the 'fundamental disciplines' must be viewed with caution and scepticism.

Within psychology, there are now many who would question the view that the basic principles of learning are well understood. Long accepted principles of association and reinforcement, gestalt principles, the theory

A. N. Chomsky: Extract from 'Linguistic Theory' in *Language Teaching: Broader Contexts*. Report of N.E. Conference on the Teaching of Foreign Languages, Menasha, Wisconsin, 1966, pp. 43–9.

of concept formation as it has emerged in modern investigation, all of these have been sharply challenged in theoretical as well as experimental work. To me it seems that these principles are not merely inadequate but probably misconceived—that they deal with marginal aspects of acquisition of knowledge and leave the central core of the problem untouched. In particular, it seems to me impossible to accept the view that linguistic behaviour is a matter of habit, that it is slowly acquired by reinforcement, association, and generalization, or that linguistic concepts can be specified in terms of a space of elementary, physically defined 'criterial attributes'. Language is not a 'habit structure'. Ordinary linguistic behaviour characteristically involves innovation, formation of new sentences and new patterns in accordance with rules of great abstractness and intricacy. This is true both of the speaker, who constructs new utterances appropriate to the occasion, and of the hearer who must analyse and interpret these novel structures. There are no known principles of association or reinforcement, and no known sense of 'generalization' that can begin to account for this characteristic 'creative' aspect of normal language use. The new utterances that are produced and interpreted in the daily use of language are 'similar' to those that constitute the past experience of speaker and hearer only in that they are determined, in their form and interpretation, by the same system of abstract underlying rules. There is no theory of association or generalization capable of accounting for this fact, and it would, I think, be a fundamental misunderstanding to see such a theory, since the explanation very likely lies along different lines. The simple concepts of ordinary language (such concepts as 'human being' or 'knife' or 'useful', etc., or, for that matter, the concept 'grammatical sentence') cannot be specified in terms of a space of physical attributes, as in the concept formation paradigm. There is, correspondingly, no obvious analogy between the experimental results obtained in studies of concept formation and the actual processes that seem to underlie language learning.

Evidently, such an evaluation of the relevance of psychological theory to language acquisition requires justification, and it is far from uncontroversial. Nor will I attempt, within the framework of this paper, to supply any such justification. My point simply is that the relevance of psychological theory to acquisition of language is a highly dubious and questionable matter, subject to much controversy and plagued with uncertainties of all sorts. The applied psychologist and the teacher must certainly draw what suggestions and hints they can from psychological research, but they would be well-advised to do so with the constant realization of how fragile and tentative are the principles of the underlying discipline.

Turning to linguistics, we find much the same situation. Linguists have had their share in perpetuating the myth that linguistic behaviour is 'habitual' and that a fixed stock of 'patterns' is acquired through practice and used as the basis for 'analogy'. These views could be maintained only as long as grammatical description was sufficiently vague and imprecise. As soon as an attempt is made to give a careful and precise account of the rules of sentence formation, the rules of phonetic organization, or the rules of sound-meaning correspondence in a language, the inadequacy of such an approach becomes apparent. What is more, the fundamental concepts of linguistic description have been subjected to serious critique. The principles of phonemic analysis, for example, have recently been called into question, and the status of the concept 'phoneme' is very much in doubt. For that matter, there are basic unsolved problems concerning even the phonetic representations used as a basis for analysis of form in structural linguistics. Whereas a decade ago it would have been almost universally assumed that a phonetic representation is simply a record of physical fact, there is now considerable evidence that what the linguist takes to be a phonetic transcription is determined, in nontrivial ways, by the syntactic structure of the language, and that it is, to this extent, independent of the physical signal. I think there are by now very few linguists who believe that it is possible to arrive at the phonological or syntactic structure of a language by systematic application of 'analytic procedures' of segmentation and classification, although fifteen or twenty years ago such a view was not only widely accepted but was also supported by significant results and quite plausible argument.

I would like to emphasize again that this questioning of fundamental principles is a very healthy phenomenon that has led to important advances and will undoubtedly continue to do so. It is, in fact, characteristic of any living subject. But it must be recognized that well-established theory, in fields like psychology and linguistics, is extremely limited in scope. The applications of physics to engineering may not be seriously affected by even the most deep-seated revolution in the foundations of physics, but the applications of psychology or linguistics to language teaching, such as they are, may be gravely affected by changing conceptions in these fields, since the body of theory that resists substantial modification is fairly small.

In general, the willingness to rely on 'experts' is a frightening aspect of contemporary political and social life. Teachers, in particular, have a responsibility to make sure that ideas and proposals are evaluated on their merits, and not passively accepted on grounds of authority, real or presumed. The field of language teaching is no exception. It is possible—even likely—that principles of psychology and linguistics, and research in these disciplines, may supply insights useful to the language teacher. But this must be demonstrated, and cannot be presumed. It is the language teacher himself who must validate or refute any specific proposal. There is very little in psychology or linguistics that he can accept on faith.

I will not try to develop any specific proposals relating to the teaching of languages—as I mentioned before, because I am not competent to do so. But there are certain tendencies and developments within linguistics and psychology that may have some potential impact on the teaching of language. I think these can be usefully summarized under four main headings: the 'creative' aspect of language use; the abstractness of linguistic representation; the universality of underlying linguistic structure; the role of intrinsic organization in cognitive processes. I would like to say just a few words about each of these topics.

The most obvious and characteristic property of normal linguistic behaviour is that it is stimulus-free and innovative. Repetition of fixed phrases is a rarity; it is only under exceptional and quite uninteresting circumstances that one can seriously consider how 'situational context' determines what is said, even in probabilistic terms. The notion that linguistic behaviour consists of 'responses' to 'stimuli' is as much a myth as the idea that it is a matter of habit and generalization. To maintain such assumptions in the face of the actual facts, we must deprive the terms 'stimulus' and 'response' (similarly 'habit' and 'generalization') of any technical or precise meaning. This property of being innovative and stimulus-free is what I refer to by the term 'creative aspect of language use'. It is a property of language that was described in the seventeenth century and that serves as one cornerstone for classical linguistic theory, but that has gradually been forgotten in the development of modern linguistics, much to its detriment. Any theory of language must come to grips with this fundamental property of normal language use. A necessary but not sufficient step towards dealing with this problem is to recognize that the native speaker of a language has internalized a 'generative grammar'—a system of rules that can be used in new and untried combinations to form new sentences and to assign semantic interpretations to new sentences. Once this fact has become clear, the immediate task of the linguist is likewise clarified. He must try to discover the rules of this generative grammar and the underlying principles on the basis of which it is organized.

The native speaker of a language has internalized a generative grammar in the sense just described, but he obviously has no awareness of this fact or of the properties of this grammar. The problem facing the linguist is to discover what constitutes unconscious, latent knowledge—to bring to light what is now sometimes called the speaker's intrinsic 'linguistic competence'. A generative grammar of a language is a theory of the speaker's competence. If correct, it expresses the principles that determine the intrinsic correlation of sound and meaning in the language in question.

It thus serves as one component of a theory that can accommodate the characteristic creative aspect of language use.

When we try to construct explicit, generative grammars and investigate their properties, we discover at once many inadequacies in traditional and modern linguistic descriptions. It is often said that no complete generative grammar has ever been written for any language, the implication being that this 'new-fangled' approach suffers in comparison with older and well-established approaches to language description, in this respect. The statement concerning generative grammar is quite accurate; the conclusion, if intended, reveals a serious misunderstanding. Even the small fragments of generative grammars that now exist are incomparably greater in explicit coverage than traditional or structuralist descriptions, and it is important to be aware of this fact. A generative grammar is simply one that gives explicit rules that determine the structure of sentences, their phonetic form, and their semantic interpretation. The limitations of generative grammar are the limitations of our knowledge, in these areas. Where traditional or structuralist descriptions are correct, they can immediately be incorporated into generative grammars. Insofar as these descriptions merely list examples of various kinds and make remarks (which may be interesting and suggestive) about them, then they cannot be directly incorporated into generative grammars. In other words, a traditional or structuralist description can be immediately incorporated into a generative grammar to the extent that it is correct and does not rely on the 'intelligence of the reader' and his 'linguistic intuition'. The limitations of generative grammar then, are a direct reflection of the limitations of correctness and explicitness in earlier linguistic work.

A serious investigation of generative grammars quickly shows that the rules that determine the form of sentences and their interpretations are not only intricate but also quite abstract, in the sense that the structures they manipulate are related to physical fact only in a remote way, by a long chain of interpretative rules. This is as true on the level of phonology as it is on the level of syntax and semantics, and it is this fact that has led to the questioning both of structuralist principles and of the tacitly assumed psychological theory that underlies them. It is because of the abstractness of linguistic representations that one is forced, in my opinion, to reject not only the analytic procedures of modern linguistics, with their reliance on segmentation and classification, but also principles of association and generalization that have been discussed and studied in empiricist psychology. Although such phenomena as association and generalization, in the sense of psychological theory and philosophical speculation, may indeed exist, it is difficult to see how they have any bearing on the acquisition or use of language. If our current conceptions of generative grammar are at all accurate, then the structures manipulated and the principles operating in these grammars are not related to given sensory phenomena in any way describable in the terms that empiricist psychology offers, and what principles it suggests simply have no relation to the facts that demand explanation.

If it is correct that the underlying principles of generative grammars cannot be acquired through experience and training, then they must be part of the intellectual organization which is a prerequisite for language acquisition. They must, therefore, be universal properties, properties of any generative grammar. There are, then, two distinct ways of approaching what is clearly the most fundamental question of linguistic science, namely, the question of linguistic universals. One way is by an investigation of a wide range of languages. Any hypothesis as to the nature of linguistic universals must meet the empirical condition that it is not falsified by any natural language, any language acquired and used by humans in the normal way. But there is also another and, for the time being, somewhat more promising way of studying the problem of universals. This is by deep investigation of a particular language, investigation directed towards establishing underlying principles of organization of great abstractness in this language. Where such principles can be established, we must account for their existence. One plausible hypothesis is that they are innate, therefore, universal. Another plausible hypothesis is that they are acquired through experience and training. Either hypothesis can be made precise; each will then be meaningful and worthy of attention. We can refute the former by showing that other aspects of this language or properties of other languages are inconsistent with it. We can refute the latter by showing that it does not yield the structures that we must presuppose to account for linguistic competence. In general, it seems to me quite impossible to account for many deep-seated aspects of language on the basis of training or experience, and that therefore one must search for an explanation for them in terms of intrinsic intellectual organization. An almost superstitious refusal to consider this proposal seriously has, in my opinion, enormously set back both linguistics and psychology. For the present, it seems to me that there is no more reason for assuming that the basic principles of grammar are learned than there is for making a comparable assumption about, let us say, visual perception. There is, in short, no more reason to suppose that a person learns that English has a generative grammar of a very special and quite explicitly definable sort than there is to suppose that the same persons learns to analyse the visual field in terms of line, angle, motion, solidity, persons with faces, etc.

Turning then to the last of the four topics mentioned above, I think that one of the most important current developments in psychology and neurophysiology is the investigation of intrinsic organization in cognition.

In the particular case of language, there is good reason to believe that even the identification of the phonetic form of a sentence presupposes at least a partial syntactic analysis, so that the rules of the generative grammar may be brought into play even in identifying the signal. This view is opposed to the hypothesis that phonetic representation is determined by the signal completely, and that the perceptual analysis proceeds from formal signals to interpretation, a hypothesis which, I understand, has been widely quoted in discussion of language teaching. The role of the generative grammar in perception is paralleled by the role of the universal grammar—the system of invariant underlying principles of linguistic organization—in acquisition of language. In each case, it seems to me that the significance of the intrinsic organization is very great indeed, and that the primary goal of linguistic and psychological investigation of language must be to determine and characterize it.

I am not sure that this very brief discussion of some of the leading ideas of much current research has been sufficiently clear to be either informative or convincing. Once again, I would like to stress that the implications of these ideas for language teaching are far from clear to me. It is a rather dubious undertaking to try to predict the course of development of any field, but, for what it is worth, it seems to me likely that questions of this sort will dominate research in the coming years, and, to hazard a further guess, that this research will show that certain highly abstract structures and highly specific principles of organization are characteristic of all human languages, are intrinsic rather than acquired, play a central role in perception as well as in production of sentences, and provide the basis for the creative aspect of language use.

26 M. A. K. HALLIDAY
Syntax and the Consumer

At the Seventh Annual Round Table Meeting, held at the Institute of Languages and Linguistics in 1956, Professor Archibald Hill read a paper entitled 'Who needs linguistics?' In it he referred to 'the kinds of people who can now be shown to be in need of linguistic knowledge for practical reasons', including among them teachers of foreign languages and of the native language, literary scholars and those concerned with the study of mental disorders. His concluding paragraph contained the words 'It is the linguists who need linguistics. . . . It is we who have the task of making linguistics sufficiently adult, and its results sufficiently available so that all people of good will, who work within the field of language, language art, and language usage, can realize that there are techniques and results which are of value to them'.

Professor Hill could, if he had wished, have added others to the list; what he was emphasizing, as I understand it, was that any benefits which those other than the linguists themselves may derive from linguistic work depends on the linguists' own pursuit and presentation of their subject. Within those areas of activity, often referred to as 'applied linguistics', in which languages are described for other than purely explanatory purposes, the linguist's task is that of describing language; and he will not, for example, attempt to tell the language teacher what to teach or how to teach it, nor claim to be a pediatrician because his work may contribute to studies of language development in children.

While recognizing the limitations on their own role, however, linguists are not unaware of the needs of the consumer. Language may be described for a wide range of purposes; or, if that is begging the question I want to ask, there is a wide range of purposes for which a description of language may be used. The question is: do these various aims presuppose different ways of using the same description, or are they best served by descriptions

M. A. K. Halliday: Extract from 'Syntax and the Consumer', *Monograph Series of Language and Linguistics*, No. 17, Report of 15th Annual Round Table Meeting on Linguistics and Language Studies, Georgetown 1964, pp. 11–18.

of different kinds? Is there one single 'best description' of a language, or are there various possible 'best descriptions' according to the purpose in view?

One of the many important contributions made by Chomsky has been his insistence that linguists should define the goals of a linguistic theory. According to his own well-known formulation, the grammar should provide a complete specification of an infinite set of grammatical sentences of the language, enumerating all sentences and no non-sentences, and automatically assign to them structural descriptions. The theory should include a function for the evaluation of grammars, so that a choice can be made among different grammars all of which fulfill these requirements. The grammar can then be validated for compatibility with the given data and evaluated for relative simplicity.

Associated with this is the underlying aim that 'the formalized grammar is intended to be a characterization of certain of the abilities of a mature speaker'; 'we would like the structural description to be the basis for explaining a great deal of what the speaker knows to be true of speech events, beyond their degree of well-formedness'. Compare also Katz and Fodor's formulation: 'Grammars answer the question: What does the speaker know about the phonological and syntactic structure of his language that enables him to use and understand any of its sentences, including those he has not previously heard?', and Chomsky's summing-up: 'As I emphasized earlier, the central problem in developing such a theory is to specify precisely the form of grammars—the schema for grammatical description that constitutes, in effect, a theory of linguistic universals and a hypothesis concerning the specific nature of the innate intellectual equipment of the child'.

The evaluation of a linguistic description means, naturally, its evaluation in the light of the goals recognized for the theory. A formalized grammar is evaluated for its success in achieving the aims of a formalized grammar or of that particular formalized grammar; the relevance of this evaluation, to any other aims will depend in part on the extent to which a formalized model yields the kind of description that is most appropriate to them. That there are other possible aims is not, I think, in question; to quote Chomsky again, 'I do not, by any means, intend to imply that these are the only aspects of linguistic competence that deserve serious study', to which I would like to add that linguistic competence is not the only aspect of language that deserves serious study: the explanation of linguistic performance can also perhaps be regarded as a reasonable goal and one that is still, as it were, internal to linguistics. But I would also wish to include, among the possible goals of linguistic theory, the description of language for the purpose of various specific applications; goals which may be thought of as external to linguistics but for which linguistics is part of the essential equipment.

This is not of course to question the validity and importance of the goals defined by Chomsky; nor is it to suggest that, given these specific goals, the model that provides the 'best description' will not be of the type he specifies. But we should not perhaps take it for granted that a description in terms of a formalized model, which has certain properties lacking in those derived from models of other kinds, will necessarily be the best description for all of the very diverse purposes for which descriptions of languages are needed.* In assessing the value of a description, it is reasonable to ask whether it has proved useful for the purposes for which it is intended; and such purposes may be external as well as internal to linguistics.

There tends no doubt to be some correlation between the model a particular linguist adopts for his own work and the place where he grew up, linguistically speaking. Nevertheless I would defend the view that different coexisting models in linguistics may best be regarded as appropriate to different aims, rather than as competing contenders for the same goal. One may have one's own private opinions about the relative worth and interest of these various aims, but rather in the same way as most of us probably like the sound of some of the languages we study better than we like that of others. Estimates of the relative attainability of different goals may be more objective, although even here the criteria for the assessment of one goal as more difficult of attainment than another can probably be made explicit only where the two are basically different stages in the pursuit of a single more general aim. It is difficult to measure the relative demands made on a theory by requirements such as, on the one hand, that 'the structural description of a sentence must provide an account of all grammatical information in principle available to the native speaker' and on the other hand that the grammar should be of help to the student learning a foreign language or to the pediatrician in his diagnosis and treatment of retarded speech development; nor is it any easier to measure the degree of success of a description in meeting these demands.

Yet in spite of the difficulty of measuring attainment linguists 'intuitively' —that is, by their experience as linguists—recognize a good description, and most of them seem to agree in their judgements. This is not in any way surprising, but it illustrates an important point: that linguistic theory is no substitute for descriptive insight. Naturally different descriptions of a language will follow when different models are used to describe it; but the differences imposed by the model tend to obscure the similarities, and also the differences, in the linguists' interpretation of the facts. It is true, in the first place, that two descriptions will differ precisely and directly because different models are being used and these impose different kinds of state-

---

* This is of course a different question from that of the relative evaluation of different formalized grammars. [Author's footnote.]

ment. In the second place, however, the descriptions may differ because the linguists disagree at certain points in their interpretations. And in the third place the models themselves may impose different interpretations, either because one solution is simpler in one model and another in the other or because they have different terms of reference and different aims.

For example, transformational grammars of English recognize a passive transformation relating such pairs of sentences as *the man eats cake* and *cake is eaten by the man*. The analogue in a 'scale-and-category' grammar (to use a name by which the version of a system-structure grammar that my colleagues and I have been working with has come to be known) would be a system at clause rank whose terms are active and passive: as for example the question transformation is paralleled by a clause system whose terms are affirmative (transformational grammar's 'declarative') and interrogative. In fact no system of voice at clause rank is introduced into our present description of English. We could say that this is because it does not represent our interpretation of the facts. But the question is: what 'facts' are being interpreted? The 'system' implies proportionality: given a system whose terms are a, b, c, then the set of their exponents $a_1 a_2 a_3, \ldots,$ $b_1 b_2 b_3 \ldots, c_1 c_2 c_3 \ldots$ are proportionally related: $a_1 : b_1 : c_1 :: a_2 : b_2 : c_2$ and so on. This holds good, it seems to us, to a reasonable extent (such that the simplicity of the general statement is not outweighed by the complexity of further statements that are required to qualify it) of affirmative and interrogative in the clause, and of active and passive in the verbal group where the description does recognize a system of voice; but not of active and passive in the clause. In other words, *John was invited by Mary, this house was built by my grandfather, the driver was injured by flying glass, John's been dismissed from his job* and *it was announced that the committee had resigned* are not explained as all standing in the same relation to a set of their active counterparts. Such a relationship is shown, but indirectly (as the product of a number of systemic relations) and not always by the same route.

But this does not necessarily imply different notions about English; it may simply mean a difference in what is being required of the description. While there may be some similarity between the system in a scale-and-category grammar and the transformation in a transformational grammar, in the sense that instances of the two often correspond, they are not and cannot be saying the same thing, because these are different kinds of model. The nature of a grammatical description, in fact, is determined as a whole by the properties of the model in which it has status, as well as being conditioned by the goals that lie behind the model.

If I were asked to characterize the work in which I have been engaged together with some of my colleagues, I would say that our aim is to show the patterns inherent in the linguistic performance of the native speaker:

this is what we mean by 'how the language works'. This presupposes a general description of those patterns which the linguist considers to be primary in the language, a description which is then variably extendable, on the 'scale of delicacy', in depth of detail. It involves a characterization of the special features, including statistical properties, of varieties of the language used for different purposes ('registers'), and the comparison of individual texts, spoken and written, including literary texts. This in turn is seen as a linguistic contribution towards certain further aims, such as literary scholarship, native and foreign language teaching, educational research, sociological and anthropological studies and medical applications. The interest is focussed not on what the native speaker knows of his language but rather on what he does with it; one might perhaps say that the orientation is primarily textual and, in the widest sense, sociological.

The study of written and spoken texts for such purposes requires an analysis of at least sentence, clause and group structures and systems, with extension where possible above the rank of sentence. The analysis needs to be simple in use and in notation, variable in delicacy and easily processed for statistical studies; it needs to provide a basis for semantic statements, and to handle with the minimum complexity grammatical contrasts such as those in English expounded by intonation and rhythm; and it should idealize as little as possible, in the sense of excluding the minimum as 'deviant'. Idealization of course there is; as Putnam has said, 'I shall assume here that some degree of idealization is inevitable in linguistic work, and I shall also assume that the question of how much idealization is legitimate is one that has no general answer. . . . Anyone who writes a grammar of any natural language is . . . automatically classifying certain sentences as non-deviant, and by implication, certain others as deviant'. For our purposes it is important that as much as possible of ordinary speech should be shown to be—that is, described as—non-deviant; in this analysis spoken English is much less formless, repetitious and elliptical than it might appear in another kind of description. But there are deviant utterances, and it is important to specify in what ways they are deviant.

For a brief, and necessarily oversimplified, illustration of one feature of the sort of description that we are attempting I shall refer to the *scale of delicacy* which, besides being of theoretical interest in providing a measure of the status of a given contrast in the language, and of the degree and kind of deviation of deviant utterances, has proved of value in textual analysis because it provides a variable cut-off point for description: the analyst can go as far as he wishes for his own purpose in depth of detail and then stop. Delicacy can be illustrated with reference either to structure or to system.

Delicacy is in effect a means of having things both ways: that is, of saying that two utterances are both like and unlike each other at the same time. Any two utterance tokens, of any extent, may be alike in one of two ways: they may be occurrences of the same formal item (tokens of the same type), or they may be different formal item exponents of the same grammatical categories (tokens of different types with the same grammatical description).

Both types of likeness are properties of the description: that is, it is the linguist who decides what are occurrences of the same item and what are different items with the same grammatical description. One possible decision of course is always to aim at maximal differentiation of tokens into types: this seems to be the point of view taken by Katz and Fodor when they write 'almost every sentence uttered is uttered for the first time', since this can presumably only mean that the criteria adopted for token-to-type assignment should be such that almost every sentence uttered will be *described* as being uttered for the first time. This would no doubt reflect a desire that the description should be capable of making all distinctions that the native speaker recognizes; this does not provide criteria, though it may be used to test their adequacy. But token-to-type assignment is one point where the native speaker's intuitions tend to be most uncertain, and this uncertainty reflects the multiple nature of the type-token relation in language: two utterances may be tokens of the same orthographic type but not of the same phonological type (the same 'expression'), or vice versa, and neither determines whether or not they are tokens of the same formal type (grammatical or grammatico-lexical, according to the model).

Whatever the criteria adopted for token-to-type assignment, the question whether these items (types) are or are not assigned the same grammatical description is one to which it may be useful to be able to answer 'both yes and no'.

In speaking about one possible approach to a particular type of pattern in language, I am not implying that we handle it more effectively than other linguists working with different models, but intending to show how its treatment links up with other features of a model conceived with the specific aims we have in view. Other models will handle such patterns differently in the light of their own goals. But while accepting, and indeed applauding, the fact that linguists today are working with models of different kinds, I would at the same time underline one point of which no teacher of linguistics needs to be reminded: that there exists a vast store of knowledge which is just linguistics, and common ground to all linguists whatever model they happen to be using.

27 WILLIAM F. MACKEY
Applied Linguistics

Among the post-war remedies for the betterment of foreign-language teaching it is applied linguistics that has attracted the greatest attention. In the training of language teachers this new discipline is gradually taking the place of philology. Every year practising language teachers are hearing more and more about 'the science of applied linguistics'. In some quarters language teaching is considered to be the exclusive province of this new science. And in certain countries national agencies have been convinced that no one not trained in the techniques of applied linguistics can successfully teach a language.

What is applied linguistics? What does one apply when one applies linguistics? How does it relate to language learning? How does it concern language teaching? Of what use is it to the teacher? What is new about it? These are some of the questions which language teachers have been asking; it is the purpose of this article to supply some of the answers, without necessarily trying, as many such efforts often do, to sell the product at the same time. Let us take the above questions in the order in which they appear.

1 *What is applied linguistics?*

The term 'applied linguistics' seems to have originated in the United States in the 1940s. It was first used by persons with an obvious desire to be identified as scientists rather than as humanists; the association with 'applied science' can hardly have been accidental. Yet, although linguistics is a science, 'applied science' does not necessarily include linguistics.

The creation of applied linguistics as a discipline represents an effort to find practical applications for 'modern scientific linguistics'. While assuming that linguistics can be an applied science, it brings together such diverse activities as the making of alphabets by missionaries and the making of translations by machines. The use of the term has now become crystallized in the names of language centres, reviews, books, and articles.

W. F. Mackey: Extract from 'Applied Linguistics: its Meaning and Use', *English Language Teaching*, Vol. XX, No. 1, 1966, pp. 197–206.

2 What does one apply?

What does one apply when one applies linguistics? What is applied may be a theory of language and/or a description of one.

If it is a theory of language, what is applied depends of course on the sort of theory being used. If the theory is based on the existence of units of meaning, for example, the results will be different from what they would be if the theory ignored the existence of such units.

There are dozens of ways in which one theory may differ from another; and there are dozens of different theories of language, several of which are mutually contradictory. Some of these constitute schools of language theory, like the Saussurian School, the Psychomechanic School, the Glossematic School, the Bloomfieldian School, the Prague School, the Firthian School, and others. When we examine the many theories of different schools and individuals we note that very few indeed have ever been applied to anything. We also notice that those which have been applied are not necessarily the most applicable. On the other hand, the fact that a language theory has never been applied to language teaching does not mean that it cannot be. Some of the more ambitious and inclusive theories, which seem to be the most relevant, have in fact never been applied.

Secondly, if it is a description of a language that is being applied, it might include any or all of its phonetics, grammar, or vocabulary. And since descriptions based on the same theory often differ there are more varieties of description than there are types of theory.

Descriptions differ in their purpose, extent, and presentation. Some descriptions aim at being concise; others at being extensive. Some analyse the language by breaking it down; others by building it up. Some are made as if the language described is unknown to the linguist; others as if it is already known to the reader. Some will present the language in two levels (grammar and phonology); others in as many as fourteen. Yet the number of levels of a description is no indication of its linguistic range; a three-level description may have a wider scope than an eight-level one which excludes vocabulary, meaning, or context. Some descriptions are based on written works; others on speech. Some may cover all areas in which the language is spoken; others may be limited to a single city. Some may be compiled from the speech of a single person over a period of a few weeks; others may be based on the writings of many authors covering a few centuries.

It is obvious, therefore, that the problem of the language teacher is not only whether or not to apply linguistics, but whose linguistics to apply, and what sort.

3 How does it relate to language learning?

In order to exist, a language must have been learnt; but in order to be learnt a language does not have to have been analysed. For the process of learning a language is quite different from the process of analysing one. Persons who have never gone to school find it difficult to divide their language into such classes as the parts of speech, despite the fact that they may speak their native language with a great deal of fluency and elegance. Foreign languages have also been successfully mastered throughout the ages without benefit of analysis.

It is the production of methods of analysis that is the business of the linguist. But if the linguist claims that such and such a method is the best way to learn the language, he is speaking outside his competence. For it is not learning, but language, that is the object of linguistics. Language learning cannot therefore be the purpose of linguistics—pure or applied. Applied linguistics is not language learning.

Therefore the units used for analysing a language are not necessarily those needed for learning it. As an illustration, let us take a sample of an analysis of English made by a representative of one of the schools of linguistics which has done the most applied linguistics in language teaching. As a case in point, let us take the description of the English pronouns. The pronouns are arranged into seven sets, which include 23 units. To explain these, 34 other units (called *morphs*) are brought into the picture, although they have no further function than to explain the first 23. Rules are then given to 'convert the abstract forms into those actually found'. For example, after having learned that the abstract form for the first person plural object is *{w-i-m}, we get the form actually found, the form *us*, by applying the following rule:

1 *we:*   {w-i-y}

2 *us:*   * {w-i-m}; {-m} after {w-i-} becomes {-s}; * {w-i-} before resulting {-s} becomes {-ə-}, a portmanteau

3 *our:*   * {w-i-r}; before {-r} and {r-z}, initial consonant and vowel are transposed, giving * {i- w-}; initial * {i-} becomes {a-} before {-w-}

4 *ours:*   * {w-i-r-z} (See rules given for 3.)

If this is to be applied linguistics, it should justify the definition of philology sometimes attributed to Voltaire, 'la science où les voyelles ne comptent pour rien, et les consonnes pour peu de chose'. One can imagine what happens when two languages are contrasted on this basis.

It is true, however, that some linguists have pointed out the disparity between language learning and language description, stating that 'a linguistic description of a language is of little help in learning the language; recently published structural accounts of European languages rebut any disclaimer to this judgement'. For two descriptions of the same language can be so different that a learner may not be blamed for wondering whether the units and categories alleged to form the essential elements of the language exist only in the minds of those who have attempted to describe it.

4 *How does it concern language teaching?*

Although the linguistic descriptions of the same language are not identical, it is now widely admitted that the linguist is the competent person to write our grammars, phonetics manuals, and dictionaries. In some quarters it is assumed that the very fact he can do this makes him qualified to form language-teaching policy and prepare language-teaching texts. In the use of applied linguistics in language teaching, it has been further assumed that if one is able to make a thorough description of the forms of a language, one is by that very fact able to teach it.

These assumptions are obviously ill-founded, for there have been outstanding language teachers with no knowledge of linguistics. And it has been demonstrated that 'the methods of the linguistic scientist *as a teacher* are not necessarily the most effective'. This can be explained by the different preoccupations of the two disciplines. Much of the present state of applied linguistics in language teaching is due to the fact that some linguists have been more interested in finding an application for their science than in solving the problems of language teaching. Some of the unhappy results have been due to a desire to apply to language teaching a one-sided technique of formal description with no universal validity, even in the field of linguistic analysis.

Much is made of the ability of the linguist to predict mistakes by comparing the native language of the learner with the language he is being taught. This differential description is sometimes confusingly called 'contrastive linguistics', a term which also means the analysis of a single language based essentially on the contrast of its units one with the other. What is the use of predicting mistakes already heard? Since anyone who has taught a language can predict from experience the sort of mistakes his students are likely to make *a posteriori*, is he any the wiser for the *a priori* and less reliable prediction which the linguist makes on the basis of a differential analysis?

It has been stated as a principle of 'applied linguistics' that all the mistakes of the language learner are due to the make-up of his native language. This is demonstrably false. Many mistakes actually made have no parallel in the native language; they are simply extensions of the foreign language patterns into areas in which they do not apply, e.g. *I said him so* on the analogy of *I told him so*. Other mistakes are due to a confusion of new material with parts of the language not deeply enough ingrained; this inhibition is a matter of order and rate of intake. Still other mistakes are due to the habit, which language learners soon acquire, of avoiding the similarities with their native language. This may result in either blind guessing or the systematic avoidance of native patterns, even though these exist in the foreign language, e.g. words like *attack* (a cognate of the French *attaque*) are stressed on the first syllable by French learners of English despite the fact that both French and English versions have the stress on the final syllable. Texts for language teaching based only on the differences between the two languages cannot take these important tendencies into account.

Even for the many mistakes due directly to interference from the native language the practising teacher is in a better position than the descriptive linguist. For although a differential description, of English and French for example, may indeed point out the fact that a French learner of English may have difficulty in pronouncing the interdental sounds of *thin* and *then* because of their absence from the French phoneme inventory, it cannot predict, as can an experienced teacher, which way a given learner or group of learners will handle the difficulty. In fact, different learners with the same native language do make different mistakes; the above interdental sounds, for example, are rendered sometimes as /s, z/, sometimes as /t, d/. But this information is supplied, not by an *a priori* comparison of English and French, but by the observations of language teachers.

Applications of differential descriptions do not produce the same type of teaching. For some teachers will start drilling the differences because they are difficult, while others will start using the similarities because they are easy (e.g. the 'cognate method').

Most of the available differential descriptions are so superficial and incomplete as to be misleading. This is because they are at best based on a unit-by-unit and structure-by-structure comparison of two languages. They fail to show all the units of the first language which are equivalent to structures in the second, and the structures in the first which are equivalent to units in the second. They also ignore the units and structures of one level that are equivalent to structures and units of another. And even with this, they are still dealing only with the make-up of the languages, not with the multiple differences in contextual usage, with the fact that in such and such circumstance a learner must say one thing in his native language but something entirely different in the foreign language. Since we do not have such complete differential descriptions of any two languages—even of the most widely known—we are likely to get better results by collecting and classifying the mistakes which the learners make than by trying to predict those we should expect him to make.

5 Of what use is it to the teacher?

It is the business of the language teacher to know the foreign language, to know how to teach it and to know something about it. It is in relation to this latter need that linguistics might be expected to be useful. But the contents of most courses in linguistics for language teachers are seldom concerned with the analysis of the material which the teacher will have to teach; they are of little direct help in the preparation of specific language lessons. At best, they are background courses in the description of the language to be taught. In practice, many such courses are devoted to proving to the language teacher that most of the grammar rules he has been taught are false because they have not been arrived at by 'scientific' methods of analysis. In some courses, the very word 'grammar' is taboo; one refers not to the 'grammar of the English language' but rather to the 'structure of the English language'. Teachers are asked to discard familiar and widely accepted terms which have a long tradition of usage, in favour of a new jargon representing one of several brands of language analysis. And after having mastered the technicalities of one brand of linguistics the language teacher encounters other brands with conflicting theories and contradictory methods of analysis. Should he then keep on believing in one without trying to understand the others? Or should he study all of them?

What is the language teacher to do when faced with the multiplicity of approaches to the analysis of a language and the different trends in descriptive linguistics? What should be his attitude when asked to give up his grammars on the grounds that they are unscientific—that they give recipes rather than formulas?

Above all, the language teacher must be interested in results; and tested recipes are often better than untested formulas. Until more complete and definitive analyses are available, language teaching will have to rely for its description of a language on those abundant and serviceable grammars of the past. For a language teacher, the completeness of a grammar is more relevant than its scientific consistency; clarity is more important than conciseness; examples more useful than definitions. If the language teacher is to wait until more scientific grammars are produced he puts himself in the position of the tanner of hides who stops tanning until the chemists have found the chemical formula describing exactly what is done. The formula, once discovered, might eventually improve the tanning operation; but until it is formulated and tested and proven more effective, the only sensible thing to do is to continue tanning hides in a way that has given the best results.

The fact is that most of the new 'linguistically approved' grammars being applied to language teaching are more difficult to use and far less complete than are the older works. Some are no more than undigested research essays on the making of a grammar. Others represent a sort of do-it-yourself grammar-making kit allegedly designed to 'crack the code' of any language in the world.

Although the ability to analyse a language may not be the most important qualification of a language teacher, some training in practical linguistics can enable him to establish with more precision than he otherwise might what is the same and what is different in the languages with which he has to deal. It can also help him understand, evaluate, and perhaps use some of the descriptions of the language he is teaching. And if the training is neither too one-sided nor doctrinaire it may prevent him from becoming the prisoner of a single school of thought and encourage him to surmount the great terminological barriers which have prevented any mutual understanding in linguistics.

Ideally, such training could put the teacher in a position to analyse each linguistic contribution and its application to language teaching, from the small details of analysis to the hidden theoretical assumptions on which the analysis is based. Such training would make it unnecessary for the language teacher to swallow a man's philosophy along with his linguistics. For the main attraction of some analyses is their consistency with certain philosophical beliefs. Is it then any advantage to deny the beliefs and admit the consistency, for consistency's sake? Or is it better to seek an analysis which is philosophically more palatable but perhaps less consistent?

Finally, the proper sort of training could enable the teacher to distinguish between the scientific status of linguistics and the scientific pretensions of linguists. For some linguists seem to be so eager to appear 'scientific' that they state or restate the most banal facts about a language in a pseudo-scientific notation and a collection of technical terms borrowed indifferently from several disciplines and heavy with scientific associations. Old ideas about language do not become better when couched in an unfamiliar jargon. This leads us to our final question.

6 What is new about it?

As far as language-teaching is concerned, there are very few ideas proposed as applied linguistics which were not familiar to teachers at one time or another. What, for example, is essentially different in practice between the 'phonemic transcription' proposed today and the 'broad transcription' used by language teachers in the past century?

Throughout the history of formal language teaching there has always been some sort of applied linguistics, as it is known today. For language teachers have always tended to apply language analysis to the teaching of a language; in fact, some of the first descriptions of a language were made for the purpose of teaching it. Yet the sorts of descriptions actually produced have varied with the needs and contingencies of the time. And some of the oldest are still some of the best. Such ancient classics as the grammars of Pānini, Dionysius, Priscian, and Donatus are not outclassed by those of today. Yet the blind application of the categories of these grammars to the description of modern European and even to non-European languages was obviously so unsuitable as to create a series of reactions which resulted in the attitude of 'scientific' superiority which afflicts contemporary linguistics.

One is the reaction against the linguistic analysis of exotic languages made in the past century—a type of analysis which superimposed the structure of European languages on the facts of the native language being described. As a reaction against this, techniques of description were developed by Boas, Sapir, and especially, by Bloomfield and his associates. These techniques were apparently so successful that they were later applied to languages, like English, with a long tradition of linguistic analysis. This in turn was a reaction against the current English school grammars which still propagated the traditional definitions of the eighteenth century. But in the process the best linguistic traditions were ignored, including the works of such linguists as Sweet and Jespersen, so that the language might be handled as if the person describing its elements were unable to understand them. And the movement, which started as an effort to prevent the analysis of exotic languages as if they were English, found itself analysing English as if it were an exotic language.

Against this trend, other reactions are beginning to take shape. These are appearing as a re-formulation of the traditional approach to grammar, a compromise with the older grammatical categories, a return to the study of ancient grammatical theory. It is now being admitted that the old universal grammatical theories were more in need of revision than of repudiation. And some linguists are beginning to consider the descriptions of 'modern scientific linguistics' as nothing more than another arrangement of the grammatical data, according to a less traditional outline, but nevertheless according to a completely arbitrary set of labels which has become fossilized within its own short linguistic tradition.

If linguistics has been applied to the language part of 'language learning', psychology has been applied to the learning part of it. The history of the application of the principles of psychology to the learning of languages is analogous to that of the applications of linguistic analysis. So is the situation today. There are almost as many different theories of learning as there are theories of language. Most of them are still based on the observations of animal learning. Although there is a promising branch of psychology devoted to verbal learning and verbal behaviour, it is still involved in solving problems related to the learning of isolated items.

In one form or another, both language analysis and psychology have always been applied to the teaching of foreign languages. In fact, the history of language teaching could be represented as a cyclic shift in prominence from the one to the other, a swing from the strict application of principles of language analysis to the single-minded insistence on principles of psychology. The history zigzags, with many minor oscillations in between, from the mediaeval grammarians to Comenius, from Plötz to Gouin. And today's interest in applied linguistics represents another swing toward the primacy of language analysis in language teaching.

Contemporary claims that applied linguistics can solve all the problems of language teaching are as unfounded as the claims that applied psychology can solve them. For the problems of language teaching are central neither to psychology nor linguistics. Neither science is equipped to solve the problems of language teaching.

It is likely that language teaching will continue to be a child of fashion in linguistics and psychology until the time it becomes an autonomous discipline which uses these related sciences instead of being used by them. To become autonomous it will, like any science, have to weave its own net, so as to fish out from the oceans of human experience and natural phenomena only the elements it needs, and, ignoring the rest, be able to say with the ichthyologist of Sir Arthur Eddington, 'What my net can't catch isn't fish'.

28 The Validity and Utility of Linguistic Descriptions

PETER S. ROSENBAUM

The growing enthusiasm on the part of many teachers of English for giving careful attention to linguistic matters is noteworthy for several reasons. It speaks well for the teacher since it suggests the birth of a scholarly concern for developments in the field of language study and a professional attitude toward linguistic insights which have potential educational value. Furthermore, this enthusiasm vindicates the many linguists who have held that linguistic science could be of importance in the teaching of English. But discussions of the relevance of linguistics to the teaching of English have been in progress for a considerable time now, and even the most cursory glance at the literature indicates a disappointing lack of progress. Few familiar with this debate and its meagre results will disagree that one of the problems has been a continuing inability to answer satisfactorily the obviously central question, namely, 'which linguistic description?'

The last thirty years has seen the development of a variety of descriptions of the structure of English. Among the more frequently mentioned proposals are the conceptions of Fries; the immediate constituent approach of Bloch, Wells, and Hockett; the phonological syntax of Trager and Smith, and Hill; Harris' morpheme to utterance procedures; and the two distinct transformational notions of Harris on the one hand and Chomsky on the other. The question of which, if any, of these linguistic descriptions might justifiably be employed in the classroom is, of course, many-sided. But one of the more frequently alluded to criteria is entirely linguistic in nature and is bound up in a general concern for the validity or correctness of linguistic descriptions. The historical emphasis on validity or correctness seems entirely appropriate even though it does no homage to the popular preoccupation with behavioural goals and outcomes as the basis for the evaluation of curricula. The issue

P. S. Rosenbaum: Extract from 'On the Role of Linguistics in the Teaching of English', *Harvard Educational Review* 35, 1965. Reprinted in *Modern Studies in English*, ed. D. A. Reibel and S. A. Shane, Prentice-Hall, 1969, pp. 467–76.

is not whether the information contained in a given linguistic description can be taught and learned successfully, for surely there is no description which is so difficult that it cannot be taught and learned in some form, but precisely one of the status of the information itself. One might hope to diminish the centrality of the content, thereby making it unnecessary, perhaps, to choose among the various linguistic descriptions, by demonstrating the utility of one or the other description in the teaching of literate skills, e.g. composition. But this hope should not be taken too seriously since the most recent account of empirical research in this area indicates the inconclusiveness of all such demonstrations:

Reviews of educational research, however, have continually emphasized that instruction in grammar has little effect upon the written language skills of pupils. The interpretation and curricular applications of this general conclusion have ranged from the view that grammar and usage should not be taught in isolation from written composition to the position that formal grammar merits little or no place in the language arts curriculum.*

Thus, the validity of proposed linguistic descriptions remains the most pertinent consideration.

The major approaches to syntactic description can be collapsed under two rubrics. The first, which is known popularly as the *structural-descriptive* approach to linguistic analysis includes the work of Fries, Bloch, Wells, Hockett, Trager, Smith, Hill, and others. The second, the *transformational* version of generative grammar, is represented, for example, by the work of Chomsky, Halle, Lees, Klima, Matthews, and Postal. If the question of the validity of linguistic descriptions is to be spoken to in any serious way, it is necessary to consider two aspects of evaluation. The first pertains to the evaluation of a particular description within a given theoretical framework. For instance, which of two transformational descriptions of the relative clause structure in English is better? The second aspect of evaluation deals with the comparison of various forms of linguistic description. Is it possible, for example, to compare the structural approach to linguistic inquiry with the transformational approach in any meaningful way? In view of the well-documented interest in the validity of linguistic descriptions on the part of those involved in the educational implementation of these descriptions, it may be fruitful to examine the major approaches to linguistic inquiry in terms of evaluation in somewhat greater detail.

Underlying the structural view of language is a set of assumptions about the goals of behavioural studies and scientific inquiry which limit the range of relevant phenomena to a corpus of observed utterances. This limitation suggests a curious contradiction since, quite invariably,

* H. C. Meckel: 'Research on Teaching Composition and Literature' in N. L. Gage (ed.) *Handbook of Research on Teaching*, Chicago, 1963, p. 974.

representatives of the structural tradition speak of language as a set of behavioural patterns common to members of a given community involving a set of verbal interchanges between two or more people. There is no non-arbitrary upper bound on the number of acceptable utterances which could comprise the speech behaviour of a given community. Thus the linguists of the structural school seem, at least implicitly, to be thinking of language as a potentially infinite set of utterances. But this position is completely contradicted by the properties of a structural linguistic description. All structural analysis is ultimately based upon observable data, i.e. data recorded by simple listening or by various instruments such as oscillographs, sound-spectrographs, and so on. If this methodo-logical requirement is taken literally, then the result of a structural analysis, the linguistic description of a language, is actually a description of only a finite corpus of events. There is clearly an equivocation on the term 'language' here which leads to two equally damaging conclusions. If an arbitrary natural language is taken to consist of an infinite set of sentences, then the results of a structural investigation do not constitute a description of language at all, but of something else. On the other hand, should a language be construed as nothing more than the corpus stored in a set of tape recordings, then the task of saying anything of scientific interest about the psychological and linguistic properties of the endless repertoire of sentences which not only define the language of a speech community but which are the personal property of every normal member of this community belongs to a branch of science other than linguistics.

The extreme preoccupation with observable data in linguistic analysis probably stems from Leonard Bloomfield's particular version of scientific inquiry, a version which most structural linguists have accepted at face value. In Bloomfield's view, science dealt exclusively with accessible events and the task of scientists was the induction of general laws from these events. Thus, the central object of investigation in a linguistic science as conceived by Bloomfield was necessarily actual speech. For Bloomfield, the only information of scientific interest was that provided by physical phonetics and the context in which phonetic data were observed. This view is implicit in all structural work and one never finds a popularization of structural linguistics which does not give prominence to assertions about the centrality of speech. For our purposes, the effects of Bloomfield's views on the goals of linguistic inquiry are more important than the causes. By restricting the domain of linguistic investigation to phonetic and contextual data Bloomfield excluded a vast range of perhaps even more accessible data as linguistically and scienti-fically useless; this data being the extraordinarily rich body of knowledge which a human speaker has about his language. We will return to this neglected aspect of linguistic information later.

The goal of linguistic science, to determine inductively the laws governing the behaviour of observable linguistic data, was unfortunately one step removed from the problem immediately confronting those linguists who were anxious to adopt the Bloomfieldian point of view. The induction of general laws from a body of data presupposes a prior classification of this data. For structural linguistic inquiry, this meant that a requirement for further research was the precise specification of the relevant facts. It was necessary to decide on the linguistic importance of the various aspects of the continuous flow of sound coming from the recording device or from the speaker directly. Thus, in a certain sense, the task before the structural linguist was 'pre-scientific': to provide materials upon which a science of language could operate productively. Central to the search for the facts of language was also a concern for the general efficiency with which these facts could be stated. The overall problem, therefore, consisted in providing a methodology which would yield the facts of language in terms of a consistent and optimally efficient classificational scheme.

The structural methodology for discovering the facts of language is now quite well known. In its most general formulation, the method involves a set of putative discovery procedures which are supposed to isolate automatically a set of linguistic units in a hierarchical arrangement and to present an inventory of the speech data which are found to represent these units. Quoting from what is probably the most widely known structural analysis of English:

> The presentation of the structure of a language should begin, in theory, with a complete statement of the pertinent linguistic data. This should be followed by an account of the observed phonetic behaviour, and then should come the analysis of the phonetic behavior into the phonemic structure, completing the phonology. The next step is to present the recurring entities—composed of one or more phonemes—that constitute the morpheme list, and go on to their analysis into the morphemic structure. In that process the division into morphology and syntax is made. After the syntax, one may go on from the microlinguistic (linguistics proper —phonology and morphemics) to metalinguistic analyses.*

Structural linguists have been more successful in proposing and employing discovery procedures which fairly effectively produce an analysis and classification of sound sequences than they have in determining the measure or measures to be used in evaluating the adequacy of these classifications in terms of efficiency. An important issue is involved in the failure of the structural linguists to come to grips with the problem of evaluation. The question of which measure of efficiency will most appropriately evaluate alternative structural descriptions has no obvious answer. How do we know what the right measure is? Is efficiency to be

---

* Trager and Smith, *An Outline of English Structure*, Norman, Oklahoma, 1951, p. 8.

defined in terms of the number of discrete symbols or entities in a description? Is it going to have anything to do with the type of symbols which the description utilizes? These questions cannot be answered without proposing a set of conditions which the measure of efficiency must meet. Suppose I am working for a grocer and he tells me to unpack a crate of oranges and to construct the most efficient display of oranges in the front window. Unless the grocer tells me the conditions that the optimally efficient arrangement must meet, my task is an impossible one. Similarly, unless a set of conditions on the measure of efficiency for linguistic descriptions is established, there is no reason to choose one measure of efficiency over another. Such conditions cannot be an aspect of the subject matter in a science of language, as conceived by Bloomfield, since they would constitute a level of abstraction which has no observable basis whatever. If, on the other hand, such conditions are taken to be theoretical constructs, laws governing the form that a linguistic description may take, then the whole business becomes circular since such laws can be inferred only from a classified set of data in the first place. Since there is no non-arbitrary measure of efficiency which can be employed in the evaluation of alternative structural descriptions of a set of observed data, it is impossible to compare and rank these descriptions.

Furthermore, the taxonomic framework provides no basis for choosing between structural and nonstructural descriptions. The fundamental problem here is that a structural linguistic description is a taxonomic classification. No such classification, whether it be of books in the library, fish in the sea, or sounds of speech, can be right or wrong, valid or invalid, true or false. Such a classification is inevitably nothing more than an arrangement of the data which makes no claims whatever about the nature of the data. A linguistic theory which is capable of evaluating the form of a linguistic description must presuppose an explicit statement of the facts which any adequate description must represent and characterize. Given such a statement it is not only possible to develop a theory which will decide on the adequacy of linguistic descriptions in terms of their ability to characterize the facts; it is absolutely necessary to develop such a theory. Without it, there is no possibility of determining the success of any type of linguistic description claiming to account for these facts.

The most readily accessible body of facts about language is the information which is available to any speaker concerning his native language. There are several aspects of a speaker's linguistic competence on which considerable consensus is found in the literature. A speaker can understand sentences which he has never heard before. Similarly, he can produce new sentences on the appropriate occasion. Second, a speaker knows implicitly that certain sentences in his language are ambiguous while others are not. Still other sentences are synonymous.

Third, he is capable of detecting differences in the relations which words have to one another in sentences even though these relations are not explicitly specified in the phonetic representations of sentences. Many other similar abilities could be cited.

Bloomfield and his followers have rejected such linguistic data with the assertion that introspective evidence involves a spurious mentalism which fails on the grounds of nonobjectivity. On this view, one's intuitions about language exist only in the private domain, in one's mind, and are thus not fit materials for a science of language. Essentially, the argument is that the mind is inaccessible to scientific investigation because the attributes of the mind, such as linguistic intuition, are not subject to objective study. Intuitions are not physical events which can be monitored and recorded. Thus the study of linguistic data dealing with the speaker's knowledge of his language necessarily belongs to some field other than linguistic science. This view has been severely criticized in the recent linguistic and philosophical literature and little new can be added to the discussion. If it is the case that any significant linguistic theory must provide evaluation criteria for linguistic description, then the consistency of the introspective data brought forth in support of such a theory is clearly a major consideration. The consistency of introspective evidence is not, however, nonempirical, i.e. incapable of being verified. Suppose one asks, for instance, how to test the judgement that the implicit subject of the complement verb *leave* in the sentence "*The boy promised his mother to leave the party early* is the same as the explicit subject of the whole sentence, *the boy*, and that the implicit subject of the same verb in the sentence *The boy told his mother to leave the party early* is the same as the object of the verb *tell*, i.e. *his mother*. This is not only an empirical question, but one with an obvious answer. This supposedly nonobjective fact will be attested to by every normal native speaker of English who understands the question. Objectivity, therefore, is not a property which a theory of the speaker's linguistic knowledge necessarily lacks and it is probably pointless to devote further consideration to such objections.

Adopting the view that an adequate linguistic description must account for the speaker's linguistic capacities, we can think of a linguistic theory as being, at least in part, a set of constraints on the form of any description which can attain this end. The constraints specify, in other words, the way in which the goals of the linguistic inquiry can be attained. The linguistic theory acquires, therefore, the capacity to evaluate possible linguistic descriptions in terms of their ability to characterize the speaker's knowledge of his language. Such a theory is said to explain the speaker's knowledge because the form of the linguistic description which most adequately accounts for the facts is a logical consequence of the constraints comprising the linguistic theory.

In this view of linguistic inquiry, the object of research is two-fold: first, to determine precisely the constraints, or laws if you will, which govern the form of the constructs employed in the linguistic descriptions which best characterize the varied instances of human linguistic ability; second, to determine the particular instances of the descriptive constructs within an arbitrary language. The latter constitutes the actual construction of a linguistic description. Recent work on the transformational version of generative linguistics represents the first modern attempt to develop a linguistic theory and a descriptive apparatus which have as a goal the explanation of the speaker's linguistic knowledge. The literature contains a substantial amount of material on both aspects of linguistic inquiry and no reiteration is called for here. The virtue of a transformation approach to linguistic research from the standpoint of the issue of validity is that if a particular version of linguistic description fails to satisfy the constraints imposed by the linguistic theory, then it can be said with justification that the description is wrong. Similarly, if the constraints on the form of the linguistic description do not result in a set of descriptive constructs which satisfactorily account for the facts, then this version of the theory is wrong. Measures for determining the validity of a particular description of a given language as well as a general form of linguistic description are consequently provided.

The discussion of evaluation procedures for contemporary versions of linguistic research provides one fruitful avenue for confronting the issue of the validity of linguistic descriptions. The basic result of this discussion is the finding that the structural approach to linguistic inquiry fails to provide a principled basis for choosing among particular linguistic descriptions and forms of linguistic description. (The fact that taxonomic linguistic descriptions can be evaluated in terms of internal consistency is irrelevant since any linguistic description can be judged in this way.) It would not seem unreasonable, therefore, to exclude structural linguistics from further consideration and to pass over to the deeper and ultimately more important question concerning the pedagogical implementation of a verifiable linguistic theory and description of the structure of English. It is natural to inquire, at this point, into the purely linguistic bases for a programme designed to incorporate the valid results of linguistic research into the curriculum. Such an inquiry may prove of little value, however, since certain considerations deriving from what is already known about the nature of the constructs employed in a transformational description of language indicate that the constructs themselves do not and cannot automatically provide any new educational insights. Rather, the ultimate value of valid linguistic descriptions in the teaching of English seems to depend entirely on the ingenuity and imagination of linguists, teachers, and educators competent in both areas.

A transformational grammar characterizing linguistic competence is a finite specification of the infinite set of pairs of phonetic signals and semantic interpretations comprising the sentences in a natural language. This specification is abstract in the sense that it is not detectable on the basis of the physical data alone. It must be inferred from the knowledge which people have about sentences in their language. The specification is, in effect, an abstract representation of this knowledge offered in terms of hypothetical syntactic structures upon which semantic interpretations and phonological realizations are defined. The necessity of positing such abstract sentence structures and the form that these structures must have is a topic to which much attention has been devoted. The formal apparatus employed in the explanation of the speaker's ability to deal with the infinite set of sentences in his language consists of a set of ordered rules which recursively enumerate the sentences of this language. The structures underlying sentences, often represented by tree diagrams, are not objects of substance having material existence in the real world; rather they merely constitute a record of the application of a particular set of rules.

The rules in a transformational grammar are quite different from the rules countenanced by prescriptive linguistic descriptions and from the instructions for sentence building found in so many textbooks. The rules postulated in the syntactic component of a transformational grammar are either those which specify a set of abstract underlying structures, upon which a semantic interpretation for the sentence is based, or those which derive *superficial*, alternatively *surface*, structures, which receive a phonetic interpretation, as a function of the underlying structure. These claims about the nature of the rules employed in an adequate description of syntax suggest that recent educational popularizations of transformational grammar have grossly misunderstood the results of transformational research. To quote from one textbook published very recently,

This chapter is a study of *transformational* grammar. *Transform* means 'to change'; thus, you will see how basic sentences are changed, or transformed, to produce other sentences that are interesting and varied.*

Ongoing work in transformational grammar shows that it is incorrect to think of two sentences as being related by a transformational rule or set of rules which somehow convert one sentence into another. Rather, when various considerations force the conclusion that two or more sentences are syntactically related, this relation is reflected in those aspects of underlying structure which both sentences share. Thus the burden of representing a common source for two or more sentences falls not on the transformational rules of the grammar which generate surface structures, but on the rules which generate underlying structures.

* Mellie John and Paulene M. Yates, *Building Better English*, 4th ed., New York, 1965, p. 463.

The abstract constructs offered in a transformational description are designed solely for purposes of description and explanation. Neither the transformational theory nor the transformational description of the syntax of English contains any implicit pedagogical recommendation. From neither does it follow that a transformational description of English should be taught in the classroom. From neither does it follow that instruction in transformational grammar will improve performance in the literate skills. With respect to the latter assertion, consider an analogy from physical education, in particular the pedagogy of the forward pass. Any instance of the physical event identified as a forward pass has certain mechanical properties which are characterized by the Newtonian theory of mechanics. The descriptive apparatus of this theory, consisting of such constructs as mass, acceleration, velocity, time, distance, and so forth, is a consequence of the theoretical constraints imposed upon a description seeking to account for the mechanics of physical events. To teach a potential quarterback the mechanics of the forward pass is to teach him how this type of event works. It is not to teach him how to make it work. The Newtonian theory itself gives us no reason to believe that instruction in the mechanics of the forward pass will affect the quarterback's becoming a good passer one way or the other. Similarly, to study and practice the constructs of a transformational grammar may result in an understanding of how the student's language works, but not necessarily in an understanding of how to make it work.

But the mere fact that the answers to various educational problems do not spring forth full blown from the linguistic research on transformational grammars does not imply that the results of this research will fail to provide a new and valuable dimension in which to consider traditional problems in the teaching of English. This fact simply asserts that a linguistic description does not enumerate educational benefits. It remains not with the linguistic theory or description, but with the informed educator, whether he is a teacher, linguist, or specialist informed in both areas, to determine the applicability of valid linguistic results to the teaching of English.

29 SOL SAPORTA
Scientific Grammars and Pedagogical Grammars

A central question in the application of linguistics to the teaching of
foreign languages involves the conversion of a scientific grammar into a
pedagogical grammar. What form the pedagogical grammar takes,
whether drills or rules or some combination of the two, is presumably
determined by some assumptions about the nature of learning in general,
that is, by principles which are not primarily linguistic. On the other
hand, the content of the grammar, that is, a specification of what it is
that is to be learned, is narrowly linguistic.

Now, in principle, the strategy for improving pedagogical grammars
might involve starting from either direction. One could take a pedagogical
grammar which is known to be only partially adequate and, given a
comprehensive learning theory, perform whatever operations of segmentation, recombination, and reordering that might be necessary to effect
maximally efficient learning of essentially the same material. Or one could
take the same partially adequate grammar and refine the linguistic description of the relevant data, leading, it would be hoped, to a closer approximation of the desired terminal behaviour. Thus, a textbook writer who
decides that examples should precede rather than follow statement of
the rule is following the first strategy, based in this case on the assumed
superiority of 'inductive' learning; but a textbook writer who treats *he
is easy to please* as representing a different construction from *he is eager
to please* is providing a description which more accurately reflects the
data and is therefore following the second strategy. Obviously, the two
are not mutually exclusive.

Strangely enough, the impact of the descriptive linguistics of the forties
and fifties on language teaching was primarily on the form and only
incidentally on the content of pedagogical grammars. I think it is not
unfair to say that with the possible exception of such features as stress
and intonation—perhaps phonology in general—linguists by and large

Sol Saporta: Extract from 'Applied Linguistics and Generative Grammar' in A.
Valdman (ed.) *Trends in Language Teaching*, McGraw-Hill, New York, 1966, pp. 81–91.

had little to say about the nature of the major languages that were being taught and somewhat more to say about how they were to be taught; with authentic models, initially via speech and subsequently via writing, through repetition, memorization, and manipulation of illustrative sentences, etc. In short, the influence of linguists was more on the goals and methods of language instruction than on the elucidation of the pertinent linguistic facts. Unfortunately, however, in keeping with the narrowly behaviouristic tenor of the times, the learning theory which has served as the basis for the pronouncements about method has been the most inflexible form of stimulus-reponse formulation, which has suggested to language teachers that the probability of acquiring the unconscious control of a set of grammatical rules is merely a function of the frequency and reinforcement associated with sentences illustrating the rules.

Recent studies in generative grammar have had two consequences of some relevance in this connexion. First, they have made explicit the kind of capacities a language learner must have if he is even to approximate the competence of a native speaker, capacities such as the ability to distinguish grammatical from ungrammatical sentences and to produce and comprehend an infinite number of the former, the ability to identify syntactically ambiguous sentences and more generally the interrelation of sentences, etc. Second, although a careful examination of these capacities does not necessarily provide an answer as to how they are acquired, it makes it clear that there are certain ways in which they are unlikely to be acquired. Specifically, it cannot be the case that learning a language merely involves successively closer approximations to the linguistic performance of some model, since this latter performance includes slips, mistakes, false starts, and a variety of nongrammatical behaviour, which the competent speaker is able to identify as such, and, more important, the corpus to which the learner is exposed is nothing more than some small sample of the linguistic universe of grammatical sentences which ultimately characterize his competence.

One distinction in the aims of a pedagogical grammar and a scientific grammar must be made clear. A scientific grammar enumerates the grammatical sentences of a language and provides each with a structural description and a semantic interpretation. The pedagogical grammar ideally attempts to develop the native speaker's ability to recognize and produce sentences. That is, a speaker can accept an arbitrarily selected sequence of elements in his vocabulary, determine whether or not it is a sentence in his language, and, if so, assign to it its correct structural description and semantic interpretation. It is difficult even to formulate the analogous problem of speech production; yet clearly the speaker's capacities include the ability to integrate situationally appropriate verbalizations. An enumeration of the grammatical sentences, therefore, is considerably short of a sentence recognizer, for example, and it is fair to say that we are far from understanding the latter operation.

In this connexion, the traditional translation grammar provided an explicit formulation of the relevant pedagogical aim by assuming that the semantic interpretation could be precisely specified by a sentence in the learner's native language. The recent tendency to distinguish translation from the skills a native speaker controls has been a healthy one, but the vague suggestion that the meaning of sentences is somehow derivable from observation of the situations in which they occur is quixotic and cannot be seriously considered as an alternative method for systematically providing the relevant semantic information. Indeed, such a proposal in effect precludes the possibility of understanding new utterances at all and hence fails by definition. One cannot help but conclude that the speaker's ability to provide a semantic interpretation for a novel sentence must somehow be related to his knowledge of the meaning of the constituent elements. This is not to imply that the meaning of sentences is derivable by a simple 'additive' process, but the implication that it is not derivable at all is an extreme case of confusing baby and bath water. The problem may be viewed as one of specifying the metalanguage in which the semantic information is to be framed. The traditional language teacher chose the most obvious candidate for such a metalanguage, namely, the speaker's native language. The disadvantages are obvious, but little is gained by legislating the problem out of existence.

We find, then, that the traditional grammarians more closely approached the aims of language teaching by attempting to match a speaker's ability to understand and produce arbitrarily selected novel sentences. Their pedagogical failure was in the assumption that such abilities could be taught by the conscious application of the relevant abstract formulations. Applied linguists have noticed the irrelevance and, at times, the interference of verbalizing such formulations, and some have incorrectly assumed that the appropriate abilities could be achieved solely by judicious performance of carefully selected and ordered examples. Others have been willing to modify the latter procedure to include formulations of some unspecified sort of some syntactic and semantic information. They have, however, failed to make explicit the form, content, and alleged pedagogical function of such formulations, and until they do, the corresponding claims are difficult to evaluate.

Before examining the more concrete proposals which might be made regarding second language learning as a result of recent studies in transformational grammar, it may be appropriate to question the validity of some of the suggestions which linguists in general have made. My impression about these claims is that linguists by and large have generated more heat than light or at least have promised more than they have delivered.

The basis of all language teaching which pays even the most superficial lip service to linguistics is the primacy of speech over writing. This linguistic fact has been utilized in two ways. Some have converted it into an educational goal, claiming that if one is obliged to reduce one's aims, then concentration on speaking is more fruitful than concentration on reading. Others, unwilling seriously to alter their aims, nevertheless maintain that listening and speaking should be taught first, reading and writing next. The arguments which have been proposed for this position are essentially the following: (1) It reflects the way children learn their native language. (2) Writing is only an imperfect representation of speech; the former includes all the relevant distinctions, such as stress and intonation in English, whereas these are only unsystematically represented in writing. (3) The transfer in learning from the spoken to the written form is greater than the reverse.

The first of these arguments is largely irrelevant. It merely demonstrates that speaking before writing is the necessary order in first language learning, not that it is the only order nor even the more efficient in second language learning. Parenthetically, it may be instructive to re-examine in this connexion the procedure by which a child acquires his native language; the argument that one might facilitate second language acquisition by reproducing in part the first language situation might backfire if, as seems reasonable, a native language cannot, in a sense, be taught at all. Evidence such as the fact that children exposed to rather different samples of a given language develop very similar linguistic capacities suggests that children are not taught their language but that rather one could not prevent a normal child from acquiring the language of his environment. What makes second language learning a problem is the fact that whatever ability, presumably innate, that the child has which permits him to perform this feat is apparently lost as he matures.

The second argument given above for teaching speaking before writing is partly an oversimplification. Writing systems are not always less explicit in marking relevant information; occasionally they include information even when it is absent in the acoustic signal. Let us consider, for example, the capitalization of German nouns or the use and position of grammatical markings like the apostrophe in *boys*, *boy's*, and *boys'*. More important, however, whatever relevance the second argument has is largely as a basis for the third; that is, it is assumed that if one form of the language makes a distinction which the other does not, it is more efficient to start with the more differentiated and proceed to the less differentiated rather than the reverse.

But when phrased in this way, a number of characteristics of the written form of a language like English emerge. Given the variety of morphophonemic alternations which can be provided by general rule, it seems quite appropriate to have different representations for the final phonological segments of *sum* and *condemn* in view of the corresponding nouns *summation* and *condemnation*. Similarly, there is nothing the matter with the orthography of forms like *electric*, *electricity*, or *democrat*, *democratic*, *democracy* since they enable the derivation of the correct pronunciation by general rules. On the other hand, the derivation of the orthographic respresentation of the unstressed vowels would be a task of some magnitude. Analogously the oft-cited French adjectives like *petit* and *gris* and German forms like *rund* and *bunt* maintain morphophonemic distinctions not present in the spoken form except, of course, in the related forms *petite*, *grise* and *runde*, *bunte*.

In any case, no matter how reasonable the assumption may be about speaking facilitating writing more than the reverse, the evidence seems to be largely anecdotal, coming from generations of language students who found little transferability from writing to speech. The attempts to demonstrate the validity of such an assumption have been inconclusive. But quite apart from the validity of the position, it is not clear that it qualifies as a narrowly linguistic principle. In making such claims, linguists have argued as much as educators or psychologists as they have as linguists.

A second concern in applying linguistic notions to language teaching is the presentation and function of grammatical rules. What is unfortunately referred to by some as 'the linguistic method' is usually characterized by basic conversational sentences for memorization, pattern-practice exercises, and grammar by induction. It is not obvious how any of these notions follow directly from any adequate theory of linguistic structure or, for that matter, from any but the most superficial learning theory. It seems clear that having somehow stored a very large number of sentences cannot be equated with having learned a language. It may be argued that no language teacher, no matter how linguistically unsophisticated, suggests that such an equation is valid. One cannot help but conclude, however, that certain methods and, indeed, precisely those methods most closely associated with linguistics do demand a considerable amount of such storage, in spite of the fact that a method which requires maximization of storage is self-defeating. This, then, is the incongruity in the alleged role of memorization as a technique for learning. The student who makes the most progress by adopting rote memory as a strategy will presumably be the most reluctant to abandon it, and failure to abandon it means failure to learn a language. One is led then to the paradox of second language learning. Language is rule-governed behaviour, and learning a language involves internalizing the rules. But the ability or inclination to formulate the rules apparently interferes with the performance which is supposed to lead to making the application of the rules automatic. The curious consequence is that linguists whose central concern is precisely the formulation of accurate grammatical statements are identified with a method in which the value of such statements is limited to 'summaries of behaviour'.

Phrased differently, underlying much of the current teaching of second languages is a confusion between the training schedule undergone by the learner and the structure of what it is that is ultimately learned. All models of learning based exclusively on imitation and reinforcement fail to account for the ability of anyone who has mastered a language to produce and understand novel utterances. The relationship between the utterances to which the learner is exposed and the universe from which the sample is chosen is complex and poorly understood, but much of what passes for applied linguistics is based on the erroneous assumption that what is learned is merely a representative sample of sentences plus some vague notion like generalization. Specifically, the view that merely presenting sentences like *I eat meat, I eat fish,* and *I eat fresh meat* will automatically lead a learner to produce *I eat fresh fish* is an empty oversimplification. Such a view does not account for the obvious fact that the learner who has also been presented with *I eat well* presumably will not produce **I eat fresh well*. To say that new sentences are produced by generalization or analogy is of little help unless one can make explicit how a learner selects precisely the correct analogy. The ability to accept *I eat fresh fish* and to reject **I eat fresh well* implies command of an abstract grammatical rule, a rule which distinguishes *I eat fish* from *I eat well* and, incidentally, which makes the distinction without appeal to the acoustic signal. In short, the correct generalization implies knowledge, perhaps unverbalized, that nouns and not adverbs may be modified by adjectives, and that *fish* and not *well* is a noun. No amount of hand waving will obscure the fact that this is what has to be learned, and the appeal to generalization is vacuous since it presupposes knowledge of precisely what it is that is to be learned. On the other hand, having made this point explicit, we are no nearer understanding what the most efficient way is of learning it.

A third linguistic claim involves the role of contrastive analysis. Any observer is aware of the interference in second language acquisition which is due to application of first language rules. It seems reasonable, therefore, to assume that the optimal pedagogical grammar for a given target language, whether in the form of drills, rules, or some combination of the two, will be determined in part by the native language of the prospective learner. There can be little quarrel with the premise, but it is not clear how a systematic comparison of adequate grammars is to be affected or that the results of such a comparison would be significantly different from what a talented teacher might derive from, say, an examination of student errors. Independent of the mechanics of contrastive analysis is the fact that another factor, namely, the simplicity of the rules involved, interacts in ways which are not clear with the similarities and differences provided by systematic comparison. The extreme position regarding contrastive analysis is that if two languages were exactly alike, then the student would have no problems, regardless of how complex the system was. But this implies, for example, that since English *be* has a particular set of forms, the easiest learning situation for English speakers would be found in a language in which the equivalent was irregular in precisely the same way, as opposed to, say, a language in which the equivalent conformed to the same rule as all other similar forms. It seems unreasonable, however, to accept the conclusion that similarities and differences completely override questions of internal consistency and simplicity.

The reservations registered above about the claims of linguists and the interpretations of these claims are more or less independent of the particular kind of grammatical description involved. Since there seems to be little question that the recent investigations by Noam Chomsky and others on the nature of language and grammar provide the most coherent view thus far proposed, it may be of interest to inquire as to what specific implications for second language learning can be derived from the view that a grammar consists of a partially ordered set of rules which enumerate the set of grammatical sentences, assigning to each sentence its correct structural description.

First, however, the main contribution of generative grammar is precisely that to the extent that it provides the most meaningful statements about the relevant data, it enables textbook writers to base their material on the most adequate description. For example, Mary S. Temperley has pointed out the inadequacy of drills which suggest that sentences like *we elected Tom secretary* are expansions of *we elected Tom*, with *secretary* somehow to be understood as a modifier of *Tom*. That such an analysis is incorrect is demonstrated by the corresponding passive, which is *Tom was elected secretary*, not **Tom secretary was elected*. If linguistics has any contribution to make to language learning, it is this: to make explicit in general and in particular what is learned. To the extent that transformational grammar provides the best description, it by definition also provides the best basis for application. It is incongruous to argue that some less adequate formulation can be successfully applied where a more adequate one cannot. On the other hand, the possibility still exists that the difference between teaching based on a correct formulation and teaching based on no formulation is minimal.

One frequently made suggestion is that ordering in the scientific grammar might have some counterpart in the pedagogical grammar. At one extreme is the trivial case in which the presence of one distinction presupposes another and hence ordering is automatic. For example, if the distinction between transitive and intransitive verbs depends on the presence or absence of noun phrases then clearly the distinction between the two types of verbs cannot be taught before the distinction between verb phrases (VP) and noun phrases (NP). At the other extreme is the obvious case in which ordering in the generative grammar cannot be understood as making a claim about pedagogy. Thus, some phonological rules presumably must be taught before some syntactic rules in spite of the fact that in general the former follow the latter.

A generative grammar does, however, make some claims about the kind of information needed in the production and recognition of certain types of sentences. For example, in English the grammar maintains that knowledge of the passives with a deleted agent presupposes knowledge of the full passive, but not vice versa. Such knowledge is the basis of making the distinction between *the snow was piled up by the wind* and *the snow was piled up by the building*. More generally, the grammar makes explicit cases in which constructions are derived by deletions, e.g. *I eat* from *I eat NP*, which is what enables a speaker to distinguish *I eat well* from *I sleep well*.

But all such discussions seem to be based on the assumption that somehow the order of presentation determines the order of application, an assumption which in its general form is demonstrably false, since no one wishes to claim that one cannot learn to use the brake on a car before learning to use the starter.

In spite of this reservation, however, it should be possible to test the proposition that it is easier to proceed in general from a formally marked distinction to a case of structural ambiguity (ambiguities resulting from deletion being a special case) than to proceed in the reverse direction. Of interest, then, is the consequence of such a position when it involves teaching infrequent or even nonoccurring forms. Thus, *John can jump higher than the Empire State Building* is ambiguous, but it is not clear what the pedagogical virtue might be of teaching *John can jump higher than the Empire State Building can jump* at all, let alone before the corresponding short form.

Presumably, the best scientific description provides the basis for the best pedagogical drills. Thus, most grammars of English would point out that whereas *the boy called up the girl* represents one structure, *the boy called up the stairs* represents another. This difference is made explicit by merely marking the constituent boundaries. Drills based on the different analyses might involve expanding the latter (*the boy called loudly up the stairs*) but not the former (**the boy called loudly up the girl*) and, conversely, permuting elements in the former (*the boy called the girl up*) but not the latter (**the boy called the stairs up*).

On the other hand, the relation between *I like amusing stories, I like raising flowers*, and *I like entertaining guests* cannot be indicated merely by marking constituent boundaries. Understanding these sentences involves knowledge of the underlying structure, where the differences are marked. A drill for exploiting the difference might merely involve insertion of the article *the*, yielding *the amusing stories* but *raising the flowers* and both *the entertaining guests* and *entertaining the guests*. But let us notice again the incongruity in all such drills. The ability to perform the drill implies knowledge of the syntax. In short, it presupposes knowledge of precisely the information it attempts to teach. But this is not just a minor quibble: this is a crucial aspect of all second language learning. A drill which derives *his amusing stories* and *his raising flowers* from *his stories amuse* and *he raises flowers* can be done automatically; since the output does not distinguish the constructions, performance of the drill does not necessarily indicate discrimination of their underlying structure; that is, performance of the drill does not ensure learning. On the other hand, a drill which does the reverse, deriving *his stories amuse* from *his amusing stories* and *he raises flowers* from *his raising flowers* can be said to test but not to teach, since performance of the drill presupposes precisely the information to be taught.

Let us consider a similar example in Spanish. *Me permite comer* ('he allows me to eat') must be distinguished from *me quiere comer* ('he wants to eat me'). *Me* is subject of the verb *comer* in the first example but object of *comer* in the second.

This is a fact that any scientific grammar of Spanish must explain. But how command of the rules which explain this fact is to be achieved is not dictated by the form of the rules themselves. Thus, a reasonable formulation of the difference in structures might include underlying structures which differ in precisely what relation the first person pronoun has to the verb *comer*, say, something like:

El quiere Comp
El me comerà $\Bigg\}$ ⇒ El me quiere comer.

but

El permite Comp
Yo como $\Bigg\}$ ⇒ El me permite comer.

But the assumption that a formulation such as the above also prescribes the form of a pedagogical drill is unwarranted. Indeed, performing such drills can be done automatically. Performing the reverse of such drills, that is, identifying the underlying structure, presupposes exactly the distinction which is presumably being taught.

The aim of applied linguistics may be viewed as specifying what the input must be to a device which yields a sentence recognizer and producer of some second language as output. Much of the discussion has centred on whether the input should be in the form of drills, rules, or both, and if both, in what combination and order. It is not surprising that these efforts have had limited success when we consider that relatively little is known about either the device or the output. The internal structure of the device, i.e. the learner, has gone relatively unexplored, except to point out that one of its components is a grammar of the learner's native language. It has generally been assumed that the effect of this component has been inhibitory rather than facilitative. In spite of claims to the contrary, we must conclude that learning principles are largely unknown. Regarding the output of such a device, studies in generative grammar have only recently suggested what the problem is in understanding the nature of a sentence analyser and describing the capacities that characterize it.

We see that we have now come full circle. The impact of modern linguistic theory must be to improve the content of pedagogical grammars. In this sense the traditional grammarians were on the side of the angels. Post–war linguists focused on the fact that ability to verbalize even adequate rules did not ensure performance and argued for the importance of practice. But the practice which has been devised is of two kinds, one of which can be performed automatically and hence may have only a minimal effect on the learner's competence and another which pre-supposes precisely the competence to be learned. The drill which serves as input to a naïve student and which is somehow converted into command of precisely the appropriate rule is an illusion.

30 PIT CORDER
Linguistics and the Language Teaching Syllabus

If the techniques of language teaching are to advance and develop, it is clearly more economical of time and money that they should do so in a principled fashion. By this I mean that change should be directed rather than random, that it should follow principles rather than trial-and-error. We want to know not just that one technique or one set of materials appears in certain circumstances to be more successful than another, but to know also *why* this might be so (or better still, but not easily proved, why this *is* so). We want to know what the principles underlying success or failure are. In other words, we want not only *descriptions* but *explanations*. The justification for theoretical studies is that in them, if anywhere, is to be found the understanding of the nature of language and how it is learned which provide these explanations.

It is sometimes maintained that language teaching has been going on a long time quite satisfactorily without teachers knowing anything about linguistics, psychology of language or the sociology of language. Now it is true that languages have been learnt from time immemorial, but how much this was due to the activities of the teacher, as opposed to those of the pupil, might be disputed. That teachers have known nothing about language is patently untrue. All of us have been learning some part of what is now called 'linguistics' from the primary school on; all of us have been talking about language since we started school, and to do so we have been using theoretical categories which can only be called linguistic in the broadest sense most of our lives. Until these categories have become systematically definable and relatable to each other they would be best called 'pre-linguistic'. We talk about *paragraphs, sentences, words, punctuation, letters, tone of voice, accent, stress,* to name only a few which are the common property of any educated person. But, of course, language-teachers through the study of the languages they teach are more sophisticated; they talk about *speech sounds, intonation, parts of speech,*

S. P. Corder: Extract from 'Advanced Study and the Experienced Teacher' in G. L. Perren (ed.) *Teachers of English as a Second Language,* Cambridge University Press, 1968, pp. 73–5 and 77–86.

nouns, verbs, adjectives, agreement, concord, prefixes and suffixes, tenses, cases, gender, number, subjects and objects, about *main clauses* and *subordinate clauses* and about *interrogative, imperative* and *declarative* sentences. These are all abstract concepts about language. Indeed, the language-teacher who has never been introduced to 'linguistics' already knows a great deal about language in what are basically linguistic terms. As J. P. Thorne has said: 'There is still incomparably more information about the structure of utterances in the average grammar book or dictionary than is to be found about the structure of visual experience, in all the books of the Gestalt psychologists put together'. Linguistics has been called the study of what a native speaker knows about his language in order to speak it; it is the more or less explicit externalization of the internalized rules he uses to speak and understand his own language. Anyone who claims that he has been teaching English for years but knows nothing about linguistics is mistaken. What he does not know is the meaning of the word 'linguistics'. It is true, as I have suggested, that most people have acquired this theoretical linguistic knowledge in a haphazard fashion through the study of their own mother tongue, or a second language, rather than through the direct study of language as an independent discipline in its own right during their initial training. But this means only that they have been learning inductively rather than deductively.

What the ordinary teacher knows, then, about linguistics is considerable, but this knowledge normally suffers from being unsystematic; the various concepts, some of which I have listed already, are not explicitly related to each other, and the categories he uses are rather ill-defined. Modern linguistics aims to offer a comprehensive, precise and systematic account of the formal aspects of language.

What I wish to suggest here is that a teacher cannot teach a language by any of the current techniques without linguistic knowledge, and that he does make constant use of what are basically linguistic concepts in his teaching. Indeed, the suggestion that a teacher can manage adequately without the sort of knowledge I have outlined, however vague, confused and unsystematic, is preposterous. Since trained teachers do invariably use linguistic notions in their teaching, whether they realize it or not, it is clearly desirable that as far as possible these should be the best available, and, because of the great amount of research devoted to language in recent years, this means the most recent.

The linguistic knowledge of most teachers derives from the theories current half a century or more ago, and nowadays often called 'traditional'. These theories were held at a time when the linguists' main interest lay in describing and accounting for historical change in language, and their methods were devised to that end. The modern interest in language as a phenomenon in itself has led to a different theoretical approach, and to different techniques. Most teachers will agree from their own experience in the classroom that their philological studies (if they did any) have not been of great direct help to them in their teaching. It is not surprising, therefore, that their knowledge has had to be considerably supplemented over the years by the pragmatic insights into language acquired by other experienced teachers. These have added considerably to the effective use of traditional linguistic notions in the work of teaching, without, however, greatly adding to their precision, coherence or systematization. It is at least partly the fault of the academic linguists that so little of the advances in their discipline in this century have found their way into the syllabuses of schools, colleges and university language departments. There are hopeful signs that this situation is being put right, and a number of universities are now including courses in general linguistics for their students of languages, both foreign and mother tongue.

For many years it was assumed that the only academic discipline which had direct relevance to language teaching was phonetics. Of all the linguistic sciences it was the earliest to achieve systematization and rigour. The reason for this was that language is superficially a physical phenomenon for which the theory and methods of the physical and biological sciences (in this case physics, anatomy and physiology) were already available. After all, in any science we start from observables, and the observables in spoken language are physical movements of the body and vibrations in the air, both of which can be measured. No one, however, did, or would now, suggest that language teaching is just applied phonetics. On the other hand, with the development of modern linguistic studies in recent years, there has been a tendency so to stress their importance in the teaching of languages that some people mistakenly considered that they were the only relevant academic studies for the language-teacher. Thus, 'applied linguistics' became a synonym for 'language-teaching studies'. The implication of everything I have said so far contradicts this narrow point of view. Linguistic studies do, indeed, have an application in language teaching, as I hope to show, and I have already pointed out that the ordinary language-teacher has always used fundamentally linguistic concepts in his work; but linguistics is not the only contributory discipline, nor does it uniquely find its application in language teaching.

If, however, linguistic knowledge had no relevance to, or use in, language teaching, then potentially any native English speaker who had general teaching ability and nothing more could teach his own language. Any such person could walk into a classroom and start teaching English. He would be able to choose what to teach and when to teach it, and he would know how to present and practise it. Merely to state the proposition in this form is to show its absurdity, and yet even now inherent in much teacher-training is the assumption that, given the ability to perform in the language, all that is needed to turn out a language-teacher is a training in what we may call general pedagogics, just as it was assumed that all one needed to teach mathematics or history was a knowledge of these subjects and a training as a teacher. Even if this were true of these subjects, and I believe recent developments would refute it, it has certainly never been true of language teaching. The reason for this lies in the nature of language as a universal feature of human behaviour. The same cannot be said of mathematics or history. These, if they are to be regarded as behaviour at all, are certainly behaviour of a different sort, and are certainly not universal in the sense that language is. Furthermore, teaching them is largely carried out through the medium of language. In language teaching we have the peculiar situation in which the teaching of behaviour must take place through the medium of what is being taught.

The problem reduces itself ultimately to the question of the difference between 'knowing' a language and 'knowing' history. This has been described by some philosophers as the difference between 'performative' knowledge and 'cognitive' knowledge. What the relationship between these is in psychological terms is something we should all like to know, particularly language-teachers. When we 'know' history we are able to talk coherently and systematically about it; to do this we must achieve a set of interrelated concepts. When we 'know' a language, on the other hand, we do not necessarily have the ability to talk systematically about it. Teachers of languages must obviously possess a 'performative' knowledge of the language they teach. But one can also have a cognitive knowledge of the language. This is the sort of knowledge a linguist has of a language, whether he can speak it or not. I have already suggested that a teacher must also possess some cognitive knowledge of the language in order to teach it. The job of language teaching is getting the learner to develop a performative knowledge of the language through the intermediary of both the performative and cognitive knowledge of the teacher.

Nevertheless, we all know of cases where teachers untrained in language teaching have had to teach a language. Quite frequently they have achieved some measure of success. How might this have been so? The answer is twofold: first, it is certain that, as educated people, they did have some cognitive knowledge of the language; but secondly, and more importantly, such teachers would have had a text-book to work with. This means that they were able to rely upon, or supplement their own knowledge from, the author's cognitive knowledge of the language, together with all that the author would have learnt as a practical teacher.

A text-book embodies the major part of the linguistic contribution to language teaching. In its preparation many decisions have to be made, by no means all of them are directly linguistic, since they have to do with the learner, the educational system and the objectives of the course. But the actual work of writing the text-book after these decisions have been made is linguistic. This does not mean that the book will bristle with the technical terminology of linguistics; after all, the terminal behaviour of a language course is not a cognitive knowledge of the language (although for some learners in some circumstances some such knowledge may be useful and necessary as a means to achieving a performative knowledge). Indeed, it is a welcome feature of most modern text-books that they are not overloaded with technical terminology. But we should be deceiving ourselves if we imagined, as some seem to, that the linguistic contribution to a text-book is measured by the amount of linguistic terminology it contains. A well-designed substitution chart, for instance, may have no technical explanations for the pupil and yet be proof of considerable linguistic sophistication in its author.

A text-book undoubtedly serves for the majority of teachers as the syllabus for the language course; few teachers yet feel able to devise a syllabus for themselves. But what are the considerations which enter into the making of a syllabus? Most of them have to do with the sociology and psychology of language: what are the learners studying the language for? what use do they expect to make of it? in what circumstances of social life are they going to use it? which particular language activities are to be provided for: speaking, or writing, or reading, for example? When all matters of this kind have been decided (and many syllabuses do not explicitly state the terminal behaviour they are intended to produce), then the linguistic work must be done. What is the linguistic description of the terminal behaviour? What vocabulary does it comprise? What grammatical features has it? What characteristics of intonation have to be taught? And other considerations of the same sort.

Linguistic theories are made to do two things: to explain language and to make descriptions of languages. It is scarcely necessary to say that our grammars of English, our dictionaries and our books on English phonetics are all descriptive and not theoretical. They are the result of the application of a theory about language in general to the description of a particular language. Ideally they enable us to do two things: to describe the English we are going to teach and to state what is and what is not a part of it, i.e. what is correct and what is not correct. I am not here speaking of the notions of good and bad English as they are sometimes used when speaking about the performance of the native speaker—these are sociological, not linguistic—but of what is, or is not, part of English, that is, what the speaker of that variety of English might be expected to do in some ordinary situation, and what he would never do except by mistake.

The description of a language, derived as it is from the behaviour of native speakers, enables us to say what is and is not part of the language, which of that learner's utterances are correct and which are not. But it does more than that: it tells us in what respect an utterance is or is not part of the language, in what way it is correct or incorrect; which rules it breaks. By doing this it enables the teacher to pin-point the source of the error and thus do something about curing or preventing it in future.

We may also wish to know why the error has taken place. We are all familiar with the phenomenon that errors made by learners are frequently (though not exclusively) related to their different mother tongues. Any good teacher quickly learns by experience to predict most of the errors each new class of learners is going to make. Linguistics, by enabling us to compare the systems or rules of different languages, permits us to predict what errors will be made. This has, indeed, been one of the major fields of the application of linguistics to language teaching. Perhaps its importance is now not so highly rated as it was. The technical linguistic problems of making contrastive analyses of this sort are, in any case, considerable, because the categories and rules of each language are in large measure peculiar to that language, and equating them with those of another on a simple one-to-one basis is rarely possible, except perhaps at a level of abstraction which precludes immediate useful results in teaching. Nevertheless, at the level of pronunciation, there is no doubt that contrastive studies do yield valuable information for the teacher.

We have here only spoken of the contrastive study of two languages as helping us to predict the errors of the learner. The projection by the learner of the linguistic rules of his mother tongue into the second language is known as interference. But it has another aspect. Where the rules of the two languages are similar we may expect the converse—facilitation. A linguistic insight into the characteristics of the two languages involved should enable the teacher to exploit the similarities as well as prepare himself for the errors arising out of the differences. We tend in teaching to be more aware of the phenomenon of interference than of facilitation, just as in the study of the development of language in children we are more aware of what they have not yet learned correctly than of the great mass that they have learned. And yet, when we consider how quickly people learn second languages, we should be more interested in what is common to all languages than we are. The linguist is now more and more turning his attention in this direction. He wishes to discover more about language universals. The teacher, too, might do well to concentrate more on the similarities which will help his pupils, than worry overmuch about the differences which hinder their progress.

Linguistics gives us the theoretical basis and the technical means to make descriptions of the languages we are teaching, and the means to compare them and contrast them with other languages. This does not mean that we propose, in any particular teaching situation, to teach the 'whole of a language' to any particular set of students. As an aim, this is impossible to realize, not only because no native speaker would claim to know the whole of his mother tongue, but because the concept of the 'whole of a language' is probably not definable. To talk about a language, say English, is to talk about an abstraction. It is an abstraction from all the utterances produced by native speakers. It can, in the first instance, be described in terms of a set of 'rules' for producing English sentences. But the knowledge of the rules does not tell us which rules are to be applied in which set of circumstances. This is the field of semantics, or the study of meaning. Linguists may one day be able to state the semantic rules of a language which govern the choice of structural rules in a particular situation, but they cannot do so yet. The teaching of the semantic rules would be what we should call the teaching of meaning; but more of this later.

An alternative and, for the moment, more useful way of thinking of 'English' is that it is made up of a number of sub-languages or varieties. What the native speaker speaks or writes on any particular occasion is a particular variety of his language, appropriate to that situation. The descriptive categories for talking about the situation are a matter of sociology or psychology, but the description of the variety chosen is, of course, a matter of linguistics. When we teach a learner a language, what we are doing is to prepare him to behave, appropriately in a number of English-speaking situations, public or private, formal or informal, technical or everyday, in one part of the world or another, in writing or in speech. This, to repeat the current jargon, is the terminal behaviour we are aiming at. I have already suggested that the tendency in language teaching at the present time is towards more closely defined aims in terms of the competence of our pupils. This competence is describable in linguistic terms.

There was a time when the terminal behaviour was described in terms of raw frequencies, i.e. so many of the commonest words in the language by a certain stage in the course; or so many grammatical patterns or 'structures' at the same stage. This type of description and the aims it implies were a great advance on what was previously available as a description of terminal behaviour. It showed awareness that the language knowledge aimed at could be described in linguistic terms rather than in vague behavioural terms like 'the ability to read Literature in the language', 'to converse freely with native speakers', or 'to ask questions in English and answer them'.

It suffered, however, from two serious defects. First, it could not achieve a useful degree of precision about the nature of the unit it was counting, i.e. 'words', and 'structures'; and secondly, it did not take into account the fact that the probability of occurrence of a 'word' or a 'structure' varied from situation to situation of language use.

To deal with the first defect. The determination of the unit, 'structure' or 'word', was not made according to any sound linguistic principle (according to any particular coherent theory). Formal linguistic studies are largely concerned with this matter: the determination of the units of the language, their constitution and their classification. Classification as an operation in any circumstances is a question of deciding what is the 'same' and what 'different'. As applied to language it is a matter of determining in respect of which features a linguistic unit is the same as or different from another of a similar sort. Any two units of a language may be simultaneously similar in one respect, and different in another. For example, the sentence *He is reading a letter* and *He is writing a letter* cannot be distinguished from each other at the level of grammar, but are distinct lexically. *He is writing a letter* and *Is he writing a letter?* are identical lexically, but are both the 'same' and 'different' at the same time in terms of grammar. They are both indicative, transitive sentences, but one is, of course, interrogative and the other declarative. Do these therefore count as two 'structures' or as one in our frequency counts? The linguist would merely enumerate the features any sentence has. He might do this in gross terms, like indicative, transitive, past, definite subject, perfective aspect, etc. This is a far cry from the now 'traditional' notion of 'structure'. The linguist, as linguist, cannot tell the teacher what are the important and what are the less important features of a sentence. These are essentially applied judgements, i.e. important for something—in this case teaching and learning the language. It is clear therefore that the teaching description of the terminal behaviour is a matter for collaboration between linguist and teacher. *Neither* can do the work satisfactorily alone. This is what we mean by *applied linguistics*: collaboration between a linguist and a specialist in another field, in this case a language-teacher. If the teacher is also a linguist, so much the better: what he then *does* is applied linguistics. One of the objects of advanced study for experienced teachers is to enable them to engage in applied linguistics.

The second defect in the method of describing the linguistic aims of language teaching in terms of the teaching of the 'most frequent' 'words' and 'structures' is quite different. The commonness, or relative frequency, of a 'word' or 'structure', however determined, used to be calculated, as far as it could be (and this was not very far), in relation to the language 'as a whole'. Since it is obviously impracticable to take the 'whole' of a language as one's data for this purpose, some form of sample must be selected. This sample must be representative of the language 'as a whole'. But since we know that the form of language varies according to the circumstances in which it occurs, we are forced to start the operation by classifying the circumstances in some way or other, and giving each some sort of weighting according to its importance, judged in relation to the needs of the learner. There are, of course, considerable technical problems in collecting spoken language data in most situations, even if we could specify which were the important ones. Consequently, frequency counts of vocabulary and grammatical items have been based upon written language to a large extent, until fairly recently. But no one would now be satisfied that the written language is in any useful way statistically representative of the language 'as a whole', let alone of the spoken language. It is only fair to say that many of those who engaged in frequency counting were well aware that there are manifest gross differences in the frequency of linguistic features in spoken and written language, and, of course, also in the different varieties of written material. But even at their most refined these techniques did not sufficiently take into account the fact that the uses learners have for the second language are likely to be very much more restricted than those of a native speaker, and that therefore the frequency of 'words' and 'structures' should only be calculated on the basis of those language varieties that the learner is going to use, e.g. scientific, written, formal, standard, etc. To describe the terminal behaviour of the learner or group of learners in quantitative terms, the needs of the learner must be determined. This is not the job of the linguist but of the teacher. So again we come back to the same point: the description of what the learner must know at the end of his course is a matter for collaboration between linguist and teacher, a matter of applied linguistics.

At the end of all this work: the choice of language varieties to be taught, the analysis and description of the varieties, i.e. the statement of the features and frequency of these features in the corpus, we finish up with a list of linguistic items in the 'language to be taught'. This is the linguistic syllabus. It is not the teaching syllabus, because the items have then to be processed, a selection has to be made and the material has to be ordered into a programme. Here again the linguist has little to say. The decision about the ordering of the linguistic material is made largely on pedagogical grounds, only one of which might be regarded as falling within the scope of the linguist. These are considerations of complexity, teachability and utility. The linguist might have something to say about complexity. He might say, for instance, that we should logically proceed in our teaching of tenses from simple to compound, or that in English we should proceed from declarative to interrogative, from positive to negative, and from active to passive sentences, since all these moves require additional rules to be learnt. He might also maintain that simple sentences should be learnt before complex and complex before compound, again on the ground that these moves involve the learning of new processes But when it comes to matters of teachability and utility which have to do with matters of motivation, method and other pedagogical principles, he has nothing to say. We are not concerned simply with teaching our pupils to emit sentences which are correct: we are teaching them to communicate. The teacher is concerned with creating situations which will encourage them to do this, even if it sometimes means ignoring the 'logic' of linguistic progression.

Let me sum up. Linguistic knowledge, that is, knowledge about language in general, and about a specific language, and consequently the ability to talk about it, has always been fundamental to language teaching. It has been, to a considerable extent, taken for granted, since it has always formed part of the normal education of an educated man in advanced societies. It is not possible to imagine that any systematic preparation of materials for teaching could be undertaken without it, unless we restrict what we mean by language teaching simply to the activities of the teacher with the text-book in his hand. It is suggested that the considerable development in linguistic studies in this century provides the means to do this work better and to understand better what others have done, by offering more rigorously defined categories and more detailed and complete descriptions of the operation of a language and of its varieties. Linguistics is now developing techniques to provide a scheme of description which goes beneath the surface form of language and enables us to gain an insight into what a person must 'know' in order to speak a language.